Why Don't American Cities Burn?

The City in the Twenty-first Century

Eugenie L. Birch and Susan M. Wachter, Series Editors

A complete list of books in the series is available from the publisher.

Why Don't American Cities Burn?

Michael B. Katz

PENN

UNIVERSITY OF PENNSYLVANIA PRESS

PHILADELPHIA

Published by
University of Pennsylvania Press
Philadelphia, Pennsylvania 19104-4112
www.upenn.edu/pennpress

Printed in the United States of America on acid-free paper
10 9 8 7 6 5 4 3 2 1

Library of Congress Cataloging-in-Publication Data
Katz, Michael B., 1939–
    Why don't American cities burn? / Michael B. Katz.
        p.   cm. — (The city in the twenty-first century)
    978-0-8122-4386-4 (hardcover : alk. paper)
    Includes bibliographical references and index.
    1. Sociology, Urban—United States—20th century.   2. Urban policy—
United States—20th century.   3. Inner cities—United States—20th
century.   4. City and town life—United States—20th century.
I. Title. II. Series
HT123.K38   2011
307.760973'0904   2011023321

To the memory of
Baruch S. Blumberg
(1925–2011)
Kayak buddy extraordinaire

Contents

Prologue: The Death of Shorty

At 1:27 on the morning of August 4, 2005, Herbert Manes stabbed Robert Monroe—known as Shorty—to death on the 1400 block of West Oakland Street in North Philadelphia. No newspaper reported the incident. Arrested and charged with homicide, Manes spent the next ten months incarcerated until his trial, which ended on June 8, 2006. After deliberating less than ninety minutes, the jury concluded that he had acted in self-defense and found him not guilty on all charges. I served as juror number three.[1]

This Prologue is the story of the trial, what it meant for me, and what it signifies about marginalization, social isolation, and indifference in American cities. It distills the essential themes of this book into an incident at once mundane and horrific. It is also the story of what I learned from Herbert Manes. It is not a neat story. Ambiguities remain unresolved, contradictions abound, ends dangle. It begins with the two main characters and where they lived.

Herbert Manes was born on June 29, 1938. His family lived south of Gerard Street, around Ninth Street, in what he says is now "upper Society Hill." His parents had migrated from South Carolina before World War II but met in Philadelphia, where, after knowing each other for only two weeks, they married. Their marriage lasted more than sixty years until their deaths in their seventies. Herbert has two brothers, one of whom has died and one who works for Blue Cross and Blue Shield. He also has a sister who works for the Youth Study Center, a secure facility for youths age 13 to 18 considered a risk to the safety of the community or at risk for flight while awaiting their hearing before the Juvenile Court. When Herbert's parents died, an aunt who lived to be 104 years old managed the family. Everyone referred to her as "the boss." Herbert spent his entire early life in the neighborhood in which he was born, attending Jefferson School and then Benjamin Franklin High School. He left school to make money at age eighteen without graduating. Money became important, because after a shotgun wedding, which he claims was common at the time, his first child was born when he was twenty. In all, Herbert has eight sons, one daughter, and many grandchildren. His former wife, from whom he was divorced in the 1990s, lives in Cheltenham, a heavily African American suburb on the edge of Philadelphia. Until her retirement, she ran the dialysis unit at a local hospital. Herbert speaks of her fondly, describing her as a "lovely lady" with whom he stays in touch. Most of his children live in the Philadelphia area, some in Willingboro (formerly Levittown, New Jersey, and currently home to many African Americans), and three or four in the South. Herbert sees his children and grandchildren only at family reunions.

For thirty-five years, Herbert's father worked for a moving company from which he received a pension. Herbert describes him as a good father and has warm memories of both parents. Herbert drove a furniture truck for the same firm for many years until, like most of the city's manufacturers, it went out of business. He then worked in steel mills, which he described as "brutal work." He retired after an injury and survives on social insurance. "Uncle Sam takes care of me," he told the jury. He also drove a gypsy cab.

Herbert looks older than his years. At 6 feet tall and 170 pounds, he stands slightly stooped; his close-cropped hair is a grizzled gray; his large lips protrude on one side of his face, almost as though he had experienced a stroke. Round, dark-framed glasses give him a quizzical look. For his trial, he wore an open-neck, long-sleeved light gray shirt, blue trousers buttoned at the top with no belt, and light tan workingmen's boots.

Shorty remains more mysterious. In Pennsylvania and New Jersey, birth and death certificates remain closed to all but relatives and their attorneys. As one of the jurors who had acquitted Shorty's killer, I could not just show up on his brother's or sister's doorstep asking for biographical information. Nor would it be safe for me to roam his neighborhood's streets in search of friends and acquaintances to interview. A friend offered to help by contacting two people with local networks. But the unpredictability that disorganizes lives on the city's mean streets intervened. One man was arrested and jailed before he could cooperate. Another potential informant was shot in the head and killed on a violent Saturday night when three other men also met their deaths between midnight and three in the morning.

This much is known: Shorty was born on August 26, 1964, in Neptune, New Jersey, where he lived until at least age ten. His brother and sister still live there. Like Herbert with his gypsy cab, Shorty was part of the informal economy found everywhere in America's inner cities. Shorty worked on the street as a freelance mechanic. In Philadelphia, many street mechanics work near auto supply stores. Customers purchase parts in the stores and bring them to the mechanics. The activity violates a city ordinance, but no one seems to care. Although only 5 feet 2 inches tall and 147 pounds, Shorty was expert in martial arts. Herbert described Shorty's strength and powerful build; he was, said Herbert, impossible to fight in any straightforward way.

Shorty was well known to the police. Between July 23, 2001, and January 29, 2003, he was charged with offenses ten times. His alleged crimes ranged from unauthorized use of an automobile and other vehicles to theft by receiving stolen property, criminal trespass, burglary, retail theft, and drug-related offenses. Remarkably, each charge was either withdrawn or dismissed. For a long time I was puzzled by Shorty's ability to escape criminal charges unindicted; he truly seemed to be a Teflon man. His history began to make sense in December 2009 when the *Philadelphia Inquirer* ran a series of articles under the banner "Justice: Delayed, Dismissed, Denied." "In America's most violent big city," the investigation discovered, "people accused of serious crimes are escaping conviction with stunning regularity." The statistics told a depressing story of administrative incompetence. "Only one in 10 people charged with gun assaults is convicted of that charge. . . . Only two in 10 accused armed robbers are found guilty. . . . Only one in four accused rapists is found guilty of rape." In most big cities prosecutors win about half their cases; in Philadelphia they win 20 percent. "It is a system that all too often fails to punish violent criminals, fails to protect witnesses, fails to catch thousands of fugitives, fails to decide cases on their merits—fails to provide justice."[2] In Philadelphia, Shorty's ability to walk away from arrests now appeared more the norm than the exception.

Despite Shorty's record, police sergeant Troy Lovell, who patrolled the area, described Shorty as pleasant, friendly, and "respectful." At the time of his death, Shorty's blood alcohol level was just shy of legal intoxication and showed that he had recently ingested a substantial amount of cocaine, which had mixed with the alcohol to form a potent new compound. One man, intimately familiar with the Philadelphia street scene, claimed that street mechanics generally were addicted to drugs. Whether or not this claim is accurate, Shorty surely did not spend much of his income on rent. He lived near the scene of his death on a tiny, desolate street of run-down row houses that angled alongside railroad tracks. Even by the standards of the neighborhood, his room rent must have been low.

West Oakland Street, where Herbert lived in a first-floor room and Shorty died, is a narrow, one-way street of small, poorly kept row houses, perhaps a slight step up from where Shorty had lived. Everyone acknowledged the neighborhood to be dangerous. It embodied the decline, decay, and abandonment that scarred much of North Philadelphia.

The house in which Herbert lived was owned by the Philadelphia Housing Development Corporation, which had purchased it for $1; its certified market value for 2007 was $8,300. Of the 6,947 people who lived in the census tract in which West Oakland Street was located, only 45 were white; the rest were largely African American; only 118 had been born outside the United States—compared to 9 percent of the city's population—and more than three of four had been born in Pennsylvania. More than two of five households consisted of women with no husband present. Nearly a third were householders living alone, with 16 percent of women and men over age sixty-five living by themselves.

Just 60 percent of households had incomes from earnings, and these averaged only $24,859 in 1999; a third had income from Social Security; 11 percent from Supplemental Security Income (SSI); 19 percent from public assistance; and 17 percent from pensions. Median household income was $16,367, and 41 percent of families fell below the poverty line. It was a neighborhood that had seen much better days.

Although in 1936 the Home Owners Loan Corporation (HOLC) slammed it for its "Negro concentration," until the 1950s the neighborhood remained more than half white with roughly half of families owning their own homes. Clothing and furniture factories, long since gone in the early twenty-first century, were nearby, as were railroad yards and other businesses. The proximity of the subway connected the neighborhood easily with the rest of the city. Mansions even lined a nearby major street. Today, abandoned houses and vacant lots appear to easily outnumber the mostly small businesses—fast food restaurants, an auto supply dealer—that remain.

Herbert's fatal encounter with Shorty began sometime during the evening of August 3, 2005. Herbert, hungry and without money, borrowed five dollars from Shorty, promising to pay him back that night or the next day. He was expecting a government check. With the money, he says, he went to a local restaurant to buy some chicken. Later, still hungry and without money, Herbert went to a friend's house where he unsuccessfully tried to borrow more money. On his way home, he ran into Shorty, who was working on a car on West Oakland Street. Shorty demanded his money on the spot. When Herbert told him he did not have any money, Shorty struck him. In the fight that followed, Shorty knocked Herbert to the ground and was punching him when two passersby intervened, pulling him off. Herbert immediately went home where, he claims, fearful for his safety, he retreated to the second floor. Shorty appeared in front of his house with a pipe three feet seven inches long. He started knocking out windows, yelling, "I want my money!"

Henry Fairlee, who lived on the second floor of Herbert's house, entered the unlocked front door—unlocked because the lock always was broken—and told Herbert to go out to talk with Shorty so he would stop breaking windows. This is Herbert's version. Fairlee tells a different story. He claims to have been one of the people originally pulling Shorty off of Herbert. He claims, too, that Herbert came tearing out of the house with a knife in hand, swinging his arms and lunging at Shorty, who had not yet picked up the pipe. At this point, according to Fairlee, Herbert stabbed Shorty, who then went to his toolbox for a pipe before returning to the house into which Herbert had retreated.

Fairlee was the only civilian witness for the prosecution, and he lacked credibility. He was in custody for two parole violations. He had a record of felonies—breaking and entering, burglary, receiving stolen goods. On the witness stand, he had trouble staying awake, his head periodically lolling against the side of the dais. Contradictions riddled his testimony, and he even contradicted his testimony at the preliminary hearing. He either erred or lied about the length of the pipe, claiming under repeated questioning that it could not have been between three and a half or four feet long. For Fairlee's version to be valid, moreover, Shorty, who had just sustained a mortal wound to his heart, would have to have been able to locate and wield the pipe. The medical examiner reported that only three inches of the six-inch knife blade had penetrated Shorty's chest, an outcome unlikely if a six-inch blade had been thrust into him with great force, as Fairlee claimed. Another witness, interviewed by the police, was waiting outside the courtroom. He had told the police he had seen Herbert run from the house with a knife that he plunged into Shorty. The prosecuting attorney, however, did not call him to the stand.

Herbert, of course, tells a different story. He denies, first of all, that Fairlee was one of the people who pulled Shorty off him at their first encounter. Herbert said he wanted to go to his brother's to borrow some money but was frightened. He could not exit the back door because the yard was so full of debris that it was impassable, and he did not have a telephone with which to call the police. Because the neighborhood was so dangerous and he feared intruders, Herbert kept a knife—an ordinary kitchen knife with a six-inch blade—above his doorway. He pocketed the knife and went outside onto the stoop. Shorty immediately knocked him down, whether with a blow from the pipe or by leaping and kicking is not clear. Herbert ended up on the ground, underneath Shorty. This was the moment when Herbert pulled the knife from his pocket and stabbed him. On the witness stand, Herbert often appeared confused; he tried to answer the questions put to him, but he seemed not always to understand them. Yet, when his attorney asked, "Did you intend to kill Shorty?" Herbert unhesitatingly responded with force, "As God is my witness, I did not."

When Sergeant Lovell—a twenty-year veteran of the Highway Patrol, six feet four inches tall, African American, handsome, and articulate—arrived, he first noticed Herbert sitting on his stoop drenched in blood. Herbert complained of his cut hand and pain in his ribs. As Lovell was tending to him, Fairlee came up behind him and told him an injured man was lying on the ground across the street. Lovell moved to Shorty and asked what had happened; all Shorty could manage was to point at Herbert. Assessing Shorty's condition as grave, Powell instructed the two officers just arrived on the scene to take him to the hospital. They drove Shorty to Temple University Hospital, a trip of perhaps a minute and a half, where he was soon pronounced dead.

Sergeant Lovell allowed Herbert to go into his house to clean up a bit. Then he placed him under arrest and ordered him taken to Temple University Hospital, where his hand was stitched. From the hospital he was brought to police headquarters at Eighth and Race, where detectives questioned him. He was, he stressed, trying to protect himself. Several people witnessed the events on West Oakland, but only Fairlee, and later the one other witness, agreed to speak with the police. Fairlee also went to the police station, where he told police his version of the story, casting Herbert as the aggressor. Herbert was charged with murder and incarcerated.

The crime scene investigating unit found no fingerprints on the knife, the pipe, or a pair of scissors of unknown provenance found under Shorty. At the trial, the police were unable to produce the knife, pipe, or scissors, which, apparently, had been lost. (I was told by an attorney that evidence often is lost.) It appears doubtful that detectives returned to West Oakland to try to persuade other witnesses to speak with them. After all, the case was about two poor black men arguing over five dollars, and they had closed it.

In 2005, 375 homicides occurred in Philadelphia, most in poor, heavily African American neighborhoods. Of the victims, 339 were men, and 308 were black. Many of the killings resulted from arguments, and most victims died of gunshot wounds. Most were younger than Shorty. On the week of Shorty's death, eleven homicides took place in the city. Only four of these made either of the major newspapers, and of these, three were odd cases: a white girl shot in a drive-by shooting; a promising young man about to start college gunned down; a white man shot by a friend while sleeping on a sofa. Only in the use of a knife rather than a gun was Shorty's death exceptional.[3]

Why was Herbert charged with first-degree murder when the evidence for murder was virtually nonexistent? Why was he incarcerated for so long? Why did the district attorney's office go to trial with so little evidence and only one witness, who lacked credibility? Why was the police work so inadequate? Was Herbert's real offense being a poor, uneducated black man living in Philadelphia's badlands? If Herbert had been a middle-class white man, I thought, he would not have spent the last ten months in jail or find himself tried for first-degree murder. Still, looked at another way, for Herbert the American judicial system worked. He had an excellent attorney, a fair-minded jury, and an exemplary judge. Was his situation unusual, I wondered. Not long after the trial, I read Steve Bogira's *Courtroom 302*, a devastating account of how criminal justice is dispensed in Chicago.[4] By the standards of Bogira's account, Herbert was lucky. These were among the questions that lingered in my mind after the trial was over. We had found Herbert not guilty, but by no means did we know or understand all that had happened.

Herbert, Shorty, and the trial haunted me. Why was I so interested in this ordinary murder case? Why did I want to know more about Herbert, Shorty, and their neighborhood? Why did the men and the trial matter? At first, these seemed easy questions, but they were not. The best I could do was to try to put myself at the center and reconstruct the trial through my own eyes and then to probe my reactions.

The jury selection had proved a bit weird. Both the DA and defense attorney were interested in my background. The DA wanted to know my children's education, where I was educated, and whether I taught undergraduates. My degrees from Harvard seemed unduly important to them—making the DA somewhat ill at ease. The defense attorney, a man, as I later learned, seventy-nine years old with years of experience defending indigent clients, asked the subject of my doctoral dissertation. I thought it a peculiar question, but I answered politely. Later, when we met (he took a shine to me and invited me to lunch) he explained that if I had answered the question in a surly or impatient manner, he would have removed me. He could not understand why the DA let me on the jury. The defendant, Herbert Manes, was of course present during the questioning. So I had my first look at him. He looked so old, sad, and beaten down that my sympathies were on his side, and I had to tell myself to try to contain my emotional reaction.

The process of jury selection seemed to drag on for hours. It was the first taste of one of the two emotions that dominated my responses through the next few days, namely, boredom. We spent hours and hours just sitting in the jury room. We were given a time to be present, and the jurors were prompt, but for reasons rarely explained to us, we had to wait. The whole process could have been completed in one solid working day.

The other emotion was responsibility. I could not escape the weight of making a decision that would determine the rest of a man's life. As a result, I found myself able to focus intensely on the proceedings. I don't have a particularly sharp memory—age is having its effect that way—but my ability to remember details was far better than I expected, far better than usual, undoubtedly a sign of motivation.

The jurors were a cross section of Philadelphia. I was the only one with a postgraduate degree. One other man was a translator who also did some adjunct teaching. None of the others had professional jobs. Two were nineteen years old—one of them immature, unable to stop babbling about his life. I worried about him. (When we went into deliberations, he shut up and said almost nothing.) One woman may have been older than I; gray, quiet, and withdrawn, she said almost nothing and conveyed an impression of not wanting to be there. The most interesting and impressive juror was a large, burly man—a mechanic with a two-day growth of red stubble who wore shorts, spoke with a tough Philly accent, and had served jail time for contempt in his divorce trial. When we were deliberating, he said, "I'm not smart, but I'm street smart." In fact, he was smart, period. He picked up important details that the rest of us had missed, and, from tending bar in the projects, he knew about street life in a way the rest of us did not. The woman who volunteered to serve as foreperson was in her thirties, a paralegal, attractive, a single mother who lived with her mother—bright, quick, and appealing. I stayed quiet in the jury room, revealing nothing about myself. I did not want them to know I was a professor at Penn. I did not want to intimidate them or have them react to me as other than someone ordinary. My cover was blown at the end when the judge, in delivering his instructions to the jury, mentioned, for some reason, that there was a professor among the jury. (When he was interviewing me and found I was a history professor, he asked me my opinion of the greatest president in U.S. history. My answer—Lincoln—pleased him; he's a Lincoln fan.)

The jury was serious. We were instructed not to discuss the case among ourselves while the trial was ongoing. And few jurors made any remarks about it. I sensed, however, that they were following it intently, an assumption supported by their recall and comments in our deliberations. As the case unfolded, I had little idea of how they were reacting. After the first day, I knew that I could not find the defendant guilty on the evidence presented and would not be swayed. So I feared we might be in for a long session in our little room. Happily, that was not the outcome.

Judge Lockwood introduced the case well. He's a friendly-looking but firm man who radiates fairness. I thought his conduct of the trial exemplary and his rulings correct. The DA, a slim, intense, expensively dressed and made-up woman, told us that it was a simple, straightforward case and not to expect it to be like murder trials on TV. I did not know exactly what she meant. It was, in fact, rather like TV, except that the police work did not seem as thorough and the one civilian witness wouldn't have made the cut. I think she meant that the real-life case was a lot messier and that we would have to reach a decision with less conclusive evidence. The other jurors did not like her. They thought she was smart, but several said she frightened them. They found her cold and hard. On the last day, when she had to deliver her closing statement, she dressed all in black, which seemed overkill. I learned much later that she erupted after the jury had left the courtroom, calling Herbert a killer and a liar, berating the defense attorney, and shouting angrily at Shorty's relatives who had criticized her handling of the case.

The defense attorney, William Gray, was, as noted earlier, nearly eighty. He has a fascinating background, having turned to the defense of indigent criminals for personal reasons partway through a successful career as a business attorney. He likes to talk (and knows it). His verbosity irritated the jurors somewhat, but they thought he was good. He sometimes uses literary allusions, and his language can be flowery. Early in the trial, he made an allusion to Lincoln, and he began his closing argument with a quote from Emerson. But he had prepared carefully and had a clear, effective strategy, at the heart of which was his daring decision to put Herbert on the stand. It turned out to be a brilliant move, for the reasons I have already explained.

Listening to the evidence, I could not fathom why Herbert was on trial for first-degree murder or why he had been held for ten months. The evidence just was not there. In fact, the witnesses, all for the prosecution, introduced more and more ambiguity and doubt. The one civilian witness, Henry Fairlee, startled me. I could not believe he had been put on the stand for the prosecution. Watching his head loll and his eyes shut, hearing his contradictions and his outright misstatement about the length of the pipe, I thought he was the least credible witness imaginable.

When the jurors finally found themselves alone, the first task was choosing a foreperson. One or two suggested me, but I deferred to the woman who had volunteered. She seemed a little less certain than she was earlier. Shorty's relatives had been watching the trial and clearly were upset and angry. But she was gutsy, and I supported her as foreperson and sat next to her in order to give her a hand if needed. We went quickly around the room to gauge opinion. Not one juror hesitated to dismiss the charge of murder one. No one found any of the evidence credible.

The next question was manslaughter. After a brief discussion, we agreed that there was no way Herbert could have avoided the confrontation. He could not have left his house through the back because the rear was blocked by trash. Because he did not have a telephone, he could not have called the police (the defense attorney probably should have brought this out). We did not believe he had used the borrowed money for food, but that was immaterial. We also thought that if he had a serious criminal record, the DA would have highlighted it at the trial. Only one juror, the sharper of the nineteen-year-olds, wanted to discuss the manslaughter possibility. But he quickly agreed that no evidence supported it. We all thought it most likely that Herbert had acted in self-defense, not intending to kill Shorty. This discussion took less than an hour and a half, which amazed the attorneys. Watching Herbert's face relax, seeing him embrace his lawyer as the decision was read, moved me deeply. After we returned to the jury room, Judge Lockwood came in to thank us. He praised our attentiveness and said we had acted correctly.

In one way, I found the trial experience frustrating. I wanted to interrupt and ask questions. As someone who makes part of his living teaching seminars, this is something I expect to do. Obviously, I could not. But at a number of points along the way, I wanted to probe more or bring up something it seemed to me the attorneys had missed. I was also frustrated by what we did not know about Herbert and Shorty. Who were these men? Only a piece of their lives was laid in front of us. What had brought them to the streets of North Philadelphia? Why were two grown men willing to kill each other over five dollars? What had made West Oakland Street a place where freelance mechanics fixed cars on the street, aging men lived in rooms with knives stashed over the door for protection, and most residents would refuse to bear witness to the killing of a likable and familiar figure?

I suppose that the law would say these questions are irrelevant. They are immaterial to what happened, and the only intent that counted was what lay in Herbert's mind at the moment his knife penetrated Shorty's chest. The only geography that mattered was the detail necessary to choreograph Herbert's and Shorty's movements. But that was not enough for me. I wanted to understand, as fully as possible, the situation and the men about whose lives and death the state required me to decide. I think like a historian or a social scientist, not a lawyer. In my world, where the goal is to comprehend rather than to judge, context matters greatly.

For decades I have tried to write about poverty, its contexts, and the ideas and policies used to explain or ameliorate it. I also have written, read, and thought a great deal about cities, especially the transformations that have produced the North Philadelphias of America. (Even here I fall into stereotypes: North Philadelphia is a complex and varied place that belies its reputation for blight and social disorganization, just as West Philadelphia, beyond Fortieth Street, belies the image of a dangerous urban frontier so prominent in the minds of a great many Penn students and maddening to its residents.) But there is an abstraction in most of the literature and in most of what I have written. This abstraction confronted me in the early 1990s, when for about five years I served as archivist to an ex officio member of the Social Science Research Council (SSRC) Committee for Research on the Urban Underclass (a title originally insisted on by the Rockefeller Foundation, which funded the committee's work), later renamed, more softly, as a committee on concentrated and persistent urban poverty. The SSRC committee brought together the leading social scientists working on poverty. It focused primarily, with few exceptions, on quantitative data.

Members were serious, responsible social scientists; for the most part, they cared about poverty. But the research, of necessity, given its method, transmuted the Herberts and Shortys of America into statistics, their characteristics the variables in equations. To have talked of their lived experience, to have allowed hearts to show on sleeves, would have been seen as violating objectivity. To have sat down with them for an evening's talk would have been unscientific and useless. There is, of course, a long history of social scientists and observers who have tried to find and reveal the lives beyond the abstractions. Henry Mayhew and Charles Booth in England come immediately to mind. In the United States, Jacob Riis's *How the Other Half Lives* remained an iconic text that was unmatched in its popular impact until Michael Harrington's *The Other America* in the 1960s. Within the social sciences, anthropologists and ethnographers such as Eliot Liebow in *Tally's Corner*, Robert Fairbanks, II in *The Way Things Work*, and Philippe Bourgois and Jeff Schonberg in *Righteous Dopefiend* have opened windows on lives never seen before by most Americans.[5] Even in reading the best ethnographies, however, a layer of experience separates me from the day-to-day reality of lives spent on West Oakland Street and thousands of streets like it. This is so even though I have lived for nearly thirty years in West Philadelphia, where diversity is the only thread uniting the individuals who pass our house every day. I have tried to enter the lives of extremely poor people in the past, reconstructing histories of the poorest New Yorkers of the early twentieth century from charity records and complementary sources. By piecing together these life stories, I have unraveled the complexity and strength, as well as the pathos and sometimes disorganization, in the lives of desperately poor women.[6] But I have never done the same for their counterparts today.

Occasionally, though, an incident concretizes what I have been writing and thinking about. It braids together strands often examined separately by social science, exemplifying the multiple and sometimes contradictory forces at play in the most ordinary lives and how powerful structural forces transforming cities, social structure, and national economies play themselves out in individual experience.

One of these moments happened a year or two after my family and I moved from Toronto to Philadelphia. It was the late spring or early summer of 1979 or 1980. I was mowing our small front lawn, which is raised a few feet above the sidewalk. Brick walls, punctuated by concrete front steps, line the block. A few yards down the street, an African American man whom I guessed to be in his thirties leaned against a car, occasionally walking up and down the block and resting on a wall. He was clearly disoriented. I watched him for some time, wondering what to do. Should I call the police? No, they might beat him up (Philadelphia police were reputedly tough on black men). Should I go in the house and get my dog and then go talk to him? After about half an hour, I was disgusted with myself. This was a fellow human being in trouble on a bright, warm afternoon. Why was I so hesitant—even afraid?

I approached and asked if he needed help. He asked for a glass of water, which I fetched. Then he said he was trying to reach his brother's apartment; the address belonged to a building around the corner. He was a Vietnam vet. He had been to the nearby VA Hospital, where he had been given either the wrong amount of medication or the wrong medication, which had left him disoriented. He had stopped in the bathroom of a church but forgot to retrieve his bag, which held his wallet. He did not know where he was. I took him to his brother's apartment; later that evening he rang our doorbell to thank me. For what did I merit thanks, I wondered.

The most disheartening part of the episode followed when I told friends and neighbors about it. Their response—that I deserved praise—seemed exactly wrong, given my long hesitation, and only underscored the distance, fear, and ignorance underlying the response of even liberal professionals and the separation of Philadelphians by class and race. So much had come together in the incident that I did not understand, but I could not find a single book that offered a comprehensive history of post–World War II American cities and explained what was then called the urban crisis. The issue was much on my mind; it was one of the factors that influenced me to take on the directorship of the undergraduate Urban Studies Program at Penn shortly thereafter and create a course that would look holistically at modern American cities. Over more than twenty years, I have taught the course many times, understanding more at each iteration, but never really the whole story.

Herbert's trial, which took place more than two decades after the incident on my street, also encapsulated what I had been struggling to understand and write about. Converging on the histories of Herbert and Shorty, although I was missing many details, were deindustrialization, white flight, racial segregation and concentrated poverty, the failures of urban education, a job market that excluded an extraordinary share of black men, the ravages of drugs, the importance of the informal economy, and a criminal justice system that in practice values the lives of black men less than mine or those of my family and friends. If I could gather more details, I thought, perhaps I could make real—more concrete—the subjects of my research.

But it is more than a matter of making experience concrete. Most research and writing plucks a thread from the fabric of experience. Historians and social scientists write about the welfare state, unemployment, single-parent families. They focus on particular problems and policies. When looked at from the experience of men like Herbert and Shorty, however, the borders of these distinctions melt into one another. Real lives do not divide into neat compartments. How to capture that lived reality is the challenge. I hoped that learning and thinking more about the men and the trial would bring me closer to an understanding.

Urbanist Mike Davis, in his book *Planet of Slums*, talks about the dramatic growth of social isolation in cities around the globe, most notable in Third World cities but clearly visible in the United States as well.[7] I had been reading Davis's book before the trial. With it in mind, the events laid before the jury brought powerful confirmation of its thesis. The events took place a few miles from my home. Similar confrontations, hardly meriting notice in the press, happen all the time even closer. Other than the frisson of fear they occasionally engender in respectable citizens, they might as well be in another city. An invisible veil reinforced in suburbs by gated communities, in cities by security systems, police, and segregation, separates comfortable Americans from what happens on West Oakland Street. They don't know, and they don't really want to. But they should. That is why the story of this mundane trial matters.

Ignorance results in stereotypes, which in turn breed contempt and easy dismissal of "the undeserving poor." It reinforces the racial and economic segregation that turn far too many Americans into second-class citizens. It lets us celebrate an alleged renaissance of American cities, conveniently forgetting vast swatches of empty factories, sites of buildings returned to fields of weeds, boarded-up houses, and lives stunted by poverty right in the shadow of shiny new office towers. The attempt to expand the meaning of Herbert's trial and to reconstruct its context is, therefore, not an academic exercise or merely a quest for personal understanding. It radiates outward, provoking questions that should trouble all Americans. We owe ourselves—not to mention Herbert and the memory of Shorty—nothing less.

I needed to talk to Herbert. I had to know more about at least one of the men cast as leads in this awful story. His attorney kindly contacted him to ask if he would talk with me. He agreed.

I had arranged to meet Herbert on Friday, June 8, 2007, at 12:30 where he lived on Hartshorn Street. I arrived early and drove around the neighborhood, both to get a sense of it and to locate some places for lunch. It is a North Philadelphia neighborhood just a few blocks south of Temple University Hospital. Hartshorn is a narrow street (about the width of one car) of old row houses. A number of vacant lots dot the neighborhood where houses have been torn down on adjacent streets. A small convenience store stands on the corner of Hartshorn and Grove. It was doing a brisk trade. The day was hot, and lots of people were hanging out on stoops and in the street. I had more than a little trepidation after parking the car on Grove Street and realizing I had to get out and walk to Herbert's front door with all eyes on me, this strange white guy with a blue short-sleeve button-down shirt and a backpack over a shoulder. It felt like walking into a scene from *The Wire*.

A small iron gate blocked the steps of Herbert's house from the street. I unlatched it and rang the bell. A woman, probably in her sixties, answered and asked me in. Herbert was in the living room; he had forgotten it was Friday. But he remembered I'd called, and he put on a shirt. The room was small, cluttered with overstuffed furniture, lived in. When I asked Herbert where he would like to eat, he said let's just go for a ride. Later he told me that his landlady, who wanted to be more than a landlady, stuffed him with food and gave him a hard time if he didn't return hungry. But once in the car he wanted to head to Fifth and Spring Garden, the neighborhood where he had grown up. He had in mind a diner that had closed some months prior—I had forgotten it was no longer open. As we headed south and east, my cell phone rang. It was William Gray, Herbert's attorney, who wanted to make sure we had met and were getting along. We ended up at Fifth and Girard at a small restaurant on the corner. I took pleasure when Herbert, a professional driver, praised my parallel parking. The restaurant worked well—cool, with a corner booth, vacant, quiet, and clean. Herbert said he had been eating there for fifty years, although not recently.

Herbert ran into trouble with the law in New Jersey. For about twelve years since retiring, he had been running an informal hack business based at the corner of Grove and Hartshorn. One day before his fatal encounter with Shorty, he drove a woman to New Jersey thinking she was going for a job interview. She turned out to be a pickpocket and was nabbed by the police. He was also blamed, although he had not left the car. To make matters worse, he made an illegal U-turn and got caught by the police. The New Jersey parole authorities confiscated his license and were holding it until he paid his fine, which was about three thousand dollars—an immense sum for him. He hoped to have it paid off by the end of the year. In the meantime, he felt bereft, trapped in the house with nothing to do. He paid the landlady three hundred dollars a month for a room, three meals, and laundry. I could not tell if they had a romantic relationship, or if she just wanted to marry him. He described her as a good woman, extremely devout, who dragged him to church every week. He did not want to incur her wrath by not going. She sang in the choir and had, he claimed, a beautiful voice. One of his dilemmas was how far to take the relationship with his landlady. He did not live with her before his trial, even though she wanted him to, because he wasn't ready to accept her domination and intense religiosity. She suffocated him sometimes, he said, and seemed more like his mother. But he liked her very much.

Herbert remained obsessed with his arrest, imprisonment, and trial. Over and over again he wanted to justify his action. He claimed to have liked Shorty and to have never seen him so completely wild. He could not believe Shorty went berserk over five dollars, and he attributed it to drugs. Shorty, he said, claimed he was going to kill him. Herbert thought he was going to die and began to resign himself, until the thought that it was a ridiculous way to die snapped him out of his resignation.

For Herbert, taking action proved a matter of self-respect as well as survival even though the arrest, incarceration, and trial proved a nightmare. He said he always believed in God, but that his acquittal had intensified his faith. When the verdict was announced, he recalled, he could have died at peace on the spot.

Faith, he asserted, is a central element of his life, and he does not take drugs or drink alcohol. His only vice is smoking. To save money for his fine, he had cut back to ten cigarettes a day. People in the neighborhood tell him he did what he had to do, but they are wary of him. Killing Shorty has given him a helpful reputation. He described the neighborhood as a "jungle" where people concerned only with pursuing money could earn tens of thousands of dollars a day. He wouldn't say exactly what people did to survive, and I did not push him. I asked him if he was safe in the neighborhood. He said yes, that because of his reputation, nobody bothered him.

He was happy to talk with me. For a long time he had wanted a chance to talk about the events and his feelings. So, as useful as the interview was for me, for him it was cathartic. He proved more articulate, with a broader vocabulary, than I had anticipated. He asked about my interest, and I explained as best I could. My sense is that he understood perfectly and sympathized. He repeated over and over again that one can't understand what it is/was like unless one has lived it. I am sure he is right about this. Yet, an implicit tension ran through our conversation. Herbert did not seem uneasy, but he was wary, willing to give information about himself, but with limits I could sense. I wanted to press him for more details or to expand on what appeared to be contradictions or improbabilities. But I knew that to press too hard would violate his boundaries and end our relationship.

After lunch—I found out that Herbert likes to eat turkey and to fish—during which he sketched his life story, we drove around the neighborhood in which Herbert had grown up. By now, he had loosened up and, I think, had begun to trust me. He enjoyed being the teacher, my shepherd through a Philadelphia I did not know. He pointed out to me where friends had lived, where local stores and bars had stood, and the former locations of small manufacturing firms. The area is a mixture of expensive gentrification and unrenovated row houses. Herbert claimed that the gentrified houses are mostly occupied by unmarried teachers, principals, and social workers. He said the neighborhood is so safe, still, that he would sleep with his windows open. He attributes the safety to the presence of the police who are responsive to the wealthy new homeowners. We encountered a street mechanic, an obviously strong man and friend, whom Herbert claims has been working at the same locale for thirty years. Herbert, like Sudhir Venkatesh in *Off the Books*, described an informal economy, a world in which people scratched out a living, doing whatever it took to make some money and survive.[8]

The tour went through the Richard Allen Homes, formerly a high-rise public housing project, now an attractive town-house development, still public housing. Herbert talked about how awful the projects were when he was growing up, with fights going on 24/7. Everyone had to join a gang to survive. Only then there were no guns; all the guys went to gyms to learn to box.

I liked Herbert a lot. I enjoyed his sly, deadpan humor. He seemed to find it increasingly easy to talk with me, and, as noted earlier, thanked me for the chance to talk. I was going to give him twenty dollars—it was in an envelope with his name on it in my pocket—but I didn't. By the end of our time together, it felt inappropriate, as though it would turn what was almost a budding friendship into something else and might violate his sense of self-respect, which clearly remains crucial to him. Herbert did not want me to drive him within sight of his street and the crowd on the corner. So I dropped him off some blocks away.

How much could I believe Herbert? He seemed immensely credible. But, then, he wanted to give me a best impression. Why, I wondered, was he hungry and in need of five dollars for food when his lady friend lived a ten-minute walk away? Why did he not ask her for the money to repay Shorty? With so many children and grandchildren, why had he remained in prison—was he denied bail? Why was he alone at his trial? Clearly, there is a lot more to his story. But it does not take away from his special charm or the urgency of his need for exculpation.

When we sat in the restaurant, across a table in a corner booth from each other, I could not help but think, "Here we are, two sixty-eight-year-old men, residents of the same city, with life histories that could not be more different" (although in one way they weren't different; we both married young and had our first child at age twenty). How, really, to explain why I live a comfortable, rewarding life as a university professor while he scrapes by on SSI on a dangerous block of North Philadelphia? It is not because I had two loving parents and he did not. So cancel that stereotype. It is not because he lacks intelligence, because he doesn't. If he is to be believed, it is not because he was unwilling to work hard. To say that he is black and I am white is not enough, although it is important. I suspect that part of the answer does lie in the barriers facing black men, especially men of his generation and older. But part, too, lies in the history of the city, whose inequalities, indifference, segregation, and economic devastation are traced in the lives of Herbert and his contemporaries. As we drove through his old neighborhood, Herbert remarked that his large circle of boyhood friends was gone. "Do you mean that they left?" I asked. "No," he answered. "They're dead."

*   *   *

The rest of this book opens up some of the themes condensed into this one story of murder and marginalization in an old American city. It is a story that cannot be interpreted apart from the transformation of American cities in the late twentieth century and the emergence of new urban forms unlike any others in history. Nor can it be understood apart from the trajectory of African American social structure, which opened up class and gender divisions among blacks, leaving men like Herbert and Shorty outside the regular labor market, relegated to semi-licit work and the charity of the state or prison, while others, like Barack Obama, ascended to heights unimaginable only a few decades earlier. It provokes an uncomfortable confrontation with questions of authority and legitimation. Why is it that black men who are unable to leave bleak inner-city neighborhoods have turned their rage inward on one another and not, as they did forty and fifty years ago, on the agents and symbols of a politics, culture, and economy that exclude them from first-class citizenship? For centuries, American discourse about poverty has divided poor people into categories based on their assumed moral worth. Herbert and Shorty belonged to the long line of the "undeserving poor." They epitomized the urban "underclass" that terrified Americans in the 1980s and 1990s. By the early twenty-first century, however, cutting-edge technologies of poverty were jettisoning pathological constructions of poor people. As new poverty warriors tossed the "underclass" on the trash heap of intellectual history, where were Herbert and Shorty left standing? Did they join the new world of the entrepreneurial poor, or did they find themselves in a no-man's-land, for all practical purposes (and except for prison) abandoned by the state and philanthropy but not invited to shop in the new store stocked with market-based plans for reducing poverty? In the end, Herbert and Shorty found themselves caught in the collision between urban transformation and rightward-moving social politics. It is this collision that underlies my attempt to expand the story of Herbert and Shorty's fatal encounter beyond the badlands of North Philadelphia.

Chapter 1

What Is an American City?

For many years I have argued that in the decades after World War II, economic, demographic, and spatial transformations in the United States resulted in an urban form unlike any other in history. Recently, I have realized that in one important way this formulation of recent urban history misleads. For it reports the outcome of history as singular when it should be plural. That is, "form," should be "forms"—an unprecedented configuration of urban places that calls into question the definition of "city" itself. One configuration is represented by the deindustrialized landscape of destitution that is a short, straight ride up Broad Street from the new, revitalized core of Center City Philadelphia. This landscape where Herbert Manes killed Shorty on the night of August 4, 2005, was one face of early twenty-first-century American cities pointed out by dystopian urban critics, but there were other faces as well.

The April 25, 2006, death of Jane Jacobs was one of the events that prompted me to rethink the assumptions underlying my narrative of recent urban history. If any one person can be anointed patron saint of Urban Studies, Jane Jacobs deserves the crown. Her 1961 *Death and Life of Great American Cities* certainly must be the most widely read and influential book ever written about American cities.[1] After half a century, it retains its powerful impact. I have often assigned it to students, who invariably find it moving and convincing. *Death and Life* resonates with their ideal of urbanism and gives them a set of criteria for identifying a good city. With the book as a yardstick, they find that today's cities come up short. Although the book has the same effect on me—new delights emerge every time I reread it—recently, I have begun to wonder if it does as much to inhibit as to advance our grasp of American cities today. Its identification of mixed-use, short blocks, multi-age dwellings, and density as the crucial ensemble of features that define a healthy neighborhood finds its model in old cities such as Philadelphia, New York, Boston, and many of the cities of Europe. At least implicitly, this makes the goal of urban reform recapturing the past. Yet the growing, dynamic, vibrant components of urban America are more like Phoenix and Los Angeles than the old East Coast cities. With Jacobs's criteria, they never can qualify as good cities; mutant forms of urbanism, they repel rather than attract anyone who loves cities. But is this a useful assessment? Is the fault with these cities or with the criteria? Did Jacobs bequeath us a core set of ideas that define urbanism, or do we need a different set of markers to characterize what makes a city—and a good city—in early twenty-first-century America? Certainly, the former—the belief in a core set of ideas defining healthy urbanism—underlies one of the most influential urban design movements of today: New Urbanism. New Urbanism does not take Jacobs's criteria literally, although her spirit clearly marches through its emphasis on density, mixed residential and commercial use, pedestrian-friendly streets, and vibrant public spaces. Its charter defines a set of core principles it considers adaptable to a wide array of places, from suburbs to shopping malls.[2] The other view, which finds New Urbanism an exercise in nostalgia that is out of touch with the forces driving urban change, is represented by Robert Bruegmann in his 2005 book *Sprawl: A Compact History*, where he approvingly cites architectural writer Alex Krieger who "persuasively argues that the New Urbanism is only the latest version of a long-standing desire by cultural elites to manage middle-class urban life."[3]

Even more than Jacobs's death, what forced me to confront the protean quality of today's urbanism and the inadequacy of singular definitions grew out of research and writing a book on the twentieth century, *One Nation Divisible: What America Was and What It Is Becoming*, coauthored with Mark J. Stern.[4] Stern and I set out to examine how the 2000 U.S. Census reflected social and economic trends during the twentieth century. We concluded that America is living through a transformation as profound as the industrial revolution—one that reshapes everything, from family to class, from race and gender to cities. Events on the ground— the trends we identified and discussed—have undermined the concepts with which we interpret public life: work, city, race, family, nationality. All of them have lost their moorings in the way life is actually lived today. Their conventional meanings lie smashed, badly in need of redefinition.

The same situation occurred during the transition from the nineteenth to the twentieth century, when an emergent industrial civilization, also based on a global economy, shattered existing ideas, producing, among other changes, a new urban form: the industrial city. "'Modern industry,' is almost equivalent to 'city life,' " observed University of Chicago sociologist Charles Henderson in 1909, "because the great industry, the factory system, builds cities around the chimneys of steam engines and electric plants."[5] The emergence of this new urban form—the industrial city—energized late nineteenth and early twentieth-century social science and reform. With their focus on applied research, social scientists in both Europe and the United States tried to figure out how to respond to the problems of housing, poverty, public health, employment, and governance posed by this new entity, which they understood only imperfectly. Others, such as Max Weber and Georg Simmel, searched for its essence as they advanced new theories of the city. In the United States, the attempt to define the industrial city culminated in the work of the Chicago School, which based its model on the interaction of industrial change, immigration, and social geography.[6] Geographer Peirce Lewis calls this urban form, described "in any sixth-grade geography book written before the [Second World] war" as the "nucleated city":

> The railroad station was the gateway to the city, and the land with the highest value clustered nearby—occupied, quite naturally, by high-bidding commercial establishments. There the biggest cities built skyscrapers, visible monuments to the high value of center-city land. Industries located near the railroad track because it was the most economical place to receive raw materials and ship out finished products. Poor people lived in disagreeable areas near the edge of the commercial district, or, more commonly, close to their place of industrial employment, often under squalid circumstances in the shadow of belching chimneys. With the help of trolley cars, affluent people moved to the outer edges of the city, or, if they could afford it, to a nearby suburb. But even suburbanites had to live near railroad stations, and even the most affluent suburbs were necessarily fairly compact.[7]

This nucleated city and its compact suburbs no longer exist. What has taken their place?

My point that we need new answers to the question "What is an American city?" is hardly original. Poke around just a little in current writing about cities, and it pops up, either explicitly or by implication. A keen observer, in fact, could find the dissolution of conventional urban form described much earlier than the closing decades of the twentieth century. In his monumental 1961 jeremiad, *The City in History*, Lewis Mumford asked, "What is the shape of the city and how does it define itself? The original container has completely disappeared: the sharp division between city and country no longer exists."[8] In the same year (which is also, remarkably, the same year Jacobs's *Death and Life* was published), geographer Jean Gottman used the term *Megalopolis*, the title of his massive book, to describe the "almost continuous stretch of urban and suburban areas from southern New Hampshire to northern Virginia and from the Atlantic shore to the Appalachian foothills." Within this territory, the "old distinctions between rural and urban" did not apply any longer. As a result, within Megalopolis, "we must abandon the idea of the city as a tightly settled and organized unit in which people, activities, and riches are crowded into a very small area clearly separated from its non-urban surroundings." Although Megalopolis was most developed in the northeastern United States, it represented the future of the world.[9] More recently, in his iconoclastic history of sprawl, urbanist Robert Bruegmann observed:

> In the affluent industrialized world since the economic upturn of the 1970s a great many cities have been turned inside out in certain respects as the traditional commercial and industrial functions of the central city have been decanted to the edges while the central city and close-in neighborhoods have come to be home to an increasingly affluent residential population and a high-end service economy. With the penetration of urban functions into the country side, the old distinctions between urban, suburban, and rural have collapsed.[10]

Pronouncements by authorities are one way to illustrate the need to redefine what "city" means in the early twenty-first century. Another emerges clearly from contrasting actual cities. Philadelphia and Los Angeles provide especially apt comparisons because they embody the old and the new urban America.

A Tale of Two Cities

In 1900, Philadelphia typified urban America.[11] The ecology of America's third-largest city was a classic example of the urban ecology codified by the Chicago School of sociologists—concentric zones based on class and economic function, dotted by pockets of ethnic and racial concentration, radiating out from a central city—or of Peirce's "nucleated city." With its diversified manufacturing base, Philadelphia was an industrial powerhouse. By 2000, Philadelphia had slipped from second- to fifth-largest American city, while Los Angeles had skyrocketed from thirty-sixth to second. At the start of the twenty-first century, Los Angeles defined American urbanization. In *The Next Los Angeles*, Robert Gottlieb and his colleagues observe, "To understand the future of America, one needs to understand Los Angeles. Nearly every trend that is currently transforming the United States . . . has appeared in some form in Los Angeles."[12] This new megalopolis was shaped by the automobile rather than the railroad, which, along with the streetcar, had done so much to define America's industrial cities in the nineteenth and early twentieth centuries. Los Angeles's heterogeneous population—far more diverse than Philadelphia's ever was—had arrived from around the globe as well as from all over America. Los Angeles's sprawling, multicentered, multiethnic regional development stood in dramatic contrast to the old, single, dense core surrounded by residential zones and a suburban periphery, exemplified by the Philadelphia region. Even though service industries dominated its economy to an unprecedented degree, Los Angeles probably was America's most important twentieth-century industrial city. At midcentury, its aerospace industry replaced Pennsylvania's shipbuilders as the heart of the military-industrial complex, while factory jobs migrated from the Northeast and Midwest to the South, West, and overseas. Los Angeles emerged as a major center in the Pacific basin and an important player in the global economy. Philadelphia, on the other hand, could not surmount its place as a second-order city on the international stage.

The contrast between Philadelphia and Los Angeles reflected not only changes in the two cities over time but America's divergent regional history. Phoenix, Houston, Las Vegas, and other Sunbelt cities more or less followed the Los Angeles model and grew rapidly. Old industrial cities, like Philadelphia, Baltimore, and Detroit, lost manufacturing jobs and population.

Although Philadelphia did not begin to lose manufacturing jobs in the aggregate until after 1950, industrial restructuring had begun to undermine its older manufacturing sectors early in the twentieth century. Philadelphia's mills started to shift to the non-union South in the 1920s, and shipbuilding, a huge industry early in the century, was a shadow of its former self in 1950. As a share of the workforce, employment in textiles dropped by nearly two-thirds between 1900 and 1940. The experience of the steel, machine tools, locomotive, steam engine, and railroad industries followed the same trajectory.

To some extent, new industries temporarily replaced the old ones. These included consumer-oriented manufacturing, such as auto assembly and food processing, as well as firms participating in the "second industrial revolution" of chemicals and electronics. The Philadelphia region also played an important role in the radio and early computer industries. But these newer industries lacked the local base of the older manufacturing firms. They were, instead, often branch plants of national or international corporations such as RCA and Westinghouse that pulled out of the region to chase cheaper land and labor in the South, Mexico, or Southeast Asia.

Philadelphia never successfully replaced its industrial economy. Service sector growth, while important, never catapulted the Delaware Valley into a competitive spot in the global economy, and its major service sector employers, like its midcentury manufacturers, are usually branch offices of corporations headquartered elsewhere. Public sector employment also became increasingly important. Employment by the federal government multiplied from 1.7 percent to 3.6 percent of the regional workforce between 1950 and 1970 before falling back to 1.9 percent as federal aid to cities declined. To some extent, employment in local government compensated for the federal withdrawal; its share of employment increased from 1.3 percent in 1980 to 1.9 percent in 2000. Where the Philadelphia region grew jobs was in education and health care. Employment in educational services jumped from 1.8 percent in 1950 to 7.9 percent in 2000. Jobs in hospitals multiplied from 1.4 percent of the regional workforce in 1940 to 4.2 percent in 2000. The Delaware Valley's universities and medical schools, not its factories, had become its anchor institutions—major economic assets. Los Angeles followed a very different economic path in the twentieth century. As happened elsewhere in America, agriculture became less important. By the middle of the twentieth century, it accounted for only 1.2 percent of employment in the city. This straightforward decline, however, masks an important change that distinguished the Southwest from the Atlantic Coast: the rise and extent of migrant labor.[13] Mexicans harvested fruits and vegetables; Japanese immigrants dominated the cultivation and trade in flowers. Los Angeles may have acquired the image of an entertainment and leisure paradise, but its reality was industrialization, which included food processing. In the 1920s, Los Angeles's population more than doubled and then increased even more with the dust bowl migration of the 1930s and the great migration of African Americans in the decades following World War II. By 1935, Los Angeles had catapulted to fifth-largest manufacturing center in the United States. Its major industries included cinema, petroleum drilling and refining, and aircraft and automobile assembly. It was second in the manufacture of tires, and fourth in apparel and furniture. With the Cold War and wars in the Pacific—Korea to Vietnam—Los Angeles emerged at the apex of the military-industrial complex. From 1940 to 1970, as its population tripled to ten million, it led all other metropolitan areas in manufacturing growth. At its peak in 1980, aircraft production accounted for 3 percent of regional employment; with military cutbacks and outsourcing, that fraction had declined to 1.3 percent in 2000. According to one informed estimate, each defense sector job generated 1.5 to 2.5 jobs in other local sectors of the economy. Los Angeles's manufacturing preeminence resulted not only from high-tech industries. A large local electronics sector consisted of assembly plants paying low wages to documented and undocumented Asian immigrant workers.

Southeast Asians dominated electronics, while Latin Americans engaged in low-wage work for new sweatshops in the apparel industry, which elsewhere had largely fled the United States.

By the late twentieth century, however, services dominated Los Angeles's economy. Banking, insurance, and various other business services became increasingly important, as they did in Philadelphia. Real estate, though, employed a larger fraction of the workforce than it did in Philadelphia, as did entertainment and recreation. Although employment in higher education and medicine also multiplied, Los Angeles—with its robust manufacturing and high-end services—did not depend on educational and health services as much as Philadelphia. Los Angeles also differed from Philadelphia in the role of public administration. In 2000, local public administration employed 1.9 percent of the region's adults—roughly half the share in the Philadelphia area. In part, the lesser importance of public employment in Los Angeles reflected the city's more buoyant private sector. In part, too, it grew out of differences in priorities, which resulted in more privatized police forces, garbage collection, and services for gated communities in greater Los Angeles than there were in the Delaware Valley.

Across the twentieth century, Philadelphia and Los Angeles differed dramatically in their ability to attract new residents. Between 1900 and 1940, no more than 26 percent of Los Angeles residents reported being born in California—most of the rest had arrived from the East, the Midwest, and Mexico. In 2000, only 45 percent were native Californians. Migration from elsewhere in the United States had slowed, but more than 16 percent had been born in Mexico, and 5 percent had been born in Central America. In 1900, Los Angeles's population was, officially, 98 percent non-Hispanic white; in 2000, the majority was Latino. Asians outnumbered African Americans. Spanish was the first language of 35 percent of Angelenos, a close second to English (42 percent), with Chinese (2.8 percent) and Filipino/Tagalog (2.2 percent) third and fourth, respectively. Los Angeles represented the multicolored, multiracial future of America.

Philadelphia, by contrast, remained to a considerable extent black and white, with shades of other hues working their way in after about 1980. The great migrations of African Americans and Puerto Ricans, when Herbert's parents arrived in the city, were Philadelphia's principal migration events in the last half of the twentieth century. In the late twentieth century, between seventy and eighty of every one hundred Delaware Valley residents had been born in Philadelphia or New Jersey. In 1900, immigrants from Ireland composed 7 percent of the region's population, followed by newcomers from England (3 percent) and Italy (2 percent).

Although after 1950 no immigrant group accounted for more than 1 percent of the region's population counted in the census, in the late twentieth century, immigrants from Asia (including India) and Latin America (mainly Mexico) had begun to transform a number of city neighborhoods and even some suburbs. By 2000, 9 percent of the city's population was foreign-born—a proportion that would be considerably larger with the inclusion of their children and undocumented immigrants. Compared to Los Angeles, Philadelphia was a low-immigrant city, lacking the opportunities that attracted newcomers to the great urban immigrant magnets. Nonetheless, by every indication, immigration, whose presence was increasingly evident, was making itself felt in the city's neighborhoods, schools, and workplaces, creating tensions not experienced for nearly a century.[14]

The contrasts between Philadelphia's and Los Angeles's economic and population histories played themselves out in space. Population density in Philadelphia, for instance, has always been much higher than in Los Angeles.[15] Its downtown high-rises surrounded by vast areas of row houses contrast with the "suburban cities" of the Los Angeles region, the latter of which inspired sociologist William Whyte, author of *The Organization Man*, to coin the term "urban sprawl." The Los Angeles region's suburban central cities have retained a relatively constant share of the area's population: 51 percent in 1940, 36 percent in 1990. Philadelphia, by contrast, lost population to the suburbs during the entire twentieth century. The fraction of the regional population living in the city declined from 60 percent in 1940 to 25 percent in 2000.

Railroads and streetcars shaped urbanization in the East and Midwest in the nineteenth and early twentieth centuries. The automobile welded together the components of Los Angeles, which led all other American cities in automobile registration and use in the 1920s. As Los Angeles's outer counties surpassed Los Angeles County in population growth during the last decades of the twentieth century, they inspired a new urban vocabulary: "regional urbanization," "exopolis," "flexcity." Both the Philadelphia and Los Angeles regions, however, remain highly segregated by class, race, and ethnicity. In the Delaware Valley, segregation still largely follows the old model of the Chicago School of sociology. Lower- and middle-income minorities live in row houses and publicly subsidized housing in the inner cities and inner-ring suburbs. In the second half of the twentieth century, much of Philadelphia's white middle class departed for the suburbs, with minorities composing the majority—45 percent white, 43 percent black, 5 percent Asian, and 7 percent Hispanic. The city of Philadelphia is much more diverse than its region, whose minorities remain concentrated at its center.

The Chicago School model does not apply to Southern California. After World War II, African Americans created what has been called the nation's "first large suburban ghetto" in South Central Los Angeles. In East Los Angeles, poor Mexicans live in detached, single-family, ranch-style homes more characteristic of suburbs than cities. The ethnic clusters known as Koreatown, Little Saigon, and a new Chinatown are distinctively suburban in population density and housing styles. At the same time, freeways, airports, and manufacturing corridors separate the suburbs populated by middle- and upper-income white workers in Orange, Ventura, and western Los Angeles County from South Central and East Los Angeles. "Los Angeles in the 1960s," urbanist Robert Gottlieb and his colleagues write, "represented an unusual mix of urban decline and suburban expansion, to the point that Los Angeles appeared to lose any appearance of the classical 'city.'"[16] Philadelphia represents a city surrounded by suburbs, Los Angeles a product of "suburban urbanization," where center and periphery meld into sprawling cities that lack a meaningful center. The stark contrasts between Philadelphia and Los Angeles—their diverse regional histories, economic and demographic differences, and divergent social ecologies—pose an unavoidable question: In early twenty-first-century America, just what is a city?

Three Transformations

Despite their differences, Philadelphia and Los Angeles experienced the common transformations of economy, demography, and space that have resulted in new American cities. The decimation of manufacturing evident in Philadelphia and other Rust Belt cities resulted from both the growth of foreign industries, notably electronics and automobiles, and the corporate search for cheaper labor. Cities with economic sectors other than manufacturing (such as banking, commerce, medicine, government, and education) withstood deindustrialization most successfully—for example, New York, Miami, Los Angeles, the San Francisco Bay area, Chicago, Boston, and Houston. Those with no alternatives—Baltimore, Cleveland, Buffalo, St. Louis, Detroit—nearly collapsed. Others—Philadelphia, Pittsburgh, the Twin Cities—struggled with mixed success. Cities such as Las Vegas, Phoenix, Albuquerque, and in some ways New Orleans built economies on entertainment, hospitality, and retirement. As services replaced manufacturing everywhere, office towers became the late twentieth century's urban factories. A broad category, service embraces both demanding and rewarding jobs and low-wage, non-unionized employment that offers few benefits. In fortunate cities such as Los Angeles, new economic functions included the production of the financial and business services and products that served the emergent international economy. They also included, again notably in Los Angeles, the reappearance of small-scale manufacturing drawing on inexpensive immigrant labor.[17]

Increasingly, "anchor institutions," notably "eds and meds," also sustained the economies of fortunate cities by becoming their principal employers. Late in the twentieth century in the nation's twenty largest cities, "eds and meds" provided nearly 35 percent of jobs.[18] These institutions—fixed in place, partnering with government, business, and civic sectors—hire thousands of workers and pump massive amounts of money through urban systems. They are often the largest employers in the cities in which they are located. And they have grown in size while manufacturing industries have failed or decamped. "Eds and Meds," concludes a 2009 report to HUD secretary Shaun Donovan by the Penn Institute for Urban Research, "are playing a crucial role in the economic vitality and competitiveness of their cities and surrounding regions. . . . Across the country, many Eds and Meds are the largest employers in their cities and also fuel local economies through construction dollars and the purchase of goods and services."[19]

The first urban demographic transformation was the migration of African Americans from the South to northern and midwestern, and even, to some extent, western cities. (As James Gregory has shown, in the same years more than twice as many white southerners also moved to the North and Midwest.)[20] From World War I to 1920, between seven hundred thousand and one million African Americans moved north, followed by another eight hundred thousand during the 1920s and five million more between 1940 and 1970. The results, of course, were profound. San Francisco's black population multiplied nearly twenty-five times between 1940 and 1970 while Chicago's grew five times, to take two examples. As African Americans moved into cities, whites moved out. Between 1950 and 1970, the overall population of American cities grew by ten million people, and the population of suburbs grew by eighty-five million.

As Herbert Gans's classic *The Levittowners* showed, even more than racial change, a severe urban housing shortage, a desire to escape urban congestion, and mass-produced suburban homes made affordable by federally insured, long-term, low-interest mortgages pulled whites from cities, where they sped to their suburban homes along the new interstate highway system.[21] However, aggressive and often unscrupulous realtors, fanning fears of racial change, played a role as well.[22] In the North and Midwest, the number of African American newcomers often did not equal the number of whites who left. As a result, city populations and density went down, returning swaths of inner cities to empty lots and weed-filled fields where once working-class housing and factories had stood—a process vividly captured by the great photographer Camilo José Vergara, who has documented the emergence of the "green ghetto" in Rust Belt America, where urban agriculture has emerged as a growth industry.[23] In the Sun Belt, in cities such as Los Angeles, population trends went in the opposite direction. Between 1957 and 1990, the Sun Belt's urban population, lured by economic opportunity and an appealing climate and boosted by annexation as well as in-migration, climbed from 8.5 to 23 million.

Massive immigration following changes to federal law in 1965 also transformed urban demography. Immigration was the human face of the economic globalization transforming cities around the world.[24] More immigrants entered the United States in the 1990s than in any other decade in its history. Three facts about this immigration stand out as especially important. First, it was diverse. Mostly from Asia and Latin America, immigrants altered the ethnic mix of America's population, most notably of its cities. They fueled most of the urban population growth that occurred during the 1990s.[25]

Four of five immigrants settled in metropolitan areas, clustering in "gateway" cities: New York, Miami, Los Angeles, and to some extent, Chicago. By 2000, although still clustered, they had begun to spread out across the nation, transforming suburbs and small as well as large cities. In 1910, 84 percent of the foreign-born in Greater Philadelphia lived in the central city. By 2006, the number had plummeted to 35 percent. Similar trends occurred everywhere. Across the nation, the suburbanization of immigration had become a major factor reshaping metropolitan geography. This suburbanization of immigration is the second important fact. Thanks to labor market networks in agricultural work, construction, landscaping, low-end manufacturing, and domestic service, Hispanics, in fact, spread out faster than any other ethnic group in American history.[26]

The third fact about the new immigration is that it is essential. In New York City, immigration accounted for all of the population growth in the 1990s. In his testimony before New York's City Council Committees on Small Business and Immigration, Jonathan Bowles, director of the Center for an Urban Future, reported on research which "concluded that immigrant entrepreneurs have become an increasingly powerful economic engine for New York City . . . foreign-born entrepreneurs are starting a greater share of new businesses than native-born residents, stimulating growth in sectors from food manufacturing to health care, creating loads of new jobs and transforming once-sleepy neighborhoods into thriving commercial centers."[27] Immigration also fueled growth and economic revitalization in small cities such as Chelsea and Lawrence, Massachusetts. Two officials of the Federal Reserve Bank of Boston reported that between 1990 and 2000, immigrants accounted for almost half of New England's population growth, and more in some states, such as Connecticut, where it was responsible for 76 percent of growth. "Overall, the region's population grew only 5.4 percent over the decade, but without foreign immigration, it would have been virtually stagnant."[28] The New Jersey Urban Revitalization Research Project reported, "*Immigration is reshaping many of New Jersey's older communities, and accounts for the greater part of the population growth of most cities experienced during the 1990s.*"[29] In metropolitan Philadelphia, immigration was the source of 75 percent of labor force growth between 2000 and 2006.[30]

Immigration, Mike Davis observes in *Magical Urbanism*, redefined urban space. "As emergent Latino pluralities and majorities outgrow the classic barrio," he writes, "they are remaking urban space in novel ways that cannot be assimilated to the earlier experiences of either African Americans or European immigrants." These Latino metropolises differ from one another in their "geometries," which Davis classifies with a provisional typology whose newest and unprecedented category, "city-within-a-city," represented by late twentieth-century Los Angeles, results from the intersection of immigration with the location of low-wage jobs.[31]

Immigration, suburbanization, and racial segregation transformed urban space. Suburban growth, which had begun much earlier, exploded in the years after World War II, with suburbs growing ten times faster than cities in the 1950s. Population, retailing, services, and industry all suburbanized. Suburbs remained predominantly white until late in the twentieth century, when African American suburbanization became an important trend, although even in the suburbs African Americans often clustered in segregated neighborhoods or dominated some suburban towns.[32]

The image evoked by the term "suburb" was never accurate. Constructed at various points in history, from the transportation revolution of the nineteenth century to the communications revolution of the late twentieth century, and reconstructed repeatedly by demographic, economic, social, and political change, places labelled "suburb" have always, in fact, varied. Long before World War II, suburbs were industrial as well as residential; they housed working-class as well as middle-class families; and they were home to many African Americans. In the post–World War II era, the massive building of new suburbs like Levittown, highway construction, cheap mortgages, and especially the GI Bill reinforced the popular meaning of "suburb" as a bedroom community populated mainly by families with children. By the last decades of the twentieth century, whatever uniformity had existed among suburbs shattered. A variety of suburban forms dotted metropolitan landscapes as social scientists and regional policy advocates scrambled to create new typologies that would capture the components of the new geography that had rendered the binary of city/suburb obsolete.[33]

Both gentrification and dramatic shifts in the balance among family types resulted in new domestic landscapes, further collapsing differences between city and suburb. Gentrification played modest counterpoint to urban renewal. Gentrification refers to rehabilitating working-class housing for use by a wealthier class. Movement into gentrified neighborhoods was not great enough to reverse overall population decline outside of select neighborhoods, but it did transform visible components of cityscapes as it attracted young white professionals with above-average incomes and empty nesters who demanded new services and amenities.

Young professionals and affluent empty nesters repopulating center cities signified transformations of family and life course that undermined old assumptions about urbanism by undermining distinctions between cities and suburbs through the creation of new domestic landscapes. Consider the revolutionary rebalancing of family types between 1900 and 2000. In both years, most people lived in one of four combinations of family and household type: married couples with children; female-headed households with children; empty-nest couples; and nonfamily households (unmarried young people living together). Over the course of the twentieth century, the relative proportions living in each household type changed dramatically. In 1900, married couples with children comprised 55 percent of all households, single-mother families 28 percent, empty-nest households 6 percent, and nonfamily households 10 percent, with a small remainder in different arrangements. By 2000, the proportions had changed: married couple households comprised 25 percent of all households, single-mother families 30 percent, empty-nest households 16 percent, and nonfamily households 25 percent.[34] (The relatively small increase in single-mother families masks an enormous change. Earlier in the century they mainly consisted of widows; late in the century they were mostly never married, separated, or divorced.)

This new balance among household types had accelerated with astonishing speed after 1970. One of its results was a new domestic landscape that changed the meaning of "suburbs." By 1970, more Americans lived in suburbs than in cities or rural areas. In these early years—captured brilliantly by Herbert Gans in *The Levittowners*—the suburbs' primary function was to provide housing for families with children.[35] During the last three decades of the twentieth century, suburban demography and function changed, with the result that cities and suburbs grew more alike.[36] Between 1970 and 2000, the proportion of suburban census tracts where married couples with children comprised more than half of all households plummeted from 59 percent to 12 percent and in central cities from 12 percent to 3 percent. By 2000, the great majority of suburbanites—including those in the Sun Belt as well as the Rust Belt— lived where married couples with children made up a small share of all families. Single mothers replaced many of these traditional families in both suburbs and cities. Between 1970 and 2000, the share of the suburban population living in census tracts where single-mother families made up at least 25 percent of all households leaped an amazing 440 percent—from 5 to 27 percent. In cities, it rose 84 percent—from 32 to 59 percent. As suburban populations aged, empty-nest households became more common. In suburbs, the share of the population aged sixty-five or older rose from 11 to 16 percent, a 45 percent increase—while it remained virtually the same, 18 percent compared to 17 percent, in central cities. The share of the suburban population living in census tracts where empty-nest households comprised more than 45 percent of all households shot up from 14 percent to 25 percent, while in central cities it dropped from 30 percent to 21 percent. In central cities, immigration combined with the increase in nonfamily and single-mother households to dampen the influence of population aging. Nonfamily households— young, unmarried people between eighteen and thirty-five living alone or without relatives—replaced traditional families in both cities and suburbs. Between 1970 and 2000, the share of the population living in census tracts where nonfamily households comprised at least 30 percent of all households rocketed from 8 to 35 percent in suburbs and from 28 to 57 percent in cities.

Figures 1.1 through 1.8 illustrate how these trends remapped domestic space. These maps show the change in the distribution of married-couple-with-children households and nonfamily households in metropolitan Atlanta and Boston between 1970 and 2000. Despite the differences between these Sun Belt and Rust Belt regions, trends were amazingly similar, showing the near disappearance of suburbs dominated by traditional families and the prominence everywhere of unrelated individuals living together.

A new domestic landscape emerged from these remapped household types. The concentration of young adults and empty nesters redefined urban economic zones. "Gentrification," in fact, is shorthand for the impact of changing family and household forms on urban space. Increased numbers of single mothers living in poverty shaped new districts of concentrated poverty in central cities and fueled a rise in suburban poverty, especially in suburbs that bordered on cities. At the same time,

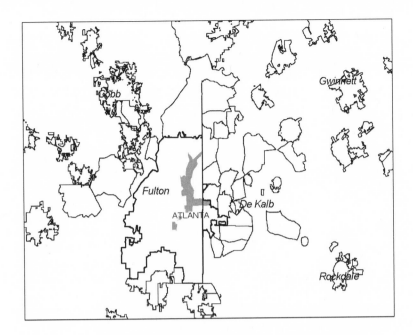

Figure 1 (*shaded areas*). Census tracts in which nonfamily households compose more than 40 percent of all households, metropolitan Atlanta, 1970.

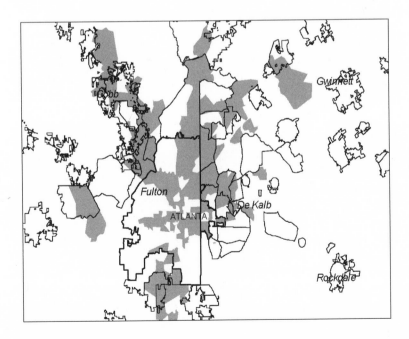

Figure 2 (*shaded areas*). Census tracts in which nonfamily households compose more than 40 percent of all households, metropolitan Atlanta, 2000.

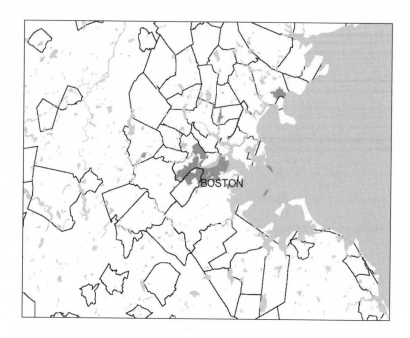

Figure 3 (*shaded areas*). Census tracts in which nonfamily households compose more than 40 percent of all households, metropolitan Boston, 1970.

Figure 4 (*shaded areas*). Census tracts in which nonfamily households compose more than 40 percent of all households, metropolitan Boston, 2000.

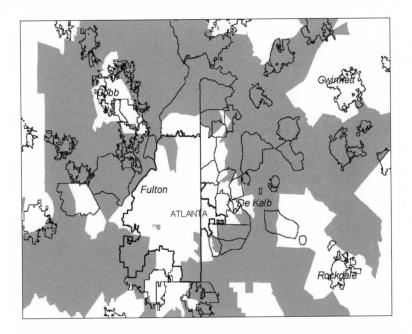

Figure 5 (*shaded areas*). Census tracts in which married couple with children households compose more than 50 percent of all households, metropolitan Atlanta, 1970.

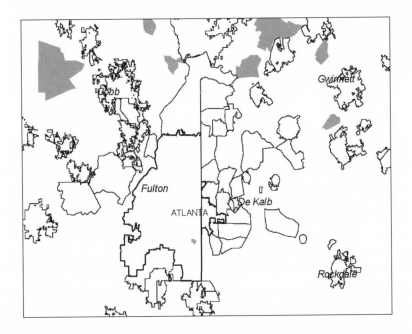

Figure 6 (*shaded areas*). Census tracts in which married couple with children households compose more than 50 percent of all households, metropolitan Atlanta, 2000.

Figure 7 (*shaded areas*). Census tracts in which married couple with children households compose more than 50 percent of all households, metropolitan Boston, 1970.

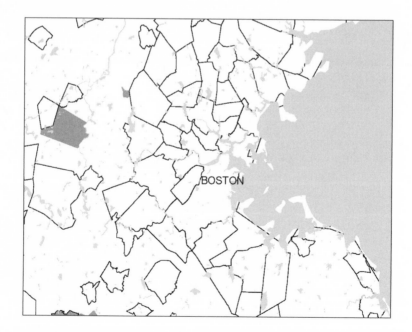

Figure 8 (*shaded areas*). Census tracts in which married couple with children households compose more than 50 percent of all households, metropolitan Boston, 2000.

by bringing young, working-class families back to several cities, immigration slowed the disappearance of traditional families and moderated the gulf separating gentrified neighborhoods from vast areas of concentrated poverty. Waves of immigration and industrial change had repeatedly rearranged the social geographies of cities. But the new domestic landscape demanded nothing less than a redefinition of suburban character and purpose. As the distinctions between city and suburb receded, the question "What is an American suburb?" emerged as the flip side of the question "What is an American city?"

Racial segregation also transformed urban space. Racial segregation was much higher in late than in early twentieth-century American cities. In 1930, the average African American lived in a neighborhood that was 31.7 percent black; by 1970, the percentage had jumped to 73.5. These were numbers never before experienced by any group, including the immigrants who poured into the United States in the late nineteenth and early twentieth centuries. Sociologists Douglas Massey and Nancy Denton described the situation, without exaggeration, as "American apartheid." Affluent as well as poor African Americans experienced extreme racial segregation. In northern metropolitan areas in 1980, Massey and Denton revealed, measures of segregation for African Americans with incomes of $50,000 remained as high as for those with incomes of $2,500. In sixteen metropolitan areas, one of three African Americans lived in conditions of such high segregation that Massey and Denton labeled them "hypersegregation."[37]

In the 1990s, although segregation in cities declined by an average of 5.5 percentage points, the average African American still lived in a census tract that was 51 percent black, while affluent African Americans were more likely to live near African Americans with modest incomes than near comparably well-off whites, and as Shorty's neighborhood underlined, many thousands of African Americans still lived in districts marked by the toxic combination of poverty and segregation.[38] Nonetheless, in the last third of the twentieth century, Massey and his colleagues show, a "new regime of residential segregation" began to emerge. Despite mass immigration from Asia, Latin America, and the Caribbean, overall levels of ethnic segregation did not rise. Measures of immigrant segregation remained "low to moderate" while, after 1970, "black segregation declined." As racial segregation lessened, "socioeconomic segregation rose, as indicated by rising levels of dissimilarity between the poor and the affluent and between the college educated and high school graduates, yielding spatial isolation among people at the top and bottom of the socioeconomic scale."[39]

Geography reflected income. After the mid-1970s, income and wealth inequality, as Chapter 2 explains in more detail, increased to levels not experienced for perhaps a century, and real wages declined despite rising productivity. "The fundamental reality," write urban scholars Peter Dreier, John Mollenkopf, and Todd Swanstrom, "is one of growing economic segregation in the context of overall rising inequality. People of different income classes are moving away from each other not just in how much income they have but also in where they live. America is breaking down into economically homogeneous enclaves." Growing economic as well as racial inequality registered on urban space as economic segregation among whites grew notably after the 1970s. Growing economic inequality marked suburbs as well as cities as inner-ring and older suburbs experienced the poverty, population decline, job loss, and infrastructure decay usually associated with inner cities. In the early twenty-first century, as many poor people lived in suburbs as in cities.[40]

In the decades after World War II, urban redevelopment also transformed city space as urban renewal displaced poor residents, usually without relocating them to alternate housing, and cleared downtown land for reuse as offices, retail sites, and homes for the affluent. Urban renewal resulted from the federal 1949 Housing Act, which authorized city governments to assemble large tracts of land by taking properties through eminent domain and selling them cheaply to developers. Its "goal was to revive downtown business districts by razing the slums, bringing new businesses into the core, and attracting middle-class residents back to the city." To rehouse families displaced by urban renewal, the 1949 law authorized 810,000 units of public housing. By 1960, only 320,000 had been built. This public housing, by and large, remained confined to segregated districts and never matched existing needs. "Between 1956 and 1972," observe Peter Dreier and his colleagues, "urban renewal and urban freeway construction displaced an estimated 3.8 million persons from their homes," rehousing only a small fraction. Urban renewal, they continue, "certainly changed the skyline of some big cities by subsidizing the construction of large office buildings that housed corporate headquarters, law firms, and other corporate activity." But it did so at a price, destroying far more "low-cost housing than it built," while doing little "to stem the movement of people and businesses to the suburbs or to improve the economic and living conditions of inner-city neighborhoods. On the contrary, it destabilized many of them promoting chaotic racial transition and flight."[41]

Destabilized cities marked by high concentrations of poverty and declining job opportunities for low-skilled workers proved fertile grounds for crime. By the late 1970s, the fear of collective violence aroused by the civil disturbances that began in the 1960s (discussed in Chapter 3) largely had given way to fears of murder, assault, and robbery reinforced by the outbreak of crack cocaine use in the 1980s, while within the segregated, impoverished cores of old cities, gangs fought each other, and black men like Herbert and Shorty killed each other (and, too often, innocent bystanders) in horrifying numbers. The number of violent crimes per 100,000 population, as reported by the FBI, rose from 160.9 in 1960 to 363.5 in 1970, 596.6 in 1980, and 729.6 in 1990 before reversing direction, declining to 506.5 in 2000 and 457.5 in 2008.[42] Although actual crime rates declined in the 1990s, crime continued to preoccupy city residents and dominate the image of city centers. After September 11, 2001, fear of terror also stoked anxieties about urban safety. One result was a preoccupation with security that transformed urban landscapes. "Fortress L.A." is the title of one chapter in Mike Davis's powerful dystopian analysis of Los Angeles, *City of Quartz*. "Welcome to post-liberal Los Angeles," he writes, "where the defense of luxury lifestyles is translated into a proliferation of new repressions in space and movement, undergirded by the ubiquitous 'armed response.' This obsession with physical security systems, and, collaterally, with the architectural policing of social boundaries, has become the zeitgeist of urban restructuring, a master narrative in the emerging built environment of the 1990s." One "universal and ineluctable consequence of this crusade to secure the city is the destruction of accessible public space."[43]

The securitization of urban space results from what geographer Stephen Graham, in *Cities Under Siege*, labels the new "military urbanism," whose technologies move back and forth between "Western cities and those on colonial frontiers." In both, "hard, military-style borders, fences, and check-points around defended enclaves and 'security zones' are proliferating. Jersey-barrier blast walls, identity check-points, computerized CCTV, biometric surveillance and military styles of access control and protected archipelagos of fortified social, economic, political or military centres from an outside deemed unruly, impoverished or dangerous." In Western cities, they are emerging "around strategic financial districts, embassies, tourist and consumption spaces, airport and port complexes, sports arenas, gated communities and export processing zones." The new military urbanism rests on a paradigm shift "that renders cities' communal and private spaces, as well as their infrastructure—along with their civilian populations—a source of targets and threats." Cities are "at war against drugs, against terror, against insecurity itself." A "complex mass of security and military thinkers . . . now argue that war and political violence centre overwhelmingly on the everyday spaces and circuits of urban life."[44] The military transformation of urban space normalizes the permanence of war as a feature of city life.

Clearly, by the early twenty-first century, economic, demographic, and spatial transformations had undercut existing definitions of "urban," "city," and "suburb." A variety of new urban metaphors competed to re-place them.

Urban Metaphors

One set of metaphors for "urban" and "city" looks inward toward central cities; another set looks outward from them; and one urban metaphor—the "fortress city" of Mike Davis and Stephen Graham—looks in both directions at once, its new spatial organization and architectural forms designed to protect against both internal insurgencies and external threats. Urban metaphors are not mutually exclusive. Sometimes the same writers use different metaphors to capture the increasingly fractured reality of "urban" or "city." All of them, however, try to make sense of the patterns of inequality that grew out of the economic, demographic, and spatial transformation of American cities in the second half of the twentieth century. The inward-looking metaphor that still very often comes first to mind is "inner city," which, since the 1960s, has served as short-hand for a bundle of problems—disorder, crime, drugs, poverty, home-lessness, out-of-wedlock births.[45] As a metaphor, "inner city" was colored poor and black. So pervasive did the image become that it spawned a new genre of popular culture, which diffused outward from inner cities to the American heartland. "Urban music," a category that includes "funk, soul and hip hop, as well as R and B" became "the biggest selling genre in the United States."[46]

"Post-industrial," another inward-looking metaphor, focused on the loss of urban manufacturing rather than, as with "inner city," demography and social structure. Political scientist John H. Mollenkopf identified a "profound transformation" that had "seriously eroded the nineteenth-century industrial city. For lack of a better term, it might be called 'the postindustrial revolution.' This second urban revolution grew out of and in many ways constituted a reaction against the first. If labor and capital concentrated into factories defined the industrial city, the postindustrial city is characterized by the geographic diffusion of production and popu-lation. The office building, not the factory, now provides the organizing institution of the central city."[47] Vivid though it was, "post-industrial's" an-alytic usefulness was limited. For it defined city by what it was not rather than by what it had become, thus limiting the idea's helpfulness in reinter-preting the emergent meaning of "urban" in the late twentieth and early twenty-first centuries.

"Dual city," a third inward-looking metaphor, focused on the social structure that had emerged from economic and demographic transforma-tion abetted by governments—federal, state, and local—that remapped the distribution of classes and functions across urban space and, through funding cuts, decimated services.[48] Growing class polarization, a problem everywhere in the nation (and, indeed, as Mike Davis shows, emerging in even more extreme forms around the globe), appeared most vividly in big cities.[49] Increasingly bereft of their middle class, city populations divided between rich and poor, the former buoyed by jobs in finance, information, and high-end services, the latter barely sustained by low-end service jobs, the informal economy, or government assistance. Writing in the *New York Times* in July 2006, economist Paul Krugman observed:

> The story of the New York economy isn't entirely a happy one. The city has essentially lost all of its manufacturing, and it's now in the process of outsourcing both routine office work and many middle-management functions to other parts of the country.
>
> What's left is an urban economy that offers a mix of very highly paid financial jobs and low-wage service jobs, with relatively little in the middle. Economic disparities in New York, as in the United States as a whole, are wider than they have been since the 1920's.[50]

This was the dual city. Its two worlds, the gleaming office towers and condos and the run-down housing and public ghettos of the poor, were not two separate spheres. Indeed, dual city theorists stressed the linkages that joined them—how they produced and depended on one another. Although the dual city metaphor, as its theorists recognized, oversimplified a very complicated situation, it had the virtue of directing attention to the new inequalities that define present-day cities, just as Jacob Riis's depiction of "How the Other Half Lives" captured the emerging industrial social structure a century ago.

Outward-looking metaphors link cities, metropolitan areas, regions, and even the world. "Historically," writes Robert Geddes, "two massive shifts of population have formed American city-regions. The farm-to-city shift after the Civil War is comparable to the massive city-to-suburb shift after World War II. Now more than half the nation's population lives in the suburbs. Although still separate legal jurisdictions, it no longer makes sense to talk of suburbs and cities as if they were separate; they are economically and ecologically joined in a new kind of human settlement, the city region."[51] A variety of metaphors—"city-region," "metropolitan area," "elastic/inelastic city," "galactic city"—try to capture the inadequacy of definitions that limit cities to their legal boundaries.

Three scholars and public intellectuals—David Rusk, Myron Orfield, and Bruce Katz—have led the effort to substitute "metropolitan" for narrowly bounded definitions of current-day cities. For them, the exercise is more than theoretical, because policies needed to counteract the baneful effects of metropolitan political fragmentation require an expanded definition of "city." No less concerned with inequality than dual city theorists, they focus more on economic and political disparities between central cities and their suburbs than on income gaps among city residents. Grossly unequal public services and tax burdens, environmental degradation, sprawl, racial segregation, job growth: these, they argue, only can be countered through metropolitan-wide actions.

Where city and suburb rubbed up against each other, they were becoming more alike. As urban problems spread outward, distinctions lessened, and the real differentiation existed between older inner suburbs and those further out on the periphery of metropolitan areas, which, themselves, could not remain immune from the urban problems attendant on growth. Just what a suburb was—what made it distinct—was no longer clear. Recognizing the inadequacy of the conventional city/suburb/rural distinction, the U.S. Census Bureau began to develop a reclassification of municipalities based on a sophisticated mathematical model.[52] A number of metropolitan metaphors tried to capture this new metropolitan configuration.

Historian Robert Fishman proclaimed the death of one metaphor—"bourgeois utopia," which represented the suburb as a sylvan residential enclave for affluent male commuters and their families. By the 1980s, he held, the classic suburb had been replaced by the "post-suburb" or "technoburb."[53] Others reclassified suburbs differently. Orfield, for one, divided them into six categories based on financial stress and age.[54] "Suburbia conceals as well as reveals its complexity," observes historian Dolores Hayden in *Building Suburbia*. "For years, when urban historians wrote about the 'city,' they meant the center, the skyline, downtown."[55] Looking closely, she identifies seven suburban patterns. Although the earliest date from before the Civil War, vestiges of all of them still exist. The most famous, or notorious, new suburban forms are Joel Garreau's "edge cities," massive configurations of office towers and malls at the crossroads of exurban highways, "A new frontier being shaped by the free, in a constantly reinvented land."[56] Recently, Robert E. Lang and his colleagues have identified "boomburbs," the "ultimate symbol of today's sprawling postwar metropolitan form." They are places "with more than 100,000 residents that are *not* the largest cities in their respective metropolitan areas and that have maintained double-digit rates of population growth in recent decades."[57] Others, focusing on the new suburbanization of immigration, have identified a suburban variant they call "ethnoburbs," "multiethnic communities in which one ethnic minority group has a significant concentration but does not necessarily constitute a majority."[58] Peirce Lewis has termed the new urban form that developed "far beyond the old urban fringe" the "galactic city," defined as "a city where all the traditional urban elements float in space like stars and planets in a galaxy, held together by mutual gravitational attraction but with large empty spaces in between. . . . This new galactic city is an urban creation different from any sort Americans have ever seen before."[59] With chain migration linking towns and villages in Latin America and the Caribbean with United States cities, Mike Davis writes of the creation of new suburban forms extending across national boundaries. "To the extent that the sending communities have become as fully integrated into the economy of the immigrant metropolis as their own nation-state . . . they are the de facto 'transnational suburbs' of New York, Los Angeles, Chicago and Miami. Indeed, they transform our understanding of the contemporary city."[60]

Metropolitan metaphors linked cities to their regions; global metaphors joined them to the world. Saskia Sassen, whose work set the agenda for debate on global cities, identifies a set of global cities at the pinnacle of new urban hierarchies, detached from their regions, connected, instead, to the world of international finance and trade. As "transnational market 'spaces,'" global cities have "more in common with one another than with regional centers in their own nation-states, many of which have declined in importance."[61] The "finance and producer services complex in each city," she asserts, "rests on a growth dynamic that is somewhat independent of the broader regional economy—a sharp change from the past, when a city was presumed to be deeply articulated with its hinterland."[62] Rather than regional centers, global cities are "command points in the organization of the world economy." Economic globalization has made great cities more relevant and important than ever, a point reinforced by a July 2006 report describing the movement of corporate headquarters *back* to New York City.[63]

In contrast to Sassen, Bruce Katz and his colleagues in the Brookings Institution's Metropolitan Policy Program emphasize economic regions that promote growth as well as higher wages. A regional industry cluster, write Brookings researchers, is "a geographic concentration of interconnected businesses, suppliers, service providers, and associated institutions in a particular field." These regional clusters "represent a powerful source of productivity and quality jobs at a moment of economic challenge." The federal government, they contend, "should play a central role in promoting cluster development and growth nationwide."[64]

Another outward-looking metaphor defines modern cities by what they produce. For Manuel Castells, the late twentieth-century "informational city" replaces the early twentieth-century "industrial city." To be sure, knowledge and information processing have been important to every mode of production. What distinguishes the informational mode "is the action of knowledge upon knowledge itself as the main source of productivity."[65] The informational city differs from Garreau's edge city, whose "primitive technological vision that sees the world through the simplified lenses of endless freeways and fiber-optic networks" misses "the core of the new urbanization process" in the United States. Unlike Garreau and Sassen, Castells stresses the interdependence of edge cities and the "functional interdependence" among "different units and processes in a given urban system over very long distances, minimizing the role of territorial contiguity, and maximizing the communication networks in all their dimensions. Flows of exchange are at the core of the American Edge City." The second point missed by Garreau's metaphor is the multiple dependencies at the heart of America's distinctive informational city: "The profile of America's informational city is not fully represented by the Edge City phenomenon, but by the relationship between fast ex-urban development, inner-city decay, and obsolescence of the suburban built environment."[66] Castells's informational city is better understood as a network than a place, a process rather than an object. A "new urban form," the informational city takes different shapes in Silicon Valley, Europe, and Asia. Across nations, however, informational cities have crystallized in a "new spatial form, which develops in a variety of social and geographical contexts: mega-cities," which, although huge, are not defined by size but as "the nodes of the global economy, concentrating the directional, productive, and managerial upper functions all over the planet: the control of the media; the real politics of power; and the symbolic power to create and diffuse messages."[67] In the United States, the information age also has given rise to a distinctive suburban form—what Margaret Pugh O'Mara identifies as "cities of knowledge," residential and high-tech industrial nodes built around major research universities.[68]

In the early twenty-first century, these metaphors—inner city, post-industrial city, dual city, fortress city, city-region, edge city, galactic city, global city, informational city, city of knowledge—compete to answer the question "What is an American city?" All are both useful and partial. Their utility depends on the angle of interest—inward versus outward, national versus global—and the concern—inequality, environmental degradation, crime, terrorism, aesthetic value, political fragmentation, the possibility of community, for instance. They are, moreover, not entirely consistent. Examples are Garreau's cheerful optimism about the role and future of edge cities contrasted with Hayden's withering attack and Sassen's emphasis on the importance of place and contiguity in global cities compared to Castells's stress on a-geographic networks. The work of assessing and reconciling multiple metaphors for cities, and of exploring their implications, is a central and urgent task for interdisciplinary twenty-first-century urban studies. Economic, demographic, and spatial transformation have exploded old ideas of cities and suburbs, turning them into encumbrances to the reformulation of helpful public policies.

*   *   *

At both ends of the twentieth century, profound economic change forced redefinitions of "city." In the late nineteenth and early twentieth centuries, the industrial city emerged as the new urban form, and a host of commentators tried to define its character. The problems they identified, and the issues on which they concentrated, are remarkably similar to those on the agenda of urbanists and public officials in the early twenty-first century. Only now, as we have seen, the model of the old industrial city clearly is gone forever. The question, then, is how to characterize what has taken its place. What is an American city? The answer, I have tried to show, remains far from clear, with various metaphors competing for dominance.

For progressive urbanists in the early twentieth century, population density or, as they more often termed it, congestion, resulting from massive immigration posed a massive challenge to public health and morals as well as to urban infrastructure and governance.[69] A century later, urbanists confronting population loss, abandoned housing, districts returned to fields of weeds, and sprawl searched for ways to turn around the city's de-densification and fill in empty suburban spaces with clustered housing and retail. Another huge and consequential difference between the early and late twentieth century lies in the response to urban redefinition. Consider the early twentieth-century example described by Peter Dreier and his colleagues:

> In the early 1900s, New York City was a cauldron of seething problems— poverty, slums, child labor, epidemics, sweatshops and ethnic conflict. Out of that turmoil, activists created a progressive movement, forging a coalition of immigrants, unionists, muckraking journalists, settlement house workers, middle-class suffragists, socialists, and upper-class philanthropists. They fought successfully for workplace, tenement, and public health reforms. Although they spoke many languages, the movement found its voice through organizers, clergy, and sympathetic politicians. Their victories provided the intellectual and policy foundations of the New Deal three decades later.[70]

Early twentieth-century urban reformers, struggling to define and tame industrial cities, grappled with the consequences of massive immigration by people with different cultures, the lack of affordable housing, the growth of poverty and homelessness, crises in public health and sanitation, and the impact of growing concentrations of wealth on society and politics. They worried about the role of privatization in municipal services, the heavy hand of state government, the weakness of mayoral executive authority, the corruption of machine politics, the inefficiencies and inequities of the courts, and the regressive and inadequate foundation of city finances on property taxes.[71]

In the late nineteenth and early twentieth centuries, cities tried to respond to these issues with active government—what historians have labeled progressivism. Despite the persistence of corruption, widespread poverty, and racial discrimination, in these decades cities increased municipal expenditures, professionalized their administrations, and constructed buildings and infrastructures that supported the most vibrant and successful era in American urban history. In the late twentieth century, by contrast, the response was the withdrawal of active government, evident in reduced federal funds, reliance on market-based solutions to urban problems, and the need to turn to private initiatives, like special service districts, to carry out public functions such as street cleaning and security. The results are everywhere to be seen, in homelessness on city streets, poverty spreading outward to inner suburbs, uncontrolled sprawl eating up open space, crumbling infrastructure, gross inequity in spending on public education, the future of urban finance mortgaged to casino gambling, and the incapacity to prevent or respond effectively to the devastation of Hurricane Katrina in 2005 or the subprime mortgage crisis of 2008. The widely heralded comeback of American cities is thin and fragile. Move away from shiny center cities, and it is not nearly so visible. Look at city budgets, and it does not seem nearly so robust. "What is an American city?" has begun to elicit both a cacophony of definitions and an array of intelligent and promising ideas about how to respond. But these have not coalesced into a new urban progressivism. Without the will to forge an effective and coordinated political response, the future of American cities, however defined, is unlikely to be as buoyant as their past.

Chapter 2

The New African American Inequality

"It is now a commonplace," observes historian Thomas J. Sugrue, "that the election of Barack Obama marks the opening of a new period in America's long racial history . . . that the United States is a postracial society."[1] In 2005, the year Barack Obama took his place in the United States Senate, Shorty, born three years after Obama, high on cocaine and alcohol, died from a knife wound on the racially segregated streets of North Philadelphia. Shorty's foreshortened life—a run-down row house on a mean street, frequent encounters with the police, work outside the regular economy as a street mechanic, violent death at the hand of another black man—screamed the stubborn salience of race in American life. "The past isn't dead and buried. In fact, it isn't even past," wrote William Faulkner.[2] Whose life—Obama's or Shorty's—more accurately represented the trajectory of African American experience in early twentieth-century America?

The question is crucial because, as Sugrue notes, "the ways that we recount the history of racial inequality and civil rights—the narratives that we construct about our past—guide our public policy priorities and, even more fundamentally, shape our national identity."[3] The narrative of racial inequality weaves together multiple threads as it recounts African Americans' struggle for political, civic, and social citizenship, to use T. H. Marshall's famous typology. What are the story's outcomes? This chapter concentrates on one thread: economic equality and mobility. It asks, "Have barriers to African American economic progress crumbled or remained stubbornly resistant to fundamental change? Has the story been similar for women and men? What mechanisms have fostered or retarded change?" These questions matter not only because they cut so close to the heart of twentieth-century American history but also because they bear on important public policy choices in the present.

The history of black economic equality and mobility does not support either the optimistic or the pessimistic version of African American history. But it does not come down in an illusory middle, either. Rather, it recasts the issue by showing that after World War II the nature of black inequality altered fundamentally. Inequality worked differently at the end of the twentieth century than at its start or midpoint. At the start of the twentieth century, pervasive, overt racial discrimination barred blacks from most jobs, denied them equal education, and disenfranchised them politically. In the course of the second half of the twentieth century, slowly and sometimes with violent opposition, the situation of African Americans changed dramatically. Courts and Congress—prodded by a massive social movement, national embarrassment on the world stage during the Cold War, and the electoral concerns of urban politicians— extended political and civil rights.[4] Affirmative action and new "welfare rights" contributed to the extension of social citizenship—guarantees of food, shelter, medical care, and education.[5] By the end of the century, legal and formal barriers that had excluded blacks from most institutions and from the most favorable labor market positions largely had disappeared. Black poverty had plummeted, and black political and economic achievements were undeniable.[6] Eight years later a black man was elected president of the United States.

Yet, for many people—both white and black—the sense remained that racism still pervaded American society, operative in both old and new ways, removing some barriers but erecting others. Observers found discrimination in racial profiling by police; verbal slips by members of Congress; disproportionate poverty, incarceration, and capital punishment; and the workings of institutions and public policies that disadvantaged blacks. Racism, they maintained, kept African Americans like Herbert Manes and Shorty residentially segregated and clustered disproportionately in the least desirable jobs, if not out of the workforce altogether, and circumscribed their opportunities for education, high incomes, and the accumulation of wealth. Far more often than whites, African Americans lived in poverty. Most black children were born out of wedlock, and a very large fraction of them grew up poor. And in the 1980s and 1990s, some indices of black economic progress began to reverse direction, accelerating downward during the Great Recession that marked the new century's first decade.

Two books captured the debate over black progress. In *Two Nations: Black and White, Separate, Hostile, Unequal*, political scientist Andrew Hacker stressed the continued force of racism in American life. In *America in Black and White: One Nation, Indivisible,* written partly in response to Hacker, historian Stephan Thernstrom and political scientist Abigail Thernstrom emphasized its attenuation.[7] Hacker highlighted the continued obstacles confronting blacks; the Thernstroms focused on black progress. Hacker intended his analysis to buttress affirmative action; the Thernstroms wanted to undercut its legitimacy.[8] Economic inequality was only one among several topics considered in each book. But it was crucial—fundamental to the story of progress, or its absence. Was the glass half empty or half full? Could past black achievement be projected into the future, or had it stalled, leaving this enduring categorical inequality etched deeply into the soil of American life?[9] What did the contrasting histories of Shorty and Barack Obama signify?

Trying to understand black inequality in the terms posed by the Hacker-Thernstrom debate, or focusing on whether America has become a post-racial society, takes us in the wrong direction. The question should not be framed in either/or terms or assessed on a single scale of progress. Rather, the historic pattern of black inequality based on social, economic, and political exclusion largely shattered during the course of the century—replaced by 2000 with its features rearranged in a new configuration of inequality. In the early twentieth century, the sources and results of America's black/white divide overlapped with and reinforced one another. What stands out about the new pattern of inequality is the *cumulative* process from which it results and the internal differentiation which is its product. Inequality among African Americans no longer grows out of a massive and mutually reinforcing, legal and extralegal, public and private system of racial oppression.[10] Rather, it is a subtler matter, proceeding through a series of screens that filter African Americans into more or less promising statuses, progressively dividing them along lines full of implications for their economic futures.

Throughout the twentieth century, despite repeated contractions and expansions in the degree of economic inequality, the income and wealth pyramid remained durable and steep, with continuities in the distribution of rewards by work, ethnicity, and gender. Yet, immense individual and group mobility accompanied this structural durability. The coexistence of structural rigidity with individual and group fluidity is the paradox of inequality; it is resolved by the process of internal group differentiation or splintering as individuals divide along lines of occupation and income. Differentiation is one of the principal mechanisms through which inequality has been, and continues to be, reproduced in modern American history.

The history of black economic inequality is also very much a story about gender—although gender has not received nearly as much systematic analysis as it deserves. Historians, by and large, have written about either black men or black women, paying only incidental attention to their comparative experiences over time. Inequality, however, has proceeded differently for African American women and men. In the middle of the twentieth century, African American women fared much worse than African American men or white women; by the century's close, they had vaulted ahead of men in educational and occupational achievement, and they closed the gaps between themselves and white women more successfully than African American men reduced their distance from white men. This story of African American inequality, thus, is not only about the relation between blacks and whites. It also traces the emergence of the gender gap between black men and black women.[11]

Public and quasi-public (privately controlled but government-funded) employment also has played a crucial role in the history of African American inequality and mobility. Especially for women, public employment has been the principal source of black mobility and one of the most important mechanisms for reducing black poverty. It has not received anything like the attention it deserves from historians or social scientists. Yet, its erosion in recent decades is one of the primary forces undermining black economic progress.

There is a widespread assumption that black men's labor market problems result from deindustrialization. This idea needs to be questioned and modified. Midcentury discrimination denied most African American workers access to steady work in the manufacturing economy. Thus, their disadvantage was evident much earlier than often assumed, and the timing of the collapse of agricultural employment played a much larger role in their subsequent labor market difficulties than historians have appreciated. Nor have writers on African American history sufficiently grasped the paradoxical role of education. Contrary to much common wisdom, education has served as a powerful source of upward mobility for African Americans, who, at the same time, have suffered, and continue to suffer, from structural inequalities that leave them educationally disadvantaged. These arguments about inequality and mobility are not intended to ignore or deny the force of racism. Many scholars have documented the persistence of racist attitudes and changes in public opinion. The intent, rather, is to shift the focus away from individualist interpretations and toward structures and processes that result from racism but, once set in motion, operate with a logic of their own.

The rest of this chapter reconstitutes the history of African American inequality through five lenses.[12] The lenses are (1) *participation*—the share of African Americans who worked; (2) *distribution*—the kind of jobs they held and the amount of education they received; (3) *rewards*—the income they earned and the wealth they accumulated; (4) *differentiation*—the distance between them on scales of occupation and earnings; and (5) *geography*—where they lived. Because it underlies the other forms of inequality, geography comes first.

Geography

Throughout American history, African Americans have clustered disproportionately in the nation's most unpromising places. Because the sources and features of inequality have always been tied so closely to where they have lived, changes in the spatial distribution of African Americans have mapped the reconfiguration of inequality among them. The consequences of African American migration have been immense as blacks, primarily a Southern and rural people at the start of the twentieth century, became, at its end, an urban population distributed far more equally throughout the nation. Movement off of Southern farms resulted in a mixed legacy for black inequality. It brought them closer to more rewarding sources of work, but, in the end, it left them isolated in America's new islands of poverty.

Black migration from the South to the Northeast and Midwest represented a shift from rural to urban living. In 1900, only 16 percent of adult blacks, compared to 35 percent of whites, lived in a metropolitan area, but by 1960, blacks had become more urbanized than whites—a distinction they retained: in 2000, 86 percent of blacks and 78 percent of whites lived in metropolitan areas.[13] Not only did blacks become more urban: over the course of the century, they concentrated more than whites in central cities. In 1900, 26 percent of white adults and 12 percent of black adults lived in central cities. This situation reversed between 1940 and 1950. By 2000, the African American fraction had climbed to 52 percent while the white share had dropped to 21 percent, a stunning reversal of metropolitan racial ecology.

In the decades after World War II, with whites leaving and blacks entering central cities, racial segregation increased, reaching historic highs by late in the twentieth century.[14] As Chapter 1 observed, segregation in 2000 was much higher than it had been in 1860, 1910, or 1930, when, except for Chicago and Cleveland, in northern cities whites still dominated the neighborhoods in which the average African American lived. This situation reversed by 1970: between 1930 and 1970, the neighborhood in which the average African American lived went from 31.7 to 73.5 percent black. Affluent as well as poor African Americans lived in segregated neighborhoods. The segregation index went down after 1980, but still remained high. At the end of the twentieth century, the typical African American still lived in a neighborhood where two-thirds of the other residents were black.[15]

In the century's last decade, black suburbanization increased modestly: the percentage of blacks living in suburbs rose from 34 percent to 39 percent. But most black suburbanization was movement to inner-ring suburbs, themselves segregated and developing the problems of inner cities. Between 1990 and 2000, there was no change in the segregation of blacks within suburbs; in both years, the average African American suburbanite lived in a neighborhood that was 46 percent black.[16] Overall, postwar configurations of segregation and inequality remained mostly in place.

Racial segregation did not just happen as a result of individual preferences, the racism of homeowners, or the venality of realtors who practiced blockbusting—although all these influences were at work. It resulted just as much from government policy and action. All levels of government share the culpability. The underwriting practices of federal agencies that insured mortgages introduced "red lining," which virtually destroyed central city housing markets, froze blacks out of mortgages, and encouraged white flight to suburbs. Governments also deployed interstate highway and other road construction to manipulate racial concentration by confining African Americans to inaccessible, segregated parts of cities. In the 1930s, when the federal government initiated public housing, its regulations forbade projects from disturbing the "neighborhood composition guideline"—the racial status quo. Thus, even before World War II, two-thirds of blacks in public housing lived in wholly segregated projects. In the years after the war, local governments found ways to use public housing to increase black isolation even further by locating developments only in segregated neighborhoods.[17]

The spatial redistribution of America's black population in the twentieth century intersects African Americans' history of economic inequality.[18] Segregation, Massey and Denton show, is itself a force that initiates a vicious cycle that concentrates poverty and magnifies its impact.[19] An overwhelming number of African Americans started the twentieth century clustered in America's poorest spaces—rural southern farms; they also ended the century concentrated disproportionately in the nation's least-promising locations—central cities, where only 21 percent of whites remained.

Participation

The geographic redistribution of African Americans focuses one lens on the reconfiguration of black inequality in the twentieth century; the altered relationship of black men to the labor market focuses another. For it is among black men, more than among black women, that these trends created a new form of disadvantage.[20]

Patterns of black women's market work varied over the twentieth century. For much of American history, black women worked out of necessity.[21] As slaves, they were forced to labor; after slavery, and in the North, they worked to supplement men's meager wages or because they were more often widowed.[22] In post–World War II cities, disincentives built into public assistance kept many of them from employment until after 1996, when new welfare legislation forced them into the labor force—for some a welcome opportunity, for others a chance to join the ranks of the working poor.[23] At the same time, better education, the impact of the civil rights movement, and the expansion of jobs in government, health care, and the social services opened more attractive work opportunities to black women. By contrast, for many black men in the late twentieth century, just a job in the regular labor market itself often proved elusive, a situation highlighted by social scientists who lamented black men's chronic detachment from the labor force.[24] The eminent social scientist William Julius Wilson titled his 1996 book *When Work Disappears: The World of the New Urban Poor.*

Between 1900 and 1960, black women of all ages listed an occupation much more often than white women,[25] and they stayed employed at ages when the white women who did work generally left the labor force.[26] (See Figure 9.) After 1960, as the labor force participation of both began its increase, the white rate grew faster than the black, and the gap between them narrowed and on occasion reversed.[27] But most striking was the frequency with which both worked. By the end of the century, only one-fifth to one-quarter of adult women—black or white—remained outside the labor force. This development, of course, reflected the swift, revolutionary rise in the number of married women at work in the late twentieth century.[28]

For black men the employment story is very different. Before 1940, very few adult black men remained outside the regular labor force, but after 1940, a stunning disparity in labor force participation opened between black and white men,[29] and black men remained outside the regular labor force much more often than white men. (Many, of course, like Herbert Manes, who drove a gypsy cab, or Shorty, a street-level mechanic, worked in the informal economy shadowing regular jobs, while others turned to illicit work such as dealing drugs.) Among black men age twenty-one to twenty-five, the proportion not in the regular labor force (defined by an occupation listed in the census) rose from 9 percent in 1940 to 27 percent in 1990, and 34 percent in 2000. Between 1990 and 2000, nonparticipation increased for black men of other ages as well. In 2000, for instance, more than one of four black men age forty-one to

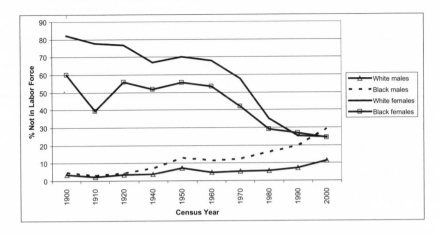

Figure 9. Labor force nonparticipation, by race and gender, persons over eighteen years, 1900–2000.
Source for figures 9–15: Author's calculations from Steven Ruggles and Matthew Sobek et al., *Integrated Public Use Microdata Series: Version 3.0.* Minneapolis: Historical Census Projects, University of Minnesota, 2003.

fifty remained out of the labor force.[30] These rates for black men, much higher than the rates for white men, increased even though official black unemployment went down.[31] The unemployment rate for black men remained about twice the rate for white men, testimony to the durability of inequality. (Official unemployment counts only individuals actively seeking work, not those discouraged, ineligible to register for unemployment benefits, or otherwise out of the labor market. This is why it is important to track the numbers outside the regular labor market with the census rather than with unemployment statistics.)[32] In fact, in 1940, the ratio of black to white nonparticipation (black/white × 100) already showed an alarming disproportion, especially for men over the age of twenty-five. Among twenty-six- to thirty-year-olds it was 185, and among forty-one- to fifty-year-olds it was 168. In the decades that followed, the situation worsened. By 2000, more than twice as many black men as white men in their prime earning years—thirty-one to forty and forty-one to fifty—were not in the labor force.

Black men's increasing absence from the regular labor force coincided with a stunning rise in their incarceration as prison substituted for a welfare state for African American men. Between 1990 and 2000, the fraction of twenty-six- to thirty-year-old African American men living in institutions—mainly prisons—nearly doubled. (See Figure 10.) In 2000, nearly 12 percent of black men age twenty-six to thirty resided in an institution.[33] This institutionalization of black men tracked the national explosion of incarceration. On June 30, 2002, 1,355,748 inmates filled

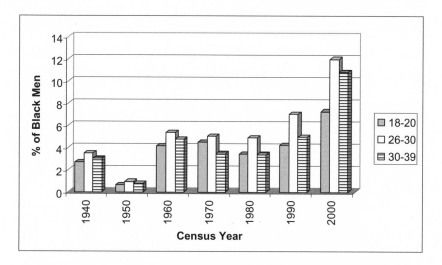

Figure 10. Percent living in institutions, by age, black men, 1940–2000.

federal and state correctional facilities—an 82 percent increase since 1990. Another 665,475 inmates resided in local jails, a 64 percent increase during the decade. The federal prison system, which grew 153 percent between 1990 and 2002, had become the largest in the nation. Most of the increase resulted from mandatory sentences for drug offenders—who represented 57 percent of federal prisoners—not from rising crime rates. In fact, in the 1990s, crime rates went down.[34] America now could boast the highest rate of incarceration in the world—702 persons per 100,000 population. In this, America surpassed Russia, whose incarceration rate had fallen to 628 per 100,000 and was still headed downward. America's incarceration rate exceeded rates in Western Europe and Canada by five to eight times.

Black men bore the brunt of America's rise in incarceration. Nationally, 49 percent of prisoners are African American compared to 13 percent of the overall population. On any given day, nearly one in three black males age twenty to twenty-nine, reports the Sentencing Project, "is under some form of criminal justice supervision . . . either in prison or jail, or on probation or parole." The rate of adult black men incarcerated on a given day doubled between 1985 and 1995, when it reached one in fourteen. These rates do not reflect increased convictions for crimes against persons or property. Rather, they result from the "war on drugs," active since 1980, which has exacerbated racial disparities by "increasing drug offenses as a proportion of the criminal justice population" and pushing up the proportion of African Americans among drug offenders.

In 2009 and 2010, the enormous cost of incarceration threatened to overwhelm state budgets strained by recession. In California, the penal system absorbed about $8 billion, or 11 percent of the state budget—more than higher education. Conditions inside prisons deteriorated as ramped-up arrests and convictions jammed them with many more inmates than they had been built to house. In a state prison "about 50 miles north of Los Angeles, where 4,600 inmates fill buildings intended for half as many. . . . a stuffy, cacophonous gymnasium houses nearly 150 people in triple-bunked beds stretching wall to wall." The combination of escalating prison costs and budget crisis provoked Governor Arnold Schwarzenegger to announce plans to reduce the inmate population, starting with a release of 6,500 nonthreatening prisoners in the next year. Criminologist Joan Petersilia of Stanford Law School, who has studied state prisons for a long time, termed the move a "seismic shift." In Pennsylvania, "three bills designed to reduce prison time for nonviolent offenders passed the state Senate [on June 9, 2010], and supporters said the measures would save taxpayer money, relieve Pennsylvania's crowded prisons and reduce crime rates." In New York, Governor David A. Paterson and state legislative leaders "reached an agreement to dismantle much of what remains of the state's strict 1970-era drug laws, among the toughest in the nation." The agreement came as the state faced a $16 billion budget deficit for the next fiscal year. In an appearance before the state legislature in February 2009, Maryland governor Martin O'Malley "made an unconventional argument that is becoming increasingly popular in cash-strapped states: abolish the death penalty to cut costs."[35] Where research and advocacy had failed to reverse America's soaring incarceration rate, unsustainable costs and budget deficits had succeeded.

This explosive growth of African American men's incarceration fueled inequality. For one thing, since 1994, Congress prohibited inmates from receiving Pell Grants with which to continue their education, and many states cut back on education for inmates, who leave prison without the skills essential for finding employment. Indeed, recent research shows, not surprisingly, that with employers reluctant to hire ex-convicts, and without job skills, former inmates have great difficulty finding work.[36] And, as Chapter 3 recounts, state disenfranchisement laws leave many permanently unable to vote, stripped of political citizenship. Not surprisingly, many return to prison.

For a series of reasons—lack of skills, incarceration, racial discrimination—black men remained over time and throughout their life course much less able than white men to find market work.[37] Black men's inability to find work in the regular labor market is not the residue of a golden age when many worked at well-paying industrial jobs. Present already in 1940, it did not result initially from deindustrialization in the 1960s and 1970s, although rates of nonparticipation increased during those years. Nor was it primarily the consequence of incarceration. Its origins, as Chapter 1 observed, lie rather, in the shift of black men out of agriculture and their relative inability to move—as white men had—into other forms of work. It remains a structural aspect of the inequality present in American labor markets for nearly three-quarters of a century. Partly on account of discrimination and partly on account of bad luck with timing—a labor market with a decreasing number of semi-skilled manufacturing jobs—black men displaced from agriculture often found themselves on the margins of the economy. The immensity of the changes in work that underlie these trends emerges unmistakably from the distribution of black men and black women among industries.

Distribution

At the start of the twentieth century, the structure of black inequality emerged from the powerful convergence of geography and work. Clustered in the rural South, African Americans worked mainly in agriculture and household service. Only a small minority escaped the simultaneous forces of racism and the demand for cheap labor to enter the skilled crafts or white-collar and professional jobs. The transformation of blacks' truncated occupational structure depended on their movement off of southern farms to cities and to the Northeast and Midwest. Thus, only with the Great Migration after World War II did black occupational mobility accelerate. Although African Americans ended the century in a far wider array of industries and jobs than they began it, theirs was a distinctive and fragile progress. Women outpaced men. Parity in the best jobs remained elusive. Upward mobility depended heavily on the public sector, and black gains were reversible, vulnerable to shifting political and economic tides.

Industry

Black women's industrial history passed through two phases: movement out of agriculture and into household service—the first major employer of black women who moved North—and, after 1940, the exchange of personal service for jobs in an array of other industries. Theirs is a story of astonishing change. In 1910, agriculture employed nearly half of black women, while most of the rest worked as servants, mainly in private households. By 1940, agricultural employment had plummeted, and in

1970 was only 1 percent (versus 0.2 percent in 2000). By contrast, the fraction of black women domestic servants rose to 58 percent in 1940 before falling to 15 percent in 1970 (1.3 percent in 2000) as a result of the replacement of live-in servants by technology, "cleaning ladies," and other help hired by the day. At the close of the twentieth century, most black women worked in the service sector or in government, health care, and education.[38]

Even during the high point of America's manufacturing era, black men often found themselves excluded from the best industrial jobs and facing a declining job market for industrial work. The timing of black men's movement out of agriculture differed from black women's. As late as 1940, 36 percent of employed black men (compared to 16 percent of black women) still worked in agriculture. But the rate of change was astonishingly fast. By 1970, agriculture only employed 5 percent of black men, and, at 9 percent, the construction industry had become their largest employer. By 2000, agricultural work had dwindled even more to a tiny 1.5 percent. Unlike women, relatively few black men ever worked in private households. Instead, construction and transportation provided many with jobs.[39]

The collapse of agricultural employment proved a more important source of joblessness among black men than the decline in manufacturing. In 1970, before the acceleration of manufacturing jobs' precipitous decline, only about 12 percent of employed black men held blue-collar occupations in manufacturing industries. By 2000, the percentage had fallen to about 8 percent.[40] In Oakland, California, for example, historian Robert Self explains that manufacturing's decline "hit black workers hard," but much "worse was the decline of employment in West Oakland, where the rail yards, docks, and warehouses once provided thousands of jobs for the community." For decades, moreover, apprenticeship programs, "the principal gateway to well-paying blue collar jobs" excluded young African American men who also were denied service sector jobs, "especially in retail and wholesale trades, restaurant and hotel work, banks and insurance companies." Only "in government service, where fair hiring" had made most progress, did they gain a significant number of jobs.[41]

Nationally, many black men moved into state-related industries, such as education, health care, social service, and public employment.[42] Federal and local public administration—employing about 8 percent—proved a more important source of jobs than health or educational services. In 2000, 19 percent of black men worked in state-related industries—that is, in public agencies or publicly funded private agencies—while retail and service industries employed 35 percent (compared to 39 percent of black women).[43] Public and quasi-public employment proved even more important for black women. At the century's end, nearly half of employed black women (43 percent) worked in state or state-related industries: 18 percent in health and hospitals, 14 percent in educational services, 7 percent in federal and local public administration, and 2 percent in welfare and religious services. Clearly, the expansion of government, education, and health care in late twentieth-century America—the growth of the anchor institutions discussed in Chapter 1—opened a plethora of new opportunities seized by African American women. Another 39 percent found work in expanding retail and service industries. For black women, America's economic transition from manufacturing to service proved a source of opportunities gained, not lost.

"The prewar black middle class," notes *A Common Destiny*, "was drawn heavily from the salaried managerial private sector; the post-1960s black middle class is much more rooted in public service."[44] Public employment, in fact, became African Americans' distinctive occupational "niche."[45] The *Brown v. Board of Education* Supreme Court decision (1954), which declared school segregation unconstitutional, the Civil Rights Act (1964), the Voting Rights Act (1965), and affirmative action policies in the 1960s and 1970s: all these increased pressure to desegregate work and expand opportunities for African Americans.[46] In some places, the federal government began hiring African Americans during World War II, but racial barriers to employment crumbled most quickly and widely in public and publicly funded jobs in the 1960s and early 1970s during the War on Poverty and Great Society era.[47] In these years, public spending on social programs escalated at an unprecedented pace. Between 1965 and 1972, federal social spending increased from $75 billion to $185 billion. In constant dollars, the rate of increase between 1950 and 1965 averaged 4.6 percent annually; between 1965 and 1976 it leapt to 7.2 percent. It accounted for 7.7 percent of GDP in 1960, 10.6 percent in 1965, and 16 percent in 1974.[48] This spending translated into the creation of jobs in government and in government-financed private programs. Within the public sector, African Americans, assisted by affirmative action, gained a disproportionate share of the new jobs. Critics often chide the War on Poverty and Great Society for lacking a jobs program. This criticism, however, is only partly valid. The expansion of public and quasi-public employment became their hidden labor market policy.[49] Operation Headstart historian Gretchen Aguiar, for instance, shows "how jobs became central to the preschool program's mission and how Head Start functioned as a hidden employment program." Paid work in local Head Start programs "represented a vital part of Project Head Start. Hundreds of thousands of poor people—most notably poor parents—have secured employment through the program since it started, and continue to do so today."[50]

Consider a statistic called the index of representation. A score of 100 on this index indicates that the representation of a group is equal to its representation in the population. A score greater than 100 indicates a disproportionately high representation. In 1960, among adult male workers, the score for both native white and African American men for public sector employment was close to 100. By 1970, the white score had dropped a little, while the black score rose to 138. From there it grew to 176 in 1980 and 1990, and 182 in 2000. Among women the story was similar: in 1960, the score for white women was a little over 100, and for black women it was 89. A decade later, the black score had risen to 180, and the white score had fallen to 91. The score for black women continued to increase to 211 in 1980 before dropping a bit to 209 in 1990, and 200 in 2000, by which time the score for white women had declined to 85.

These were good jobs. On the whole, they paid more than self-employment or jobs in the private sector. In 1970 (in 1990 dollars), the median earnings of black self-employed men were $13,730; those employed in the private sector earned $17,120; and in the public sector, $20,510. In 2000, the corresponding earnings were $18,800 in self-employment; $17,597 in the private sector; and $26,320 in the public sector. Put another way, in 2000, the median income of black men in the public sector was 50 percent higher than among those who worked in the private sector. Among black women, the differences were even wider: in 2000, $14,481 in self-employment, $13,536 in the private sector, and $24,064 in the public sector—a difference of 78 percent between median private and public sector earnings. Public and publicly funded employment has been the most powerful vehicle of economic mobility for African Americans and the most effective antipoverty legacy of the War on Poverty and Great Society.

The statistics of industrial employment tell an important story. Black women negotiated a series of transitions—first, from agriculture to private household service; then, from private household service to expanding opportunities in state-related industries and in retail and business services. Black men took longer to leave agriculture. When they finally made the last transition, industrial opportunities had dried up, and they found themselves less able than black women to enter government, education, or the social services, or, even, to find any work at all.

Occupation

For most of the twentieth century, the majority of both blacks and whites held agricultural or blue-collar jobs.[51] As black men left agriculture, they moved into the manual working class: 61 percent in 1960 (compared to 48 percent for white men) before declining to 44 percent in 2000.[52] The more important distinction is the racial division of occupations within the manual working class: black men less often were skilled craft workers and were more often laborers than white men.[53] Few black women were ever craftsmen or laborers, but a substantial number moved into semiskilled work as operatives after World War II, reaching a high point of 18 percent in 1970 before declining to 9 percent in 2000.[54]

Black women substituted white-collar jobs for agricultural, domestic service, and blue-collar jobs. (See Figure 11.) Movement into clerical, professional, and technical jobs proved stunning for both black women and black men. Between 1940 and 2000, the proportion of black men and black women in clerical jobs jumped, respectively, 908 percent and 2,297 percent, and in professional/technical jobs the proportion jumped 718 percent for black men and 1,394 percent for black women. "Once consigned to mostly menial work," observe reporters Ellis Cose and Allison Samuels, "black women (24 percent of them, compared with 17 percent of black men) have ascended to the professional-managerial class."[55] These changes were real, not simply products of population growth or shifts in the occupational composition of the workforce. In 1900, employed white men held white-collar jobs almost seven times more often than employed black men (20 percent compared to 3 percent); by 2000, the white lead had plummeted: 52 percent for white and 39 percent for black men. The share of black women in white-collar work increased from only 2 percent in 1900 and 7 percent in 1940 to about 63 percent in 2000—an astonishing record of change.

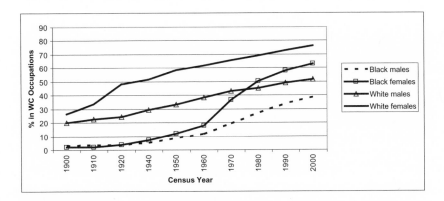

Figure 11. Percent in white-collar occupations, by race and gender, employed persons over eighteen years of age, 1900–2000.

As a result, blacks began to close the occupational distance between themselves and whites. Larger proportions of whites than blacks still held the most desirable jobs, but by 2000 the gap was much narrower than it had been at the start or middle of the twentieth century. In 1900, employed white males were more than three times as likely as blacks to hold professional/technical jobs. In 1940, the distance had widened slightly; by 2000, it had narrowed to one-third. In 1940, white males were about twelve times more likely than black men to be managers, officials, or proprietors. In 2000, they were just over twice as likely. However, this decrease in the white lead did not result from a greater share of black men in the most prestigious professions, for a disproportionate share of the professional and managerial jobs held by them were in the public sector.[56] Similar patterns marked the experience of women. In 1900, white women were six times more likely to work in clerical jobs; in 1940, the distance had increased to more than twenty times. By 2000, however, the percentages were nearly identical. In 1940, white women were about six times more likely to work in professional/technical jobs than black women. By 2000, their advantage had shrunk to one-fifth.

Broad occupational categories mask important differences based on sex and race. For instance, a growing number of black women—a five-fold increase between 1940 and 2000—worked as technicians, the lowest rung on the professional/technical ladder.[57] Only a small fraction of women professionals, either black or white, worked in law and medicine at any time in the twentieth century. Instead, for the most part, women professionals worked in human services: 81 percent of women in 1900, 89 percent in 1940, and 70 percent in 2000. These fractions, which remained similar among white and black women, reflected the importance of teaching as a woman's occupation and, later in the century, of social work and nursing.[58]

By 2000, the differences between the fractions of black women and white women in professional and technical occupations had become insignificant. This was not the case with men. White men were found much more often in law and in scientific and technical work and less often in human services than black men. In 1940, white men with professional and technical occupations were thirteen times more likely than blacks to be lawyers or judges; in 2000, the odds had fallen to just under three times. By contrast, since 1940, black professional men have been about twice as likely as white men to work in human services (in 2000, 29 percent of white men and 47 percent of black men worked in human services).

Improved occupations meant higher incomes. In 2000, the median incomes of black women professionals and managers were more than 1.5 times higher than the incomes of clerical workers and 1.9 times higher than those of service workers. For black men, upward occupational mobility also brought economic rewards, although the income differences among occupations were not quite as large as for women. The dependence on government for occupational mobility left African Americans vulnerable. Reductions in public employment and spending struck them with special ferocity and undermined their often fragile achievements.[59]

Within this story of occupational transformation, the comparative experiences of women and men remain especially puzzling and consequential. Why did black women enjoy more occupational mobility than black men? The answer lies partly in history—the kinds of work available and open to blacks when their employment in southern agriculture collapsed. In part, the answer is also incarceration, which leaves huge numbers of black men, for all practical purposes, unemployable, or employable only in low-wage, often temporary work. Another part of the answer points to the preference of employers, who, surveys and interviews demonstrate, prefer to hire black women over black men.[60] Not only do black women appear less threatening, they display more of the "soft skills" required by work in an economy based on service and information. Still another component to the puzzle's answer lies in school. One major source of black progress was education. Expanded educational achievement was the precondition for the white-collar jobs that a transformed labor market, civil rights legislation, and affirmative action had opened up. While African Americans of both sexes acquired more education, black women's achievements outpaced black men's.

Educational Attainment

In the last half of the twentieth century, African Americans made stunning educational progress. Both black men and black women began to catch up with whites, although black women moved forward more quickly. It has been customary to argue that education did not deliver on its promises to blacks because racism blocked them from the jobs for which they were qualified. This undoubtedly happened often. But education also made possible the mass movement of blacks, especially black women, into the world of white-collar work. Nonetheless, consequential educational inequalities did not disappear, and education continued to stratify, as well as help, black Americans.[61]

In 1940, more than four of five blacks had at best an elementary education, compared to about one of two white men and women. These figures did not reflect lack of commitment to education among African Americans, who showed an intense interest in their children's schooling. Rather, it resulted from their poverty and from the dreadful underfunding of black schools in the South, which received only a small fraction of the money allotted to white schools.[62] In early twentieth-century Georgia, for example, per capita spending on black children was 7 percent of spending on whites in counties where African Americans comprised 75 percent or more of the population.[63] Throughout the next sixty years, with the expansion of educational facilities and the movement of blacks to the urban North, where they attended better-funded schools, almost all African Americans received an elementary education.[64] (See Figure 12.) In 1940, only about 10 percent of blacks age twenty-six to thirty had completed high school, compared to 40 percent of whites. After 1960, the pace of African American high school attendance picked up. At the end of the twentieth century, about 90 percent of twenty-six- to thirty-year-old blacks and whites had finished at least twelve years of schooling. This percentage overstates black progress, however, because it equates the GED, a high school equivalency diploma, earned more often by blacks, with high school graduation, which leads more frequently to higher education and income.[65]

College graduation is another story. The first pattern has been persistent white advantage. In fact, the difference in college graduation rates between blacks and whites was greater in 2000 than in 1940.[66] (See Figure 13.) Among whites, the relative position of women and men reversed after 1980. Until 1980, white men graduated more often than women. In 1990, graduation rates converged, and then women pulled ahead.[67] Even though the fraction of white men graduating from college increased in the 1990s, women's share accelerated faster, leaving them substantially ahead of men. Unlike white women, black women began to graduate from college more than black men in the 1950s, and their lead gradually

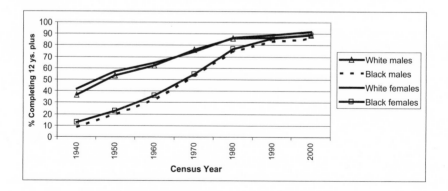

Figure 12. High school completion rate, by race and gender, persons twenty-six to thirty years of age, 1940–2000.

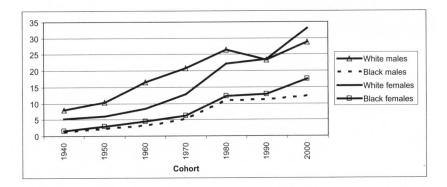

Figure 13. College graduation rate, by race and gender, persons twenty-six to thirty years of age, 1940–2000.

widened until the 1980s when they began to pull away more sharply. In 2000, 25 percent of black men age eighteen to twenty-four attended college, compared to 35 percent of black women; of those in college, 35 percent of black men and 45 percent of women graduated.[68] Still, in 2000, only 15 percent of twenty-six- to thirty-year-old African American women had graduated from college, compared to about 33 percent of white women. For men, the difference was proportionally larger: about 29 percent for white men and a very low 12 percent for blacks.

Why do black men achieve less education than black women? Undoubtedly, there are a variety of reasons. For one thing, black women can see jobs at the end of the school tunnel more readily than can black men— at least that was the situation in the past, and expectations formed over decades die slowly. Peer group influence, socialization patterns, and teachers' expectation certainly play a major role as well.[69] "Researchers," reports the *New York Times*, "say the obstacles to keeping black men from earning college degrees include poor education before college, the low expectations that teachers and others have for them, a lack of black men as role models, their dropout rate from high school and their own low aspirations." These influences, "common to disadvantaged minority students regardless of their sex," strike black men especially hard because they "have the special burden of being pigeonholed early in a way that black female students do not."[70]

Two points about educational attainment need emphasis. The timing of black and white progress in education differed. Whites began to go to high school and college earlier than blacks. Their families more often could forgo income from their work and had the money for tuition. Whites could see the link between advanced education and jobs, while blacks, whatever their education, unable to crack entrance to the better jobs, garnered lower returns for staying longer in schools. Blacks needed the intervention of the state—courts and legislatures—to help them over the hurdles that blocked their access to high school graduation and college and, then, to force open restricted doors to jobs that matched their educations.[71] The first white cohort in which a majority reached twelve years of schooling had been born between 1926 and 1935; the first black cohort to pass the same milestone, born a decade later between 1936 and 1945, reached high school in the 1950s. The initial African American cohort to send at least a third of its members to college for a year or more was born in the next decade, 1946 to 1955—they were the first African Americans to benefit from the Civil Rights Movement, affirmative action, post-1954 increased funding for historically black colleges, and the expansion of community colleges.[72]

The other point about the history of educational attainment is this. Despite great progress, blacks still remained well behind whites where it counted most. This, in fact, always had been the case. Earlier in the century, only when elementary and, then, high school education no longer were of much use in landing a good job did blacks reach parity with whites. In the late twentieth century, when a college degree had replaced a high school diploma as the key to the best work, blacks again lagged well behind. Educational progress had failed to erase the durable inequality that marked the history of race in America.[73]

Rewards

In the last half of the twentieth century, blacks closed some of the income gap that separated them from whites. Once again, women proved more successful than men, but the pace of improvement, among both women and men, was uneven. Even more, the increased incomes of individual blacks could not erase black/white disparities in family income and wealth. Economic inequality proved a cumulative process that left African Americans closer to whites, but still at a distance that showed no sign of shrinking anytime soon.[74]

Earnings

Consider, first, earnings trends from 1940 to 2000.[75] Were blacks under- or over-represented at different points along the earnings scale?[76] Three principal conclusions emerge from the data. First, blacks were over-represented among the lowest (poorest) quintile and under-represented in the highest. Second, the degree of over- and under-representation changed notably between 1940 and 2000. In other words, blacks closed a substantial fraction of the earnings gap that separated them from whites. Third, black women reduced more of the earnings gap than did black men.[77]

Here are some examples. Between 1940 and 2000, in the poorest quintile, the representation of black men fell from 255 to 147 (from 2.5 to 1.5 times), while in the highest quintile it increased from 9 to 51. For women, representation dropped from 251 to parity (102) in the lowest quintile and rose from 12 to 74 in the top quintile.

There are two ways to look at these trends: by 2000, black men were only 51 percent and black women were only 74 percent as likely to be in the top economic quintile as white men and white women. Or, in the sixty years since 1940, the likelihood that black men and black women would be in the top quintile had risen six times, while the probability that they would be found among the poorest had dropped by more than half. However we evaluate the data, demographer Reynolds Farley emphasizes that *"Never in our history has there been a time when the majority of blacks were members of the middle economic class.* The majority of blacks remain poor or near poor."[78] But the share in poverty has varied over time. In fact, trends in poverty among African Americans also allow multiple interpretations. Although poverty rates plummeted for all groups, including African Americans, the disparities—the degree of difference between them—remained surprisingly durable. Black poverty plummeted from 75 percent in 1939 to 24 percent in 1999. Nonetheless, it was about twice the white rate (39 percent) in the first year and triple (8 percent) in the second year.[79] During the recession that began in 2008, poverty rates increased among blacks more than whites, reaching 25.8 percent in 2009, the highest rate since 1994.[80] Poverty, like earnings, highlights the coexistence of progress with durable inequality.

In the late twentieth century, high black poverty rates did not result from deindustrialization. Aside from Detroit and Chicago, African Americans did not find extensive work in manufacturing in major cities and were denied the best industrial jobs. Even where blacks worked in manufacturing, service jobs remained the core of black urban employment. Black industrial workers did not earn higher wages or work more steadily than African Americans employed in other sorts of work. Among fifteen representative cities in 1949, Buffalo, New York, had the largest fraction of black industrial workers, except for Detroit, but its black poverty rate remained among the highest. In cities with the lowest black poverty rates, relatively few African Americans worked in industrial jobs. Government employment reduced poverty and proved the best predictor of African American poverty rates, accounting for 60 percent of the variance in black poverty rates across the fifteen cities. Public employment reduced poverty by providing steady, well-paid employment. African American access to public employment also signaled increasing black political influence, which, in turn, encouraged local welfare bureaucracies to respond more generously to black need. The amount of black public employment explained 33 percent of the effectiveness of cities' public assistance programs in reducing African American poverty. Overall, the correlation between the African American poverty rate and employment in government was a striking −0.7.[81]

Another measure of black economic progress is the relation of black to white median earnings.[82] The story is again one of remarkable progress, this time in reducing the earnings gap between blacks and whites, with women once more leading the way. Between 1940 and 2000, for men age forty to forty-nine, the black/white earnings ratio increased from about 41 percent to 69 percent; in the same years, for black women of the same age, it more than doubled from just under 40 percent to 96 percent—near parity. The earnings gap that separated black and white women fell first among women who came of working age in the prosperous post–World War II years—the cohort born between 1926 and 1935. It dropped further for black women who joined the workforce in the 1960s, very often children of migrants to the North who had experienced improved education and other advantages growing up outside the rural South and the children of African Americans who had moved to Southern cities, where education and opportunities also improved in these years. These earnings gains, however, proved precarious because they began to erode in the 1980s and 1990s, not because the absolute earnings of black women dropped, but because the earnings of white women rose faster. Still, black women's relative earnings remained far higher than they had been in 1940.[83]

Among men, the black/white earnings ratio increased at a steadier pace, without dramatic leaps until it reversed direction and actually declined slightly between the cohorts born from 1946 to 1955 and 1956 to 1965—a cohort that came of age amid the economic hard times of the 1980s, when most workers' incomes—regardless of race or ethnicity—went down.[84] (Figure 14 shows earnings ratios by age groups.) Although they usually earned more than women, men were not as capable of sustaining earnings gains across cohorts when the economy soured. With their hold on jobs less solid than white workers', blacks proved especially vulnerable to the forces eroding wages, job stability, and upward mobility.[85] Earnings went down especially steeply for black men born after 1945. In 2000, median earnings, in 1990 dollars, increased from $15,975 for thirty- to thirty-nine-year-old men born between 1926 and 1935 to $20,510 for men of the same age born between 1936 and 1945. Then they

A. Males

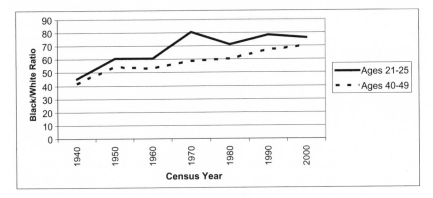

B. Females

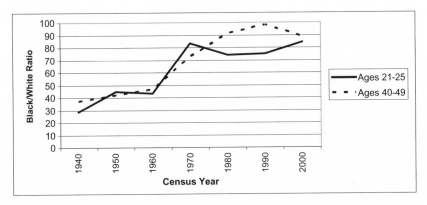

Figure 14. Black/white earnings ratios, by race, selected age groups, 1940–2000.

started to go down: for men born between 1956 and 1965, who came of working age in the 1980s, they were $18,500. The recession that began in 2008 hit blacks—both women and men—hard. Between 2000 and 2009, the real median household income of African Americans dropped by $4,368, compared to $2,365 among whites.[86]

Individual and *family* earnings are not the same.[87] Individuals draw on the total earnings of family members who live together. Family earnings, in fact, modify the trends in individual earnings: they reduce the earnings gap between black and white men and increase it between black and white women. By the end of the twentieth century, the earnings of families headed by black men were about three-quarters of those headed by white males—a ratio higher than for men considered individually. The same pattern marked earlier years, too, and for similar reasons: married black women worked for wages more often than married white women. Among women, prior to 1960 black women household heads appeared to be earning more than white, probably because they worked more. By 2000, however, the trend had reversed: for households headed by women, the earnings of black families had dropped to 74 percent of the earnings of whites as married white women increasingly entered the labor force.

Black women made stunning economic progress. In most occupations, they earned as much, or nearly as much, as white women. By 2000, there were essentially no differences in individual earnings between black and white women in the same occupational categories. Black men fared much less well. Although they reduced the earnings gap with whites, sharp differences separated the earnings of black and white men in the same kinds of work. Between 1940 and 2000, for instance, for men the earnings ratio increased from 45 to 73 in professional/technical occupations and 30 to 76 for managers, officials, and proprietors. (These earnings gaps reflect the differences in the specific kinds of jobs black and white men held within the same occupational category. The professional/technical category, for instance, includes, on the one hand, physicians and lawyers and, on the other, social workers in public human service agencies. White men, as noted earlier, disproportionately held the better jobs.) Within the blue-collar world, the earnings of black men grew still closer to white: in crafts from 52 to 86 percent. But no group erased the advantages of white men. This white male advantage was not the result of differences in education; it persisted across all groups, regardless of level of education.

Whether African American men experienced economic mobility during their prime working years depended in part on when they were born. Men born earlier in the century made the most dramatic gains. The post–World War II economic boom combined with migration off Southern farms to boost the earnings of African American men throughout their working lives. The median earnings of black men born between 1906 and 1915 more than doubled in the twenty years between 1936–1945 and 1956–1965. Men born ten years later benefited from similar influences, although their earnings did not spike as sharply. Men who entered their prime working years during the difficult years from the mid-1970s to the mid-1980s did not experience the same economic mobility. Their adult earnings hardly budged over time, while younger men struggled to stay afloat during the recession that began in 2008. From just 2008 to 2009, the median income of black households dropped 4.4 percent, compared to 1.6 percent for white households.[88]

Earnings depend on age, sex, race, and education—as well as on historical events and economic climate. Because education mediated their influence, the impact of sex and race varied substantially with educational attainment. In both 1940 and 2000, earnings increased with education for all groups. Nonetheless, in 1940, the influence of race was so strong that being black decreased the earnings of black college graduates relative to whites. During the next sixty years, the influence of education heightened. By 2000, education overrode the influence of race on earnings. For instance, the earnings difference between a black woman high school graduate and a black woman college graduate increased from $2,716 in 1940 to $14,288 in 2000. The gap between a white woman high school graduate and a white woman college graduate rose in the same period from $4,135 to $12,032.

Race mattered, but more in 1940 than in 2000.[89] Earnings of the most well-educated blacks and whites grew closer to each other over time, even though blacks generally still earned less. The standard for comparison here—and in all the comparisons—is white male high school graduates; all earnings are in 1990 dollars. In 1940, blacks with college degrees earned substantially less than white high school graduates. In 2000, they earned a lot more. In 1940, black men who had graduated from college earned $1,259 *less* than white high school graduates; in 2000, they earned $19,776 *more*. Black women college graduates improved their relative standing in the same way: in 1940, they earned $4,185 *less* than white men who had graduated from high school; in 2000, they earned $5,246 *more*. Among both men and women who had reached similar educational levels, the ratio of black to white median earnings increased. Only the increase was much steeper among women than men. In fact, by 1980, black women generally earned the same as, or more than, white women with comparable educations.

In 1940, racial discrimination prevented blacks with a college education from earning as much as whites with a high school education. By 2000, this anomaly had disappeared. But the earnings of white men, more than of any other group, benefited from college graduation. No other group even came close.[90] In 1940, among white men, college graduates earned $7,641 more than high school graduates. By 2000, their advantage had more than doubled to $17,296. The earnings advantage of other college graduates—black and white women—trailed well behind. No matter how long they had stayed in school, no group matched the earnings of white men. White men had successfully parlayed college education into a strategy for retaining and advancing their historic spot at the top of the earnings ladder.

The increased importance of education heightened economic differences between blacks and sharpened the dividing lines within black social structure, whose organizing principles came increasingly to resemble those among whites. Education, however, did not erase the cumulative economic disadvantages of African Americans, who remained unable to combine individual earnings within families as successfully as whites. This resulted partly from lower male wages and partly from the greater number of single-member, female-headed households among blacks. At work, a black woman earned as much as the white woman with a similar education who sat next to her. But she more often went home to a husband who earned less than the white woman, or to no husband at all. She also lived in a household that had fewer assets other than earnings.[91] This is the message underlined by trends in the ownership and value of homes.

Homeownership

Earnings are only one component of family wealth. Others consist of real property, savings, and securities—assets held much less often by blacks than whites, as the research of Melvin Oliver and Thomas Shapiro and of Dalton Conley has shown.[92] Using the census, only one measure of assets—homeownership—is consistently available across the century. Fortunately, it is, in fact, a useful measure because it constitutes such a large share of the wealth of most families. Since 1940, it has also been possible to examine the value of the homes that families owned.

Throughout the twentieth century, blacks owned homes much less often than whites. (See Figure 15.) Among both whites and blacks, homeownership rose after 1940—for whites from 45 percent in 1940 to 72 percent in 2000, and among blacks from 23 percent to 47 percent in the same years. In 2000, the ratio of black to white homeownership was 66, certainly an advance since 1940, but still a major difference. The homes that blacks did own were worth less than those owned by whites, although their relative value increased over time. In 1940, the median value of blacks' homes was only 20 percent of whites. It rose quickly to 56 percent by 1960 and ended the century at 67 percent. With assets the measure, the economic gap between whites and blacks emerges greater than with earnings alone. In 2006, the median value of the assets held by black middle-class families, excluding their homes, was $500, a decline from $700 in 2000.[93] According to the Institute on Assets and Social Policy, between 1984 and 2007 the "wealth gap between whites and African Americans increased more than 4 times, from $20,000 to $95,000." Middle-income white households had accumulated an average of $74,000 in assets, compared to $18,000 for a high-income African American family. "At least 25 percent of African American families had no assets

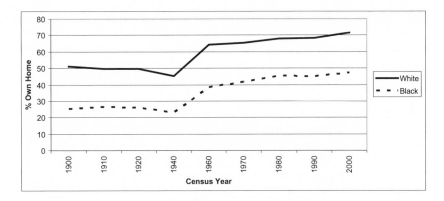

Figure 15. Percent owning property, by race, household heads, 1900–2000.

at all to turn to in times of economic hardship."[94] In fact, a view that combines earnings, education, and property qualifies the record of black economic progress. Blacks less often acquired a four-year college education—the key to the highest earnings; men (but not women) who did enter the most remunerative jobs earned less than whites; whatever their jobs or educations, they could not bundle individual into family earnings as large as those of whites; more of them were poor; they lacked assets other than homes, and they owned homes less frequently; the homes they did own were not worth as much, and when recession hit, more of them lost them. The Center for Responsible Lending calculated completed foreclosures between 2007 and 2009 per 10,000 loans made to owner occupants; the numbers were African Americans, 790; Latinos, 769; Non-Hispanic whites, 452.[95] Economic inequality was a *cumulative* process. It did not result from a single form of inequity or discrimination but from a series of screens that filtered blacks into less-favored compartments whose cumulative result was a new configuration of inequality.[96]

Differentiation

The configuration of economic inequality separating blacks and whites shattered and then recomposed between the end of World War II and the turn of the century. Differentiation became the hallmark of the African American social structure that emerged. Differentiation provides a more precise and objective way to talk about the process of change than to cast it in terms of the emergence of a black middle class—a common trope in discussions of recent trends in black social structure but one lacking precise features and difficult to track over time.[97] Applied to blacks, differentiation underscores the importance of disaggregating experience by gender and class. Only disaggregation exposes the persistent and novel in African Americans' history of work, income, education, poverty, and mobility—a point that becomes obvious from viewing the data discussed earlier in this chapter through the lens of differentiation.

First is geography. From a population three-quarters concentrated in the South, blacks spread throughout the other regions of the nation. By century's end, they had become far more diversified by geography than at its start or even its midpoint. Blacks also replaced their rural concentration in 1900 with metropolitan residence. As blacks moved to cities, and then to suburbs, segregation put a brake on their differentiation by residence and helped concentrate blacks in central cities and inner suburbs.

Differentiation also marked the history of black labor force participation, but mainly for black men. For most of the twentieth century, married black women worked for wages far more often than married white women, who caught up with them toward the century's end. It was male labor force participation that bifurcated most dramatically with the emergence of a large share of jobless adult black men in the 1970s and 1980s. Black men had divided into those in and out of the regular labor market.

Differentiation also proved the hallmark of black industrial and occupational history in the twentieth century. In 1910, just two industries—agriculture and private household service—employed nearly ninety of one hundred black working women. In 1940, the same two industries still accounted for seventy-five of one hundred. By 1970, however, it took seventeen industries to encompass the same share of working black women—a number that remained approximately steady for the rest of the century. Among black men, only eight industries accounted for three-quarters of employment in 1910, a number that grew to sixteen in 1940, and thirty-two in 2000. Clearly, here, too, differentiation was a major theme.

The same pattern marked the history of occupations. The occupational structure of black women bifurcated as they left agriculture and domestic service, with nearly two of three in white-collar jobs in 2000 but a third still employed in manual work and lower-level services. Among men, the occupational story also revealed dramatic differentiation. In 1900, nearly eighty of one hundred black men were laborers, farm owners or tenants, or farm laborers. By 2000, black men entered a variety of other occupations as their occupational structure bifurcated. At the end of the century about thirty-nine of one hundred held white-collar jobs.

Manufacturing played a relatively minor role in the differentiation of African Americans among industries and occupations. When their agricultural employment disappeared, not even one of five black men found alternative employment in manufacturing. Often disadvantaged by a prison record, lacking the education or skills needed for government or other white-collar jobs, and without a clear new economic niche, many remained—and remain—chronically detached from the labor market. Black women, by contrast, found in domestic work an alternative to agricultural employment that served to tide them over until, helped by their educational advance, they began to populate white-collar and government-related jobs.

In 1900, few African Americans had received more than an elementary education. By 2000, a substantial fraction graduated from college, equalizing the share of the black population with and without some college experience. As for earnings, in 1940, black women and black men clustered in the two lowest economic quintiles. By 2000, 36 percent of African American men and 24 percent of African American women had reached the top two economic quintiles, and poverty rates had plunged. By itself, race influenced earnings much less in 2000 than it had in 1940. Instead, education had emerged as the major engine driving economic differentiation. The evidence pointing to a population bifurcated by earnings is reinforced by the differentiation of blacks by homeownership, an important achievement in its own right and a surrogate for the accumulation of assets.

It was through this process of differentiation—the accumulation of many small and not-so-small distinctions—that black social structure came to increasingly resemble whites' and that black inequality endured despite individual and group mobility. Differentiation constitutes a powerful analytic tool for understanding stratification because it addresses the paradox of inequality: the coexistence of durable inequalities with individual and group mobility. It limns the process through which social mobility reinforces, rather than challenges, economic disparities. And it highlights the limitations of policies that focus only on access to jobs or education without addressing the factors that structure and reproduce inequality.

Because inequality is a historically contingent process, the way it works varies with time and place, and "either/or" interpretations of racial progress run the risk of turning a very complicated history into a scorecard diverting attention away from the most important issues. The question is not whether Hacker or Thernstrom wins a debate but how and why the characteristics of black inequality have changed during the twentieth century and what those changes imply. One implication points to the limits of individualist solutions to group problems. Solutions that promote individual social mobility without attending to the processes that reproduce inequality lead to differentiation—the mobility of a fortunate minority who pull away from the rest. They are supply-side solutions to demand-side problems. And they are the way American public policy usually works.

One of those demand-side problems remains the availability of work for black men. The history recounted in this chapter shows that deindustrialization does not shoulder all, or even a large part, of the trouble African American men face finding work. The problem needs to be cast, first, as the conjunction of the disappearance of agricultural work with a changing opportunity structure for which black men's education had prepared them poorly. Persistent racial discrimination, draconian drug laws, extraordinary rates of incarceration, and other influences compounded the problem and resulted in the stubbornly high fraction of black men outside the regular labor market. The flip side of demand, this history shows, has been the role of public and quasi-public employment that provided African Americans with a distinctive occupational niche, served as their primary escalator into the middle class, and reduced poverty among them. Only it was an escalator ridden more easily by women than men, and it reinforced the growing gender gap that the data so clearly reveal. It was also an escalator that more or less stopped, and even reversed, in the century's last decade, accelerating downward in the new century's first decade, fueled by the declining wages and weak labor market undercutting the well-being of most American workers.

The history of education, it might be thought, contradicts this demand-side interpretation. For among African Americans, as among whites, the links between education and income grew tighter in the late twentieth century. Education, of course, facilitated the social mobility of a great many African Americans, but it also left many behind. It was, that is, a powerful engine of differentiation. And the fraction of blacks reaching education's pinnacles remained quite small. Opportunity had opened, but whites held on to their lead. Individualist solutions to black inequality relying *solely* on education were very likely to fail. But the role of education suggests an advantage to understanding inequality as a process—a series of screens sifting girls and boys, women and men into more or less promising economic and social positions. Interpreted this way, the analysis of inequality highlights the need for multifaceted policy and points where policy interventions are most needed, and most likely to be successful.

The new black inequality that emerged in the last decades of the twentieth century resulted from powerful technological, demographic, economic, and political forces. It was facilitated by massive social movements and abetted and shaped in every way by the state. And it left

African Americans divided among themselves. Large numbers were peculiarly vulnerable to political retrenchment and economic reversal because they were employed in public or publicly funded jobs; a disproportionately high fraction lived in poverty; and many others enjoyed the benefits of upward mobility. While race remained a live force in American life, it worked in some new ways, sifting African Americans through a series of screens—residential, penal, occupational, educational, economic—that advantaged some and left others progressively behind.[98] Familiar forms of inequality remained, and an alarming gender gap had opened between black women and black men. Large differences in labor force participation and earnings separated black and white men; blacks were poor about three times more often than whites; neither black women nor black men finished college as often as whites; and a much higher fraction of whites owned property and other assets. Nonetheless, inequality had been transformed. Earlier, the embodiment of ubiquitous, converging forces of oppression, late twentieth-century black inequality was the product of a sequence of differentiating experiences. Barack Obama and Shorty were two of its products. The new inequality was harder to pinpoint or characterize, more diverse, easier for an outsider to miss—but no less real.

Chapter 3

Why Don't American Cities Burn Very Often?

In October 2005, rioting erupted in at least three hundred cities and towns across France. The riots were the worst France had experienced since 1968. They were touched off by the October 27 deaths by electrocution of two teenagers of North African and Malian origins who were climbing a fence to escape police pursuit. The riots were stoked a few days later by the discovery of an unexplained tear gas grenade inside a prayer hall in Clichy. Over two weeks, immigrant youths from working-class suburbs burned nine thousand cars as well as "a theater, some social centers, day care centers, gyms, even a post office or two."[1] Mass joblessness, spatial isolation, and cultural discrimination fueled anger at the police that erupted on French streets.

As in France, immigrants are transforming U.S. cities, which, already highly segregated by race, contain zones of exclusion characterized by poverty and joblessness. But American cities do not burn. Even the botched response to Hurricane Katrina in 2005 did not provoke civil violence. In fact, with the exception of Liberty City, Miami, in 1980, and South Central Los Angeles in 1992, American cities have not burned since the early 1970s.[2] Violence, however, has not disappeared from them. It has turned inward—witness the fatal encounter between two poor black men, Herbert Manes and Shorty, when a dispute over five dollars erupted on the streets of North Philadelphia. Anger and frustration explode in gang warfare, homicide, and random killing in drive-by shootings.[3] But civil violence—burning, looting, sniping at police—actions aimed largely at symbols and agents of exclusion and exploitation, remain part of urban history, not live possibilities in the urban present. What accounts for the absence of civil violence on American city streets?[4]

I refer to these events—the burning, looting, and sniping at police—as civil violence for two reasons. One is to sidestep the politically charged debate over whether to refer to them as riots or rebellions by using a term that is at once less evaluative and more analytically precise. The second reason is to distinguish these events from individual violence, terrorist violence, and criminal violence. In practice, all these forms of violence overlap; distinctions between them remain far from neat. Most violent activities, however, fall mostly under one heading. "Riots," terrorism, and gang warfare are instances of collective violence—in Charles Tilly's definition, "episodic social interaction" that

> immediately inflicts physical damage on persons and/or objects. . . . involves at least two perpetrators of damage; and
> results at least in part from coordination among persons who perform the damaging acts.[5]

The components of collective violence combine in endless varieties and explode in myriad forms. But, always, these three features remain its core.

Civil violence differs from both terrorist and criminal violence, even though the latter two fall neatly under Tilly's definition of collective violence. Terrorism—such as bombing the World Trade Center and the federal office building in Oklahoma City, as well as the events of 9/11—usually is carefully planned in advance and orchestrated by individuals and groups from outside the site attacked. Its purpose is to punish, seek revenge, and strike fear; killing is central, not incidental, in its mission. In all these ways it differs from the civil violence that erupted on the nation's streets. I call the drive-by shootings, gang warfare, and violence accompanying drug dealing "criminal violence."[6] Criminal violence differs from civil violence in one crucial way: it does not make claims on the state. The shift from collective to criminal violence after about 1970 is why American cities can be at once so violent and so tranquil.

To explain why something did not happen is both presumptuous and a tricky sociological problem. It is presumptuous because it assumes that civil violence was to be expected, not exceptional. It is a tricky sociological problem because theories usually try to explain events, not their absence. But, in the case of urban civil violence, the question is legitimate for two reasons. First, it can be reframed positively as an attempt to locate the mechanisms of social control in the United States. In the years after the civil violence of the late 1960s and early 1970s, an official commitment to universal citizenship rights and equal opportunity confronted widening economic inequality and continued racial disparities. In this situation, civil peace depended on effective social control.[7]

Second, the question "Why has widespread civil violence failed to recur?" is legitimate because a number of the conditions thought to have precipitated the eruption of civil violence in the 1960s either persisted or grew worse. What were the conditions? Consider the 1968 analysis of the National Advisory Commission on Civil Disorders (the Kerner Commission), appointed by President Lyndon Johnson. The commission unequivocally—and to the intense displeasure of the president—dismissed the idea that civil disorders (its term for civil violence) resulted from Communist agitation.[8] In almost every instance, police actions had ignited long-standing grievances whose roots lay in racism and economic deprivation. The commission's "basic conclusion" offered an ominous prediction for the future of American society: "Our nation is moving toward two societies, one black, one white—separate and unequal."[9]

A sense that institutions had failed compounded these grievances, point out historians Thomas J. Sugrue and Andrew P. Goodman. Government, schools, police, the economy: none of these delivered on their promises. In the 1960s, the stunning disjunction between the ideals of equal justice and opportunity embodied in American political rhetoric and the reality of everyday life undercut the legitimacy of institutions, loosening the hold of social control, facilitating the eruption of rage and frustration on the nation's streets. Writing about Plainfield, New Jersey, Sugrue and Goodman observe:

> Plainfield's formal political institutions had failed, the city's civil rights organizations were struggling, and efforts to reform the police department, integrate the school district, and institute a local War on Poverty all fizzled. In the context of multiple, reinforcing institutional failures, many black Plainfielders grew increasingly discontented. West Enders' sense of grievance and outrage mounted—and in the process, young people in the neighborhood began to fashion an alternative politics of resistance and rebellion.[10]

In the decades following the Kerner Commission, most of the conditions identified in its report as precipitating civil violence did not disappear. Comparing conditions in Los Angeles before the civil violence of 1965 and 1992, a team of scholars pointed to the continuities: "a division between the suburbs and central city, the loss of decent-paying blue-collar jobs in the service economy that was replacing the industrial one, growing income inequality, and the demographic transformation of the region through Latino and Asian immigration [compounded by] the persistent racism of the Los Angeles Police Department."[11] Nationally, between 1940 and 1967, as earlier chapters also point out, income inequality drifted lower before reversing direction after 1973. After 1973, as real working-class wages spiraled downward, income inequality jumped. By 2000, income inequality had increased approximately to its level in the late 1940s. In 1982 dollars, the average weekly wage of production and nonsupervisory workers on nonfarm payrolls dropped from $315.38 in 1973 to $254.87 in 1993 before moving modestly upward and peaking just before the recession that began in 2007.[12] In September 2010, the U.S. Congress Joint Economic Committee summarized the trajectory of income inequality:

> After remaining relatively constant for much of the post-war era, the share of total income accrued by the wealthiest 10 percent of households jumped from 34.6 percent in 1980 to 48.2 percent in 2008. Much of the spike was driven by the share of total income accrued by the richest 1 percent of households. Between 1980 and 2008, their share rose from 10.0 percent to 21.0 percent, marking the United States as one of the most unequal countries in the world.[13]

Even worse, as Chapter 2 showed, the proportion of African American men out of the regular labor force soared. Among twenty-six- to thirty-year-old black men, labor force nonparticipation leaped from about 9 percent in 1940 to 30 percent in 2000.[14] As we also have seen, the number incarcerated skyrocketed, jumping 82 percent during the 1990s; 49 percent of prisoners compared to 13 percent of the overall population were black. On any given day, one of three black men age twenty to twenty-nine was either in jail or on probation or parole.[15] Nor did allegations of police violence disappear; two examples are reactions to the 1997 brutalizing of Abner Louima while in the custody of New York City police and the fatal shooting in Cincinnati of nineteen-year-old Timothy Thomas by a white police officer during an on-foot pursuit. Indeed, alleged police brutality directed toward motorist Rodney King sparked the 1992 civil violence in Los Angeles. "Particularly in the 1990s," writes Janet L. Abu-Lughod in *Race, Space, and Riots*, "the issue of police brutality" reappeared time and time again "in cities all over the country."[16] New episodes of police brutality only underlined continued institutional failure. Police departments professionalized; waves of reform swept across urban schools; job training programs proliferated; new government incentives promised to re-create markets in inner cities. But city schools by and large continued to fail; the police were still problematic; chronic joblessness increased; and inner cities remained bleak.[17]

Other conditions that had contributed to the 1960s civil violence also worsened. Although African American poverty rates declined, within cities the spatial concentration of poverty intensified. "Between 1970 and 1980," points out sociologist Paul Jargowsky, "the spatial concentration of the poor rose dramatically in many U.S. metropolitan areas. The number of poor people living in high-poverty areas doubled; the chance that a poor black child resided in a high-poverty neighborhood increased from roughly one-in-four to one-in-three; and the physical size of the blighted sections of many central cities increased even more dramatically."[18] Among individuals, poverty declined from 22.4 percent in 1959 to a low of 11.1 percent in 1973 before its trajectory reversed, reaching 13.0 percent in 1980 and then dropping again to 11.3 percent in 2000. Fueled by recession, the poverty rate for individuals reached 14.3 percent in 2009. Rates, of course, varied along ethnic lines: in 2009, the poverty rate was 9.4 percent for non-Hispanic whites, a staggering 25.9 percent for blacks, and 25.3 percent for Hispanics.[19]

Racial segregation increased until the 1990s, reaching historic highs. In *American Apartheid*, as noted in Chapter 1, sociologists Douglas Massey and Nancy Denton coined the term "hypersegregation" to describe the areas where a third of African Americans lived.[20] Segregation increased partly because African Americans migrated in huge numbers to northern, midwestern, and far western cities where they faced housing discrimination; it increased, as well, because whites fled cities in huge numbers. Recall that by 2000, only 21 percent of white Americans remained in central cities. Ethnic transition added to urban tensions as immigration, primarily from Asia and Latin America, soared after 1980, accounting for one-third of population growth in the 1990s.[21]

After 1980, cities confronted the problems that resulted from poverty, inequality, segregation, and ethnic transformation with fewer resources than in the 1960s and early 1970s. The federal government slashed direct aid to cities; other programs—such as public assistance—took major hits; the real value of the minimum wage spiraled downward. The safety net increasingly spread under Americans in the Great Society years contracted, heightening vulnerability and insecurity. Between 1980 and 1990, the share of big-city expenses covered by federal aid dropped from 22 percent to 6 percent while state aid held constant. Between 1970 and 1996, in real dollars, the median AFDC (Aid to Families with Dependent Children) benefit dropped 51 percent while the minimum wage sank to its lowest value since 1955.[22]

Poverty, inequality, chronic joblessness, segregation, police violence, ethnic transition, a frayed safety net: surely, these composed a combustible ensemble of elements, which a reasonable observer might have expected to ignite. In 1985, two sociologists who studied crime and violence observed: "the ghetto poor were virtually untouched by the progress that has been made in reducing racial and ethnic discrimination. . . . We thus face a puzzle of continued, even increasing, grievance and declining attempts to redress grievance through collective protest and violence."[23] Writing in 1988, Tom Wicker pointed to the same puzzle. The "urban ghetto is, if anything, more populous, confining, and poverty-ridden than in 1968." Yet, the "urban riots that generated so much alarmed attention twenty years ago have long since vanished—rather as if a wave had risen momentarily on the sea of events and then subsided."[24] In her 2007 book, *Race, Space, and Riots*, Janet L. Abu-Lughod reports:

> Given the obdurate persistence of racism in American culture, and the widening divides in the racial/ethnic/class system over the past three decades . . . one might have expected more collective responses, especially in the major cities of the nation, where their effects are felt most profoundly.[25]

Why did no one light the match?

No single reason explains why American cities did not burn. Rather, the relative absence of civil violence resulted from the concatenation of several factors. These fall under three broad headings: the ecology of power, the management of marginalization, and the incorporation and control of immigrants.

The Ecology of Power

Throughout modern American history, in many cities informal but widely recognized boundaries have separated hostile groups—Catholics and Protestants in nineteenth-century Philadelphia, Irish and Jews in early twentieth-century Boston, and blacks and whites everywhere. Attempts to breach these boundaries have triggered collective violence. Boundary change, writes Charles Tilly, "strongly affects the likelihood, intensity, scale, and form of collective violence."[26] Boundaries matter because they guard both identities and interests. They reinforce relations—"you-me and us-them"—that structure identities, which, in turn, solidify over time. At the same time, cross-boundary inequalities accelerate the accumulation of advantages and resources—such as housing values in segregated neighborhoods—through a process Tilly calls "opportunity hoarding." That is why attempts to violate boundaries inevitably result in conflict.[27] Throughout the history of American cities, boundary challenges often precipitated collective violence—for example, when white Protestants attacked Irish Catholics in antebellum Philadelphia and Boston or when African Americans tried to breach racial segregation in 1920s Detroit and 1940s Chicago.[28]

The northward migration of African Americans after World War II constituted the greatest challenge yet to ethnic boundaries within predominantly white cities. Recall that between 1950 and 1970, the black population of many cities skyrocketed: in Newark from 17 percent to 54 percent, in Chicago from 14 percent to 34 percent, and in Detroit from 16 percent to 44 percent.[29] Between 1940 and 1970, the number of

African Americans in Los Angeles soared from 63,744 to 763,000. The city's African American population spiked so rapidly, writes historian Josh Sides, "that even the most determined could not ignore it. Whites were now forced to interact with blacks to a degree unimaginable in prewar Los Angeles, a situation that generated unprecedented racial conflict."[30] To many white residents, black migrants threatened to raise taxes for social services, overwhelm public schools, depress property values, and inject a rough new culture into daily life. To preserve existing boundaries, whites often turned to violence—a response documented with painful detail by historians.[31] Civil violence erupted when huge numbers of African Americans had moved in to American cities and whites had not yet moved out—that is, when boundary challenge was most intense.

In the years following the Great Migration, as boundary challenges receded, the ecology of urban power was rearranged. Whites left central cities for suburbs where they found ways to erect new and effective borders, and many cities became majority or near-majority minority. Where they did not—as in Boston, whose African American population increased only from 5 percent to 16 percent between 1950 and 1970—where the white working class remained strong, civil violence sometimes burst out, especially in protests over school busing, but it remained spatially contained and narrowly targeted.[32] Elsewhere, whites decamped for the suburbs and ceded effective political control of cities to African Americans, retaining only a hold on commerce and finance and gentrified pockets of downtown. After the Voting Rights Act of 1965, the number of black elected officials jumped from 100 to 1,813 in 1980.[33] Between 1970 and 2001, the number of African American county and municipal officials rose 960 percent and 619 percent, respectively.[34] "Across the nation," reports historian Kevin Mumford, "Americans . . . elected black mayors in sixty-seven cities with populations of more than 50,000 from the 1960s to the early 1990s, and by 1972 the state of New Jersey alone had four black mayors."[35] African Americans also made inroads into the police, the most visible and, often, hated agents of the local state. Cities hired African American police chiefs only in the years after the 1960s collective violence—for instance, in Cleveland in 1970, Detroit in 1976, and Chicago in 1983. In the same years, city police forces hired more African Americans, although not in numbers that matched their share of the population. In Detroit, to take an example, African Americans as a fraction of the police force increased from 22.3 percent in 1975 to 48.0 percent in 1987, while African Americans made up 64.2 percent of the city's population.[36] A survey of 254 American cities found that minorities, as a share of police, increased between 1970 and 1981 from 5.1 percent to 11.6 percent, while minorities as a share of total population rose from 16.7 percent to 27.6 percent—an improvement in the ratio, but still a decided under-representation.[37] The irony, of course, is that African Americans inherited city governments at the moment when de-industrialization, cuts in federal aid, and white flight were decimating tax bases and job opportunities while fueling homelessness, street crime, and poverty. Newly African American–led city governments confronted escalating demands for services and the repair of crumbling infrastructure with shrinking resources and power curtailed by often hostile state governments. They were, as a political scientist described in 1969, truly a "hollow prize."[38] Nonetheless, with so many whites gone, boundaries became less contentious, eroding one major source of civil violence.

In the United States, rural-to-urban migration had inverted a worldwide pattern. Elsewhere, in the Third World as well as in France and some other European nations, the massive post-1960s rural-to-urban migration of the landless poor found its stopping point not in city centers, home to elites and middle classes, but on their peripheries in vast shantytowns or *banlieus*. Where the poor inconveniently remained in central cities, governments—often in the face of violent resistance—helped remove them through slum clearance and other perfectly legal methods of social cleansing.[39] Everywhere, however, the trends reorganized urban space with, in Mike Davis's words, "a dramatic diminution of the intersections between the lives of the rich and poor . . . middle-class secession from public space—as well as from any vestiges of a shared civic life with the poor."[40] Davis focuses mainly on Asia, Africa, and Latin America, but his observation applies to the United States and Europe as well as to Nicaragua and Hong Kong. The implication for the problem of civil violence is clear enough. The new ecology of urban power dampens the potential for civil violence by pairing class and racial segregation with the devolution of control over space to previously marginalized groups. Limited though it is, African American urban political power exceeds that available to residents of Third World shantytowns or Parisian *banlieus*.

In the 1980s, massive immigration from Latin America and Asia reignited urban boundary conflicts, particularly in the gateway cities where most immigrants entered. The civil violence that exploded in southwest Los Angeles in 1992 marked the first major boundary conflict since the 1960s. As the nation's major immigrant city, with Los Angeles International Airport the Ellis Island of the late twentieth century, Los Angeles was the natural site for civil violence reflecting the nation's new demography. Despite widespread fear, however, events in Los Angeles proved singular, not the first spark of a long fuse stretching across urban America. Why did it prove so hard to ignite civil violence throughout the nation? The answer lies partly in a set of mechanisms that complemented the new ecology of urban power. Collectively, these mechanisms deflected civil violence by managing marginalization.

The Management of Marginalization

In one way or another, most civil violence in American history has included marginalized populations, both as objects of attack (as in lynching) and as active participants (as in Watts in 1965). By "marginalized," I mean groups largely excluded from the prerogatives and rewards that accompany full citizenship, including employment, housing, consumption, social benefits, and equal justice. Before the 1950s or 1960s, nearly all African Americans remained marginalized in one way or another. In the last half of the twentieth century, as Chapter 2 described, a significant fraction moved into the American middle class. But a large share lacked work in the regular labor market, access to the best benefits of the welfare state, and the ability to match white Americans in the consumption of housing, education, and other goods. The same can be said of Puerto Ricans and many immigrants. Since the 1960s, however, deprivation rarely has translated into civil violence. Americans have learned to manage marginalization. Five mechanisms have proved crucial: selective incorporation, mimetic reform, indirect rule, consumption, and repression and surveillance. Together, they set in motion a process of depoliticization that undercuts the capacity for collective action.[41]

In recent decades, gateways to better education, jobs, income, and housing have opened to a significant fraction of African Americans and other minorities. This is what I mean by "selective incorporation." As a result, African American social structure resembles the social structure of white America, albeit with a smaller middle class and fewer wealthy. Incorporation did not happen unaided. It did not result from the inevitable play of market forces or the working of America's democratic institutions and assimilative processes. Rather, it resulted from government and private sector sponsorship. The civil violence of the 1960s, the Civil Rights Movement, and affirmative action all encouraged selective incorporation, which depended heavily on public or quasi-public employment (that is, employment in private agencies largely dependent on public funds). Recall that these proliferated as a result of War on Poverty and Great Society social spending. Municipal bureaucracies increasingly controlled by African Americans provided many jobs, as did state and federal governments, where affirmative action took hold most quickly. In 2000, approximately 43 percent of African American women and 19 percent of African American men worked in public or quasi-public sector jobs. Among Mexican Americans born between 1945 and

1954, the share in public or publicly funded employment was 37 percent for women and 17 percent for men. In 1970, government jobs, many funded by Great Society programs, employed 57 percent of black male college graduates and 72 percent of female college graduates.[42] Many private sector firms, prompted by affirmative action and the commercial value of diversity, also increased minority employment.

For the most part, selective incorporation constructed limited ladders of social mobility.[43] African American men entered professions, for example, clustered largely in the human services, not in law, medicine, or the top ranks of corporate America. African American women professionals worked disproportionately as technicians, the lowest rung on the professional ladder.[44] Nonetheless, these limited ladders of mobility proved crucial, fracturing African American communities along lines of class and gender (women fared far better than men) and eroding the potential for collective protest by holding out the promise of economic and occupational achievement and spreading a modest prosperity more widely than ever before—a prosperity, it should be noted, that was extremely fragile because it depended so heavily on public sector jobs.[45] For example, in 1981 when President Ronald Reagan abolished the Community Service Administration (successor to the Office of Economic Opportunity, which administered the War on Poverty), 60 percent of the nine thousand workers who lost their jobs were black.[46]

Mimetic reform also dampened the potential for collective violence. By "mimetic reform," I mean measures that respond to insurgent demands without devolving real power or redistributing significant resources.[47] Mimetic reform cools out insurgencies; it does not resolve the problems that underlie them. Consider, for instance, Ira Katznelson's account of how, in New York City in the late 1960s, the Lindsay administration redirected demands for community control of schools in northern Manhattan to conservative ends. With two new institutions, the Neighborhood Action Program and the District School Board, the administration "refocused neighborhood politics in traditional directions . . . by appearing to be responsive to the period's demands for community control. But their activity, at a moment of social and political crisis, not only absorbed the energies of insurgents, it also transformed their protests and rendered them harmless." The triumph of the "mimetic policy formula" substituted decentralization for community control, elections for protest, and "modest but sufficiently tantalizing distribution" for redistribution. "The noise of schooling now signified nothing."[48] Another example is Rebuild LA, which promised to reconstruct South Central Los Angeles after the 1992 civil violence but delivered very little.[49]

Together, white abandonment, selective incorporation, and mimetic reform resulted in indirect rule.[50] Like colonial British imperialists who kept order through the exercise of authority by indigenous leaders, powerful white Americans retained authority over cities through their influence on minorities elected to political office, appointed to public and social service bureaucracies, and hired in larger numbers by police forces. Despite African American ascension to public office, real power lay elsewhere. In law, first of all, cities are creatures of state government.[51] State legislatures retain effective control of city finances, a situation underlined by the appointment of financial control boards when New York and other cities faced bankruptcy. States exercise control over cities in many other ways as well, as in education when the Illinois legislature mandated radical change in Chicago's school system or when the Pennsylvania legislature replaced Philadelphia's school board. In Pennsylvania, the state legislature in the 1990s also overturned a modest gun control law passed by the Philadelphia City Council. Cities are profoundly influenced, too, by federal spending and regulations. In the mid-1970s, to take one instance, the federal government flexed its muscle by setting stringent conditions for urban fiscal bailouts and drastically cutting money for public housing.

Corporations also limited the autonomy of city governments by threatening to exit, taking with them needed jobs. City leaders remained trapped between the constituents who elected them and the state, national, and corporate authorities who supplied funds for their campaigns and circumscribed their actions. Indirect rule meant that civil violence or other claims on city government would be directed toward African American elected officials, African American public bureaucrats, and African American police.

The private sector also helped dampen the potential for civil violence by incorporating potential insurgents into America's "Consumers' Republic."[52] In the 1960s, corporate America discovered the newly urbanized black consumer. Between 1940 and 1960, the proportion of African Americans living in urban areas increased from 48.6 percent to 73.2 percent. Corporations, recognizing a new market, quickly responded. The 1960s, writes Robert E. Weems, Jr., in *Desegregating the Dollar*, "witnessed a virtual explosion of 'how-to' articles in various advertising and trade journals offering advice on selling to African Americans." Advertising revenues in *Ebony* magazine tripled from $3,630,804 in 1962 to $9,965,898 in 1969.[53]

With more spare cash than ever before, targeted by advertising, African Americans bought the material symbols of the good life. By 1993, the black consumer electronics market had reached $2,582 million. In the late twentieth century, African American spending patterns did not differ very much from whites' (although blacks did spend less per capita on alcoholic beverages). Blacks had less income but spent it in roughly the same way. In the early twenty-first century, the average income of white "consumer units" was $50,742, compared to $35,994 for blacks. Blacks spent $4,186 on food, $1,124 on entertainment, $488 on personal care products, and $1,704 on apparel, compared to $5,349, $2,148, $529, and $1,716, respectively, for non-Hispanic whites.[54]

In their turn toward consumption, African Americans joined post–World War II Americans who had created what historian Lizabeth Cohen calls the Consumers' Republic, an "economy, culture, and politics built around the promises of mass consumption, both in terms of the material life and the more idealistic goals of freedom, democracy, and equality." The story is full of irony. Consumption demands—equal access to public accommodation, entertainment, shopping, and transportation—comprised key goals in the Civil Rights Movement.[55] They also, as Alison Isenberg has shown, helped precipitate the civil disorders of the 1960s.[56] The National Welfare Rights Movement made full membership in the Consumers' Republic—the means to enjoy an American standard of consumption—a key demand. "The Consumers' Republic," claims Cohen, "in prizing broad participation in mass consumer markets, provided a wide range of black Americans—differing in locale, class, and ideology—with an available and legitimate recourse for challenging racial discrimination, particularly as other avenues—such as desegregating neighborhoods, schools, voter registration lists, and jobs—were often blocked." But the Consumers' Republic also undermined black protest. Its "focus on winning access to public accommodations and markets inevitably limited the civil rights movement, particularly in the North, because it favored those demands that grew out of, and intersected with, the mainstream discourse and assumptions of the nation, braiding the experience of black Americans with those of whites." In the process, alternatives based on black nationalism or social democratic visions of economic justice receded. "Articulating black discontent in the language of a liberal struggle to pursue individual rights in a free capitalist marketplace and then successfully securing those rights . . . only reinforced the legitimacy of the capitalist order as a way of organizing economic life."[57]

The Consumers' Republic embraced not only the black middle class. Corporations responded to the bifurcation of black social structure with segmented products and advertising. "This market segmentation," claims Weems, "prompted corporate marketers to develop class-specific advertising aimed at African Americans." In the 1970s, "blaxploitation" films, for example, "stimulated conspicuous consumption as young black males sought to emulate the lifestyles of these dubious film icons." Although the blaxploitation films proved "an extremely effective means to more fully incorporate blacks as American consumers," concludes Weems, "the millions of dollars spent visiting a fantasy world of African American triumph and achievement might have been better spent trying to effect changes in the real world."[58] As it defined the good life in terms of the endless acquisition of material goods, this relentless pursuit of consumption turned Americans, both white and black, away from politics and, especially, the politics of the common good. "If integration and desegregation were the call to arms of the civil rights movement," points out anthropologist Elizabeth Chin, "self-esteem claims equal prominence in contemporary discussions of racial problems and their solutions." What she terms the "commodification of race and the racialization of commodities" have accompanied "a turning away from the emphases of civil-rights oriented movements."[59] Among both black and white Americans, consumption masked widening inequality, environmental degradation, and heightened insecurity with a blanket of inexpensive clothes, jewelry, and electronics, available to nearly everyone through the magic of credit. The result was the blossoming of consumer debt and bankruptcy—which reached previously unimagined heights— rather than mobilization expressed through politics or collective violence. Between 1999 and 2005, credit card debt almost tripled. The average African American debt was $8,319, compared to $8,992 for whites, who had higher incomes. In 2005, 84 percent of African American cardholders, compared to 50 percent of whites, carried a balance.[60] This disparity highlights one more irony in the relationship of African Americans to the Consumers' Republic: the inability of formally equal access to consumption, like formally equal access to schools or housing, to overcome historic inequalities of class and race. Full participation in the Consumers' Republic required not only desegregated shopping but the means with which to enjoy it. As long as African Americans remained economically behind whites, they would remain second-class citizens, disproportionately dependent on plastic to acquire not only luxuries but the very means of survival.[61]

In important respects, this sketch of African American consumption is too crude. It abstracts consumption from its context in social and family relationships, neglecting its crucial role in their maintenance, as described, for instance, by Chin in her account of consumption among poor black ten-year-olds in New Haven, Connecticut. Her emphasis on consumption as a collective, not just an individual, act also highlights the diversity of consumption among African Americans, its defiance of stereotypes of extravagance, and its capacity to resist and transform the intentions of marketers. Nonetheless, she argues, the aggressive promotion of consumption touches every aspect of African Americans' lives, creating near-irresistible pressures toward a preoccupation with self that undermines the will for collective struggle.[62]

Chin wrote before the surge of predatory lending and deceptive mortgage tactics undermined not only the possibilities for collaborative political action but the foundations of material well-being as well. In the end, of course, easy credit morphed from the means of survival into the agent of destruction, a Faustian bargain when, in the Great Recession, more and more families, unable to meet credit card or mortgage payments and pushed into bankruptcy, lost everything, including their homes. A disproportionate share of these families, as we have seen, was black.

By facilitating the rise of the Consumers' Republic, the private sector developed an indirect mechanism for deflecting the potential for civil violence. Public authorities deployed more direct mechanisms that relied on law enforcement. In 1968, Congress passed the Omnibus Crime Control and Safe Streets Act, which created the Law Enforcement Assistance Administration (LEAA), "the largest and longest federal effort to respond to the problem of crime in America."[63] Prompted by an increasing crime rate in the early 1960s, the Johnson administration had sought unsuccessfully to pass a crime bill. Civil violence on the nation's streets quickly changed the political calculus.[64] The LEAA, according to one historian, "provided a law-and-order alternative to the social, cultural, and economic perspective of the Kerner Commission."[65] The LEAA, operating mainly through block grants to states, gave money to police forces and other parts of the criminal justice system.[66] The legislation specified that no more than one-third of federal grants go to personnel—a requirement that excluded manpower-intensive programs, including "most . . . community-based or social work-oriented programs." "The police, on the other hand," point out criminologists Alan R. Gordon and Norval Morris, "could easily meet the requirements through expenditures on hardware, such as vehicles, helicopters, computers, communications equipment, and antiriot gear."[67] Thus, much LEAA money supplied technologies of repression and control. Lynn A. Curtis, president of the Eisenhower Foundation, reported:

> In its early days, LEAA distributed many grants for police hardware and command-and-control systems. The San Diego police acquired a submarine to patrol the waterfront, and Mobile, Alabama, received tanks for crowd control. . . . in our crime-control policy as in our policy in Southeast Asia, we sought to resolve problems that were social and communal in nature through high technology and big money.[68]

In 1970, an amendment to the LEAA, one of several before its abolition in 1980, abolished the one-third requirement. Although the LEAA spent about $7.5 billion between 1969 and 1980—an unprecedented federal commitment to law enforcement—its funds, at their peak, never amounted to more than 5 percent of total spending on criminal justice.[69]

State and local governments continued to bear most of the responsibility and expense for law enforcement. Like the federal government, in the aftermath of the 1960s civil violence, they also ramped up spending. Local spending on police protection leapt from $2,001 million in 1965 to $3,803 million in 1970 and $6,813 million in 1975. By 1995, it had reached $58,768 million.[70] More money allowed local police to adopt military practices, as historian Robert Fogelson describes:

> In addition to employing the rhetoric of the "war on crime" and stressing the martial arts in the training academies, these [police] departments ordered grenade launchers, infrared screening devices, and other weapons that were more appropriate for a military or paramilitary outfit than for a civilian police force. Chief Ed Davis even asked the Los Angeles City Council to appropriate funds for two jet helicopters. . . . In the aftermath of the 1960s riots, which overwhelmed the police forces in Los Angeles, Newark, Detroit, and several other cities, many departments attempted to turn groups of ordinary officers who were accustomed to working on their own into highly centralized and tightly disciplined riot control units. Following recommendations proposed by the FBI and the army, the departments taught these units how to form lines, circles, diamonds, wedges, and other formations that were designed to disperse unruly crowds.[71]

While local governments paid most of the cost of police, state governments picked up the largest share of the escalating cost of incarceration, which, notes criminologist Elliott Currie, since the mid-1970s has been "the strategy most consistently adopted against crime in America."[72] State costs for correction increased from $632 million in 1965 to $1,051 million in 1970, $2,193 million in 1975, and $4,258 million in 1980.[73]

What impact did increased funding and militarized policing have on crime? Most analyses claim that the LEAA failed to reduce crime.[74] As for incarceration, even optimistic accounts, claims Currie, leave us "at best, with a remarkably meager payoff for the enormous, costly, and disruptive investment of social resources involved."[75] Indeed, crime rates, which had been increasing during the early 1960s, soared *after* the episodes of civil violence. Despite increased federal, state, and local funding, violent crime went up, per 100,000 population, from 160.9 in 1960 to 200.2 in 1965, 363.5 in 1970, 487.8 in 1975, and 596.6 in 1980:[76] Nonetheless, with few exceptions, the civil violence of the 1960s did not recur. Did the militarization of policing and mass incarceration help authorities break up potential insurgencies, respond more effectively to ones that occurred, and prevent them from spreading to other cities?

Even without clear answers to these questions, the "war on terror" that followed the September 11, 2001 attack on the World Trade Center and Pentagon, and the newly proclaimed "war on Terror" gave political authorities the opening to ramp up the militarization of urban life. In his powerful book *Cities Under Siege: The New Military Urbanism*, Stephen Graham focuses with frightening detail on the linkages between military and civilian uses of "advanced technology—between the surveillance and control of everyday life in Western cities and the prosecution of aggressive colonial and resource wars" that he finds at the core of the "new military urbanism." "Fundamental to the new military urbanism," Graham emphasizes,

> is the paradigmatic shift that renders cities' communal and private spaces, as well as their infrastructure—along with their civilian populations—a source of targets and threats. This is manifest in the widespread use of war as the dominant metaphor in describing the perpetual and boundless condition of urban societies—at war against drugs, crime, and terror, against insecurity itself. This development incorporates the stealthy militarization of a wide range of policy debates, urban landscapes, and circuits of urban infrastructure, as well as whole realms of popular and urban culture. It leads to the creeping and insidious diffusion of militarized debates about "security" in every walk of life. Together, once again, these work to bring essentially military ideas to the prosecution of, and preparation for, war into the heart of ordinary, day-to-day city life.[77]

In *City of Quartz*, Mike Davis limns a connection between police repression and the end of civil violence. In what he calls the August 1965 "festival of the oppressed," Davis claims, "formerly hostile [gang] groups forgot old grudges and cheered each other on against the hated LAPD and the National Guard." To everyone's surprise, the "ecumenical movement of the streets and 'hoods lasted for three or four years. Community workers, and even the LAPD themselves, were astonished by the virtual cessation of gang hostilities as the gang leadership joined the Revolution." This "aspiration for unity and militancy" did not sit well with authorities. Together, "the FBI's notorious COINTELPRO program and the LAPD's Public Disorder Intelligence Division . . . concentrated on destroying Los Angeles's Black Power vanguards." In this, they succeeded, but the result was not what they had hoped or predicted. "As even the *Times* recognized, the decimation of the Panthers led to a recrudescence of gangs in the early 1970s." This, Davis emphasizes, "was not merely a gang revival, but a radical permutation of Black gang culture" led by the Crips, who "blended a penchant for ultra-violence with overweening ambition to dominate the entire ghetto." In the 1970s, Davis writes, the Crips evolved "into a hybrid of teen cult and proto-Mafia."[78] The "recrudescence of gangs," he argues, also contributed to the depoliticization of ghetto youth. "Teenagers, who today flock to hear Easy-E [*sic*] rap, 'It ain't about color, it's about the color of money, I love that green'—then filled the Sports Arena to listen to Stokely Carmichael, H. Rap Brown, Bobby Seale and James Forman adumbrate the unity program of SNCC and the Panthers."[79]

In August 1992 in Los Angeles, two major gangs, the Crips and the Bloods, entered into a truce with the hope of lessening violence and opening work opportunities. For a time, the truce held. Measured against 1991, homicides had dropped 88.2 percent June 1992, attempted murder had dropped 45 percent, and robberies had dropped 13.2 percent. "As far as I know," said Los Angles police lieutenant John Dinkin, "there have been no drive-by shootings between gangs in south and central Los Angles since the riots."[80] A barbecue chef whose restaurant had been under siege reported, "It's a big change in only 100 days. People can walk and not be scared of being hit by the spray."[81] The truce even extended beyond African American gangs and South Central Los Angeles, embracing Latino gangs in the San Fernando Valley while "individual efforts to initiate and maintain the truce soon developed into community-based organizations." One gang member observed, "Instead of shooting each other, we decided to fight together for black power."[82]

Instead of welcoming the truce, officials reacted skeptically, with law enforcement authorities claiming the truce "was an excuse for young gang members to unify against the police." The police constantly harassed truce leaders, even arresting a "respected leader of Homidos Uniodos, a truce organization" in violation of a city order that prohibited police from arresting someone solely because they suspected a federal immigration violation. The police handed him to the INS, which sought to deport him. (He successfully fought the charge.)[83] Nor did authorities get the message about opportunity. Job progress remained virtually nonexistent for youths over the age of twenty-one. One commentator warned that gangs "made the first step to come together in peace, to stop the madness, to stop the killing. Now they have to have some help, some training, some educational assistance."[84] He might as well have been talking to the wind, as the sad failure of Rebuild LA, the effort to reconstruct violence-torn neighborhoods solely through the private sector, soon revealed.[85]

Since then, public authorities have worked to prevent any resurgence of legitimate political activity by gangs. In 1993 and 1994, when gang summits met in a number of cities to discuss joining together around issues of economic justice, politicians and the media quickly dismissed their actions as nothing more than transparent ploys by criminals. Commenting on the response to a gang summit in Chicago, a newspaper reporter observed, "Most reports of the gang meeting have been negative. Chicago's local and national politicians have called the peace effort a joke. . . . Alderwoman Dorothy Tillman called the new movement a scam."[86] But Jesse Jackson proved supportive. In Chicago, he "embraced the leaders of the gang peace movement . . . calling their efforts 'the centerpiece of a new urban policy.' "[87]

Fewer black men, in fact, could participate in politics, even if they wanted to. That is because they were felons. Felony disenfranchisement laws had long been on the books in most states, but their consequences became more severe as aggressive law enforcement, including draconian drug laws, created an unprecedented number of felons, who were disproportionately black. Adding together incarcerated felons and former inmates who were barred from voting effectively disenfranchised about 1.4 million, or 13 percent, of African American men—a rate seven times the national average. Looking ahead to younger men, the situation appears even bleaker. The Sentencing Project points out that with the current rate of incarceration, at some point in their lives 30 percent of the next generation of black men will face disenfranchisement—a fraction that rises to a possible (and stunning) 40 percent of black men who live in states that permanently bar ex-offenders from voting.[88] Moreover, many black men, evading warrants or just fearful of potential arrest, avoid the institutions and agents of the state, thereby eliminating themselves from participation in political action.[89] The fatal encounter between Herbert Manes and Shorty—two black men in a bleak, impoverished urban neighborhood—has become the archetype of violence in America's cities, not collective violence against perceived injustice or organized political protest.

That public authorities bear a share of the responsibility for depoliticization among young African Americans remains a hypothesis—intriguing, explosive in its implications, and in need of much research. Indeed, the lack of research on the question—and on the social history of post-1960 policing—remains stunning and surprising. Clearly, though, the turn from politics also reflected other influences, of which disillusionment with the achievements of civil rights liberalism and Black Power were among the most important. In his history of civil rights and Black Power in Philadelphia, Matthew J. Countryman writes, "A decade after it began, the Black Power movement dissipated as African Americans experienced a series of clear lessons about the limitation of their ability to change public policy at the national and local level." At the heart of the matter, observes Countryman, "Black Power advocates were never able to convince other elements of the New Deal coalition to bear the cost of its agenda for racial justice."[90] In his ethnography of the informal economy in a Chicago neighborhood, Sudhir Alladi Venkatesh shows how, even at the height of Harold Washington's administration, poor Southside Chicagoans learned a similar lesson as they found their political influence and patronage cut off by the city's black administration, which depended increasingly on a coalition of black middle- and upper-class supporters. The result was the "gradual withdrawal of grassroots persons from the mainstream black political scene."[91] In the 1970s and 1980s, as the spread of black poverty turned vast areas of cities into reservations for the black poor, as fewer black men found work in the regular labor market, as mass incarceration locked away unprecedented numbers of them, young African Americans had reason to look with skepticism at civil rights liberalism, Black Power, and, indeed, politics in general.[92]

For a moment in 2008, Barack Obama promised to reverse the cynicism and apathy that many young Americans, both white and black, had toward politics. On a block in West Philadelphia where no presidential candidate in memory had ventured, huge numbers of people of all ages—black and white—turned out to hear Obama. Black parents held their children high above their heads to catch a glimpse, telling fidgety youngsters that they were witnessing history.[93] An aging white woman said the scene reminded her of the Civil Rights Movement. When Ohio put Obama over the top in the electoral college, a spontaneous rally broke out at the corner of 47th Street and Baltimore Avenue in the heart of West Philadelphia. Within two years, much of the fervor and passion had slipped away. Whether Obama could rekindle it, turning it once again into a powerful progressive mobilization, remained one of the most crucial questions for the future of American politics.

Other factors already discussed—the Consumers' Republic, selective incorporation, and indirect rule—also facilitated depoliticization, without which the management of marginalization would have proved far more difficult. In the 1960s, black Americans lacked channels through which to make effective claims on the state. They were underrepresented in Congress, state legislatures, city councils, police forces, and in influential positions in private corporations. Other than through collective action—whether sit-ins or violence—they had few ways to force their grievances onto public attention or to persuade authorities to respond. This changed as the new demography of urban politics, the victories of the Civil Rights Movement, and affirmative action combined to open new channels of access. As selective incorporation bifurcated African American social structure, unprecedented numbers of African Americans found themselves elected public officials, public bureaucrats, and administrators of social service agencies. New channels of access removed one powerful justification for violent protest. African Americans who once might have led protests now held positions from which they could argue that civil violence was both unnecessary and counterproductive. Others remained in America's inner cities, struggling to get by, disenfranchised, wary of the state, disillusioned with politicians, and lacking leadership or vision strong enough to mobilize them once again to make claims on the state.

The Incorporation and Control of Immigrants

This chapter has asked why the explosions that rocked African American ghettos in the 1960s failed to recur despite the persistence, and in some instances the intensification, of conditions—joblessness, racial segregation, unequal justice, institutional failure—that had helped fuel them. We have found answers in an ensemble of factors: ebbing border conflicts as whites, fleeing central cities, ceded control of urban space to African Americans; techniques for managing marginalization—selective incorporation, mimetic reform, consumption, indirect rule, repression, and surveillance; and the process of depoliticization. Important as these have been, they leave the discussion framed better to fit the past than the present and future, myopic in an international context, only partially helpful in contrasting American with European experience. For the civil violence that rocked Paris and frightens other Europeans is a product of recent immigration, not of the grievances and frustrations of historically marginalized citizens.

Both European and American cities have experienced recent massive immigration.[94] Both have had to cope with infusions of low-skilled workers from different cultural traditions. But there the parallels begin to end as immigrant incorporation and control take different routes. The results have important implications for the turn toward collective violence.

Two events framed the 2005–2006 academic year. In October 2005, immigrants in Parisian *banlieus* and the working-class suburbs of other cities took to the streets for two weeks of collective violence. In April and May 2006, immigrants across the United States, outraged by proposed federal legislation that would turn illegal immigrants into felons and criminalize efforts to assist them, also took to the streets. But their protests were coordinated, massive, and completely peaceful. On May 1, 2006, more than one million marched in protest rallies in cities across the United States. Most of the four hundred thousand marchers in Los Angeles waved American flags.[95]

The two events—civil violence in France, peaceful protest in the United States—highlight divergent relations of immigrants to the state and economy. America's immigrants sought redress through government. Their protests assumed they could realize their goals through the nation's political institutions. Despite the xenophobic wing in Congress, they approached government as a potential ally, not an enemy. They wanted nothing so much as the rights of American citizens. Their faith

in the ameliorative capacity of American government marked their as-
similation more effectively than their ability to speak English or whether
they sang "The Star-Spangled Banner" in Spanish—an important point
lost to opponents who relentlessly prophesized the submersion of American nationality in an alien sea. They were also largely employed. Labor
force detachment, by and large, has been an African American problem, not an immigrant problem. Paradoxically, the most exploited
immigrants—the undocumented—have been the most closely attached
to work. They risked crossing the border—too often at the cost of their
lives—precisely to work at jobs for which they had been recruited or
which they knew were waiting, even though those jobs paid poorly and
offered no benefits or protections.

In Paris, immigrants showed no such faith in the state, and the labor
market lacked places for them. The state, after all, had pursued a relentless policy of nationalization, rejecting even benign symbols of immigrant culture, such as wearing headscarves in school—a prohibition
unthinkable in the United States. Their protests, neither planned nor
coordinated, reflected frustration, rage, and alienation, as well as a lack
of confidence in, and inability to access, official political channels.[96] In
this, they resembled African Americans in the 1960s more than immigrants to the United States late in the twentieth century. These contrasting national modes of protest echoed historic relations between the
working class and the state in Europe and the United States. Ira Katznelson and Margaret Weir, for example, argue that in the nineteenth-
century United States early white male suffrage built trust between the
white working class and the state, leading workers to look to government
for the resolution of grievances and to trust it with the education of their
children. A very different situation, they contend, prevailed in Europe,
where workers, distrusting governments that denied them the right to
vote, formulated demands against, rather than through, governments.[97]
In France, many immigrants and their descendants are former colonial
subjects (a plurality of them are Algerian), once imported as cheap labor,
marked by memories of fierce anticolonial wars, and subject to prejudice
and discrimination. From the outset, this history defined their relation
to the state very differently than among most immigrants to the United
States.[98]

The two protests—in France in the fall and the United States in the
spring—underlined differences in the relative success with which the
two societies incorporated their immigrants into the life of the nation,
or, more accurately, in the United States, the bifurcation between incorporation and control. In the United States, references to the second
generation consist of compounds joining ethnic designations, as in
Mexican American. In Europe, as Mark Leon Goldberg has pointed out,

the second generation, even those born in Europe, are called "immigrants." "The term 'immigrant' connotes different things in continental Europe than in the United States. Generally speaking, in Europe it refers not just to emigrants from foreign countries, but to their children and in some cases grandchildren as well."[99] The U.S. record, of course, was far from unblemished. Beginning with the Chinese Exclusion Act of 1882 and culminating with nationality-based quotas of the 1920s, legislation inscribed racism into immigration policy.[100] Immigrants frequently encountered hostility, discrimination, and exploitation. In the 1990s, federal and state legislation cut many of them off from important social benefits. Armed militias now roam borders in the Southwest. But the United States also has always taken some justifiable pride in its history of diversity and celebrated the contribution of its immigrants. Multiculturalism is now public policy.[101] And post-1965 immigrants, despite concentrations in gateway cities, dispersed throughout the nation faster than any immigrants in the past.[102] The astonishing ascendance of immigration as a national political issue in the spring of 2006 centered on immigrants who entered the nation illegally or had overstayed their visas, not on the desirability of immigration itself.

Naturalization laws both reflected and reinforced divergent paths to immigrant incorporation. In the United States, naturalization remains relatively easy – easier than in most European countries —it takes, basically, five years of legal residence and a clean record, while children born on U.S. soil are automatically citizens at birth.[103] Differences in requirements for citizenship show up in naturalization rates, which are much lower in France. For individuals over eighteen, the annual rate of naturalization is about 2.75 percent in France, compared to 4.8 percent in the United States. After fifteen to nineteen years of residence, naturalization rates are 20 percentage points lower in France than in the United States, and after twenty-five years, 30 percentage points lower.[104]

In the United States, however, not all immigrants are on a fast track to citizenship. For the huge numbers of undocumented, the road to economic and civic incorporation is very different—its end is difficult, if not impossible to reach, and is in fact deliberately blocked. As is well known, U.S. immigration policy is schizophrenic. Large segments of the economy run on cheap immigrant labor, as they once did on cheap black labor. Business interests demand and abet the flow of undocumented immigrants across borders. Undocumented immigrants are, after all, an ideal workforce—hard working, terrified, and exploitable. At the same time, public anger at undocumented immigration, long simmering, has exploded with stunning velocity, demanding still more border militarization and punitive polices toward immigrants themselves and those who employ, house, or assist them. Under the Obama administration, deportations have surged to record levels—nearly four hundred thousand per year. The result, of course, undercuts potential immigrant protest. Whatever else they do, the twin threats of deportation and unemployment constitute an effective mechanism of social control that dampens the potential for collective violence among a large fraction of the nation's newcomers.[105]

Comparative immigrant incorporation and control is a much larger issue than this chapter can take up in depth or detail. But the evidence sketched here points to three conclusions. First, discussion of the potential for collective violence, or its absence, in American cities must move beyond a black/white frame to include immigrants. Not only has immigration irrevocably smashed the black/white frame; it is the source of civil violence in European cities and, as such, an essential focus for comparative analysis. Second, and a point which follows, international comparisons of current-day unrest within European and American cities should focus on the process of immigrant incorporation and control. Both European nations and the United States have experienced massive immigration, but they have responded differently, with immense consequences for the integration of newcomers. Third, the discussion of immigration needs to include both the positive elements that dampen the possibility of violence by facilitating incorporation and the darker story in which civil peace results in part from schizoid public policies that promote the vulnerability of a large fraction of the nation's newcomers.

The nation's avoidance of civil violence in its segregated ghettos has one other lesson for Europeans concerned about urban unrest. That lesson consists of modern techniques for managing marginalization—for keeping the peace in the face of persistent, and growing, inequality. In this, America is a world leader.

Chapter 4

From Underclass to Entrepreneur: New Technologies of Poverty Work in Urban America

> Behind the [ghetto's] crumbling walls lives a large group of people who are more intractable, more socially alien and more hostile than almost anyone had imagined. They are the unreachables: the American underclass.
> —*"The American Underclass,"* Time *(August 29, 1977)*

> If we stop thinking of the poor as victims or as a burden and start recognizing them as resilient and creative entrepreneurs and value-conscious consumers, a whole new world of opportunity will open up.
> —*C. K. Prahad,* The Fortune at the Bottom of the Pyramid *(2006)*

The "underclass" is yesterday's idea. From the late 1970s through the early 1990s, "underclass" stood as shorthand for black poor people dominating the crumbling core of the nation's inner cities. It was an explosive yet comfortable term. "Underclass" drew on the heritage of the "culture of poverty," a concept covering up the old idea of the "undeserving poor" with a veneer of social science. The language of poverty pathologized poor people, locating the source of their poverty in their own behavior and deficits. "Underclass" also was a strangely gendered idea, tinged with apprehension at the dangers posed by violent black men and alarmed by the passivity of black women who shunned work, gave birth to children out of wedlock, and lived on the public charity of the welfare state. Poor black women were the dependent poor, at the heart of an epidemic of dependence eroding the nation's morals and draining its treasury.

By the early twenty-first century, however, hardly anyone talked or wrote about "underclass" anymore. Instead, from Bangladesh to New York, writers celebrated the entrepreneurial energy and talent latent within poor people who were waiting for the spark of opportunity to transform their lives. Writers such as Muhammad Yunus in Bangladesh and Michael Sherraden in the United States celebrated the assets held by poor people individually and in their neighborhoods. As the market-oriented models reshaping public policy in housing, health care, education, and everywhere else reconfigured ideas about poor people and antipoverty policy, the underclass became entrepreneurs. By contrast, updated to account for shifts in the composition of poverty, mainstream social-science-based antipoverty research and policy moved forward along well-worn tracks—for instance, the role of family structure, parental employment, and workforce development—hoping to influence the federal government to haul the poverty policy wagon at a more active clip. In mainstream poverty policy and research, the microfinanciers and asset builders did not exist. Research-as-usual missed, if it did not dismiss, the new paradigms, and it paid little attention to experiments and programs that fell outside the usual boundaries of mainstream poverty work. In mainstream poverty policy, the state remained the lead actor; in the new market-based technologies of poverty work, the private sector seized the initiative from a diminished state and offered innovations that, according to their sponsors, were less demeaning and more effective. Not unimportantly, they also cost less and made no heavy claims on public money. They also rejected the pathological and cultural interpretations of poverty that underpinned fears of an underclass menacing the safety, health, and prosperity of America's inner cities.

The Rise and Fall of "Underclass"

By the late 1970s, the specter of an emergent underclass permeated discussions of America's inner cities. The term "underclass" offered a convenient metaphor because it evoked three widely shared perceptions: novelty, complexity, and danger. Conditions in inner cities were unprecedented; they could not be reduced to a single factor; and they menaced the rest of us. "Underclass" conjured up a mysterious wilderness in the heart of America's cities; a terrain of violence and despair, a collectivity outside politics and social structure, beyond the usual language of class and stratum, unable to protest or revolt.[1]

Open debate on the underclass accelerated in 1977 when *Time* magazine announced the emergence of a menacing underclass in America's inner cities. Drugs, crime, teenage pregnancy, and high unemployment, not poverty, defined the "underclass," most of whose members were young and minorities. "Behind the [ghetto's] crumbling walls," wrote *Time*, "lives a large group of people who are more intractable, more socially alien and more hostile than almost anyone had imagined. They are the unreachables: the American underclass. . . . Their bleak environment nurtures values that are often at odds with those of the majority—even a majority of the poor. Thus the underclass produced a highly disproportionate number of the nation's juvenile delinquents, school dropouts, drug addicts and welfare mothers, and much of the adult crime, family disruption, urban decay, and demand for social expenditures."[2]

With the 1982 publication of Ken Auletta's *Underclass*, the term secured its dominance in the vocabulary of inner-city pathology. Auletta reinforced the image emerging in the mass media. For him the underclass was a relatively permanent minority among the poor who fell into four distinct categories: "(a) the *passive poor*, usually long-term welfare recipients; (b) the *hostile* street criminals who terrorize most cities, and are often school dropouts and drug addicts; (c) the *hustlers*, who, like street criminals, may not be poor and who earn their livelihood in an underground economy, but rarely commit violent crimes; (d) the *traumatized* drunks, drifters, homeless shopping-bag ladies and released mental patients who frequently roam or collapse on city streets."[3] A new social stratum identified by a set of interlocking behaviors as well as by poverty dominated the wastelands that were all that remained of America's urban-industrial heartland. Herbert Manes and Shorty were two of its members.

Critics worried that arguments for the existence of a new underclass represented a resurgence of old images of the undeserving poor, an attempt to mask recurrent poverty with an argument that blames the victim. Attempts to divide poor people into categories and to distinguish invidiously among them go back centuries. Before the late eighteenth and early nineteenth centuries, poor-law officials tried to distinguish between the "able-bodied" and the "impotent" poor, a distinction that reflected the need to distribute scarce resources rather than the attempt to make a moral judgment.

Nineteenth-century writers moralized the old distinction between the able-bodied and the impotent poor into the worthy and the unworthy or the deserving and the undeserving. In the 1820s, the Philadelphia Guardians of the Poor asserted, "The poor in consequence of vice, constitute here and everywhere, by far the greater part of the poor." In the terminology of the time, "paupers"—those individuals dependent on charity and public assistance—became synonymous with the "undeserving poor."[4] Nine years later, Walter Channing, a prominent minister, pointed out that the "popular mind" regarded poverty "solely as the product of him or of her who has entered its dreadful, because dishonored, uncared for, or unwisely cared for, service. Let me repeat it, the causes of poverty are looked for, and found in him or her who suffers it."[5]

By the second quarter of the nineteenth century, the vocabulary of poverty had acquired two of its lasting features: the division of the poor into categories of merit and the assumption that the roots of poverty lay in individual misbehavior. Over the years, writings about poverty by the political left as well as the right frequently reflected these ideas. Marxists talked about the "lumpenproletariat," and even reformers in the Progressive Era who began to criticize individual-centered explanations of poverty in the 1890s used the old distinctions.[6]

Stripped of their period features, nineteenth-century discussions of urban poverty sound remarkably contemporary. Nineteenth- and early twentieth-century writers portrayed the undeserving poor as clustered in inner cities, where they formed slums that threatened to infect the respectable poor and the middle classes. Observers worried about the consequences of social isolation and the growing concentration of poverty. In 1854, in his first annual report as head of New York City's Children's Aid Society, Charles Loring Brace argued that the growing density of America's cities had eroded the character of their inhabitants. "The very *condensing* of their number within a small space, seems to stimulate their bad tendencies." He defined the "greatest danger" to America's future as the "existence of an ignorant, debased, and permanently poor class in the great cities. . . . The members of it come at length to form a separate population. They embody the lowest passions and the most thriftless habits of the community. They corrupt the lowest class of working-poor who are around them. The expenses of police, of prisons, of charities and means of relief, arise mainly from them."[7]

Housing reformers of the nineteenth and early twentieth centuries argued that the unsanitary, congested housing of the poor bred immorality, crime, and disease. Slums, they contended, were viruses infecting the moral and physical health of the city districts that surrounded them. In their writing, urban poverty acquired its lasting association with disease, embodied in the 1980s in the melding of drugs, AIDS, and poverty into metaphors of epidemics threatening to leap the boundaries of the inner city.[8] "We must deal with [pauperism]," claimed New York City's Charity Organization Society in its fourth annual report in 1886, "as we would with a malarial swamp, draining and purifying it instead of walling it about, or its miasma will spread and taint neighborhoods like the plague."[9]

By the latter nineteenth century, poverty, crime, and disease blended to form a powerful, frightening, and enduring image. As was the case in the late twentieth century, its dimensions were novelty, complexity, and danger. Among the urban poor, an undeserving subset, dependent on account of their own shiftless, irresponsible, immoral behavior, burdened honest taxpayers with the cost of their support, threatened their safety, and corrupted the working poor. Increasingly concentrated within slum districts, they lived in growing social isolation, cut off from role models and oversight once provided by the more well-to-do, reproducing their own degradation. No single factor explained the emergence of the underclass, which was at once a product of economic, demographic, spatial, and cultural influences intersecting to produce a perfect storm.

Social policy had failed to prevent the emergence of the late nineteenth century's version of the underclass. For instance, poorhouses, an early nineteenth-century innovation, had met none of their sponsors' goals. Despised and neglected, they moved to the backwaters of social policy, increasingly transformed into public old-age homes by the removal of special classes of inmates (children, the mentally ill, and the sick). Public school systems, once the hope of urban reformers, had developed into huge, unresponsive bureaucracies that, critics argued, delivered education less effectively than had the smaller schools of the past. Riddled with graft, outdoor relief (public welfare) demoralized the poor and fueled a meteoric rise in taxes.[10]

As reformers and legislators cast about for new policies, they did not abandon the distinction between deserving and undeserving poor. Nor did they redefine its dimensions. The deserving poor fell into two classes: the first, clearly helpless and pathetic people who on account of age or infirmity could neither care for nor support themselves. The other met dual criteria: they had suffered circumstances beyond their own responsibility (the death of a husband or a seasonal layoff, for instance) that had rendered them dependent, *and* they proved themselves willing to work for whatever small support public and private charity might offer. Most deserving were widows who kept their children clean, taught them manners, sent them to school, managed their tiny incomes effectively, and spent hours every day sewing or scrubbing for miniscule wages. The other able-bodied poor were family men out of work, sober and responsible, willing to chop wood or break stone. However, they always remained slightly suspect because they had failed to save for the episodes of dependence that predictably upset life among the working class.[11]

In their emphasis on race, gender, and culture, the major themes in late nineteenth-century discussions of urban poverty also resemble those in late twentieth-century writing about the underclass. In popular impressions (although not in fact), the color of the underclass was black. Despite the continuing racism that has scarred American history, this association of urban poverty with race is relatively new, a product of the massive migration of African Americans into northern and midwestern cities after World War II. Before then, of course, most African Americans lived in rural areas, and racial ghettos within northern cities, as Chapter 1 showed, remained relatively small. At the time, the most visible extreme poverty occurred within the vast tenement-house districts inhabited by second-generation white ethnics and new European immigrants. Observers, fearful of cultural differences, which they equated with inferiority, very often framed discussions of poverty in racial terms and applied them to nationality groups. This scientific racism culminated in the eugenics movement of the early twentieth century and in the 1924 nationality-based immigration quotas. In this way, stigmas of cultural difference, race, and poverty blended very early in images of the undeserving poor.[12]

Images of alcoholic, immoral, incompetent mothers unfit to raise their children also extend far into the past. Nonetheless, throughout most of American history, widows remained the quintessential deserving poor. Most despised and distrusted have been unmarried men, like Herbert Manes and Shorty, unable to support themselves. Public officials and charity reformers waged long, tough, and only partially successful campaigns to drive them from the relief rolls and out of poorhouses. (In the 1980s, they tried to purge them from the rolls of state General Assistance. By late in the twentieth century, as incarceration rates soared, prison became the main form of welfare for out-of-work black men.) In the 1870s, a new noun—"tramp"—entered the language to identify this most visible element among the era's underclass equivalent, and commentators invariably referred to them as men.[13]

When the first federal welfare program for women with children, Aid to Dependent Children (ADC), entered public policy as part of the legislation creating Social Security in 1935, its sponsors assumed it would apply to a relatively small group of widows. In the 1950s, as the recipients of ADC (later AFDC, Aid to Families with Dependent Children) increasingly were unmarried and black, public attitudes shifted. Race and sexuality fused with the usual stigma attached to welfare, and African American women raising children by themselves became the new undeserving poor.[14]

Sentiment, however, did not shift in favor of dependent men. Increasingly, nonworking males divided into two groups—adults out of work because of plant closings and economic restructuring, and young minority men, unskilled, unwilling to work, and dangerous. What defined them was their behavior, especially their alleged responsibility for crime and irresponsibility to the children they fathered. Together with African American women supported by welfare, they became the core of the underclass. They could be found throughout the nation's bleak ghettos, on many streets like the one in North Philadelphia where Herbert Manes killed a drunk and stoned street mechanic called Shorty over five dollars.

In the 1960s, writers who tried to interpret the growth and persistence of poverty formalized long-standing arguments about behavioral pathology into a theory of culture, which, despite shifts in its political connotation, has proved remarkably tenacious.[15] Anthropologist Oscar Lewis injected the concept of a "culture of poverty" into academic social science and popular commentary. Like the underclass, the "culture of poverty" did not mean simply economic deprivation. Rather, it referred to a "way of life . . . passed down from generation to generation along family lines." Lewis viewed the culture of poverty as adaptive, useful in coping with "feelings of hopelessness and despair which develop from the realization of the impossibility of achieving success in terms of the values and goals of the larger society." In his definition, "the lack of effective participation and integration of the poor in the major institutions of the larger society," along with a long list of behavioral pathologies, characterized the culture of poverty.[16]

Lewis and others, like Michael Harrington in *The Other America*, who adapted the concept of the culture of poverty to particular issues, hoped to put the idea to liberal political purposes as a force energizing activist, interventionist public policy.[17] They did not intend to reproduce the old distinction between the worthy and the unworthy poor. Nonetheless, others with more conservative agendas turned the concept's original politics on its head. The "culture of poverty" became a euphemism for the pathology of the undeserving poor, an explanation for their condition—an excuse, as in the writing of political scientist Edward Banfield, for both inaction and punitive public policy.[18]

The culture of poverty fused with racial politics in 1965 with the leak of a confidential report to President Lyndon Johnson by a young assistant secretary of labor. Daniel Patrick Moynihan's *The Negro Family: The Case for National Action* did not use the phrase "culture of poverty," but its language, especially its metaphor, "tangle of pathology," reflected similar ideas.[19] Moynihan's report coincided with the crest of the Civil Rights Movement. Indeed, Johnson drew on it for his famous Howard University speech of June 4, 1965, in which he lashed out at the persistence of black poverty. However, civil rights leaders and others found Moynihan's analysis, as reported in the press, offensive, empirically flawed, and denigrating, deflecting blame from the source of poverty to its victims.[20]

Black scholars drew from a different intellectual stream to explain the persistence of poverty. Around the globe, previously dependent people were asserting their right to liberation. As they fought guerrilla wars, organized against dictatorships, or, in the United States, struggled against racism and segregation, they revealed the bankruptcy of ideas that portrayed them as passive, incapable of self-assertion, unable to generate indigenous leadership. Their leaders developed theories of dependence and internal colonialism to explain poverty and underdevelopment in the Third World. In radical American writing, the ghetto became a colony, and exploitation and racism the explanation for persistent black poverty. Neither the culture of poverty nor the undeserving poor made sense, other than as mystifications that hid the dynamics of power and subordination. This alternative to long-standing themes in American writing about poverty flourished only briefly. Its association with the Black Power movement, location outside the academic mainstream, lack of intellectual polish, and the diminishing energy of the Civil Rights Movement all contributed to its failure to alter the framework that constrained discussions of poverty.[21]

For the most part, the assumptions underlying the War on Poverty during the same years fit within the prevailing framework. Only community action, the emphasis on the participation of the poor in the design and implementation of programs to serve them, rejected conventional approaches. The most controversial part of the poverty war, community action challenged the power of the state and local politicians, who quickly goaded Congress and the president into blunting its impact and denaturing its meaning. For the most part, the War on Poverty rested firmly on supply-side views of poverty. It emphasized opportunity, not by focusing on the labor market, as the Department of Labor at first advocated, but by improving individual skills through education and job training.[22]

The War on Poverty and the expansion of related government programs created poverty research as a field in social science, because legislation mandated evaluation. Leadership fell to economics, which alone among the social sciences seemed to offer the necessary tools, theories, and prestige. The aftermath of the culture of poverty tarnished sociology and anthropology, which had failed to develop compelling alternative perspectives or ways of answering legislators' and administrators' questions about the results of programs. Policy research itself became a new field, grounded in economics, located within new schools in universities and in the new world of independent centers and institutes. Poverty research developed sophisticated new methods, especially large-scale social experiments, applied most notably to tests of income maintenance programs, but it contributed few new ideas and little in the way of theory.[23]

By and large, academic economists of the time did not consider the implications of their research for assessing the distinction between the deserving and the undeserving poor and its relation to the existence of a culture of poverty. By the early 1980s, however, conservative writers drew the connection. The questions asked in the conservative political climate of the era were: Why, despite all the new social programs of the War on Poverty and Great Society, had poverty worsened? What explained the explosive growth of female-headed African American families, the unemployment of African American men, and the crime, violence, and social disorganization within inner cities? Spending on social welfare had risen dramatically; segregation and other barriers to African American economic and political advancement had lowered; and the country had enjoyed unusual prosperity and economic growth. Given this context, what could account for the rise in social pathology, especially among inner-city African Americans?[24]

In *Losing Ground*, Charles Murray gave the most widely cited answer, although many others offered similar arguments. The culprits became the social programs themselves. Well intentioned though they were, they had eroded the will to work and the incentives for stable family life. Murray and other conservative writers fueled renewed interest in the culture of poverty and the undeserving poor. Social programs had fostered a new, demoralized way of life among minorities clustered within inner cities. They reproduced welfare dependence between generations. They reinforced values and behaviors at variance with those of the rest of American society. They were the underclass.[25]

Social scientists counterattacked by showing how Murray and others were wrong. Critics have subjected the evidence and methods of few books to such withering and authoritative criticism as they meted out to *Losing Ground*. But Murray and the conservatives had tapped the issues that troubled many Americans and then had offered clear answers. Many remained predisposed to believe them, despite evidence to the contrary. Indeed, for the most part liberal social scientists failed to move beyond criticism of data and methods. They addressed themselves to the same questions about the results of welfare and offered different answers. But they could say little in answer to the basic questions posed by conservatives.[26]

It was not surprising, therefore, that when "underclass" surfaced in *Time* and other magazines, and in Auletta's book, few liberal social scientists objected. They had no alternative framework. With no other language in which to describe or comprehend what had happened within inner cities, "underclass" became a new neutral ground on which to debate. What were its characteristics? Its sources? Its prognosis? As leading liberal social scientists tried to appropriate the concept from both the media and conservative commentary, they faced one especially delicate obstacle. How could they reinsert culture and the African American family onto the agenda of social science without conceding the argument to the conservatives? No realistic analysis of inner-city poverty could ignore family, which, in fact, had emerged as a key concern within African American communities. But in politics and social science, conservatives had appropriated family and culture in the 1960s. Indeed, most subsequent commentary on the underclass used imprecise definitions that stressed family and individual behavior and rested on implicitly moral concepts of class structure.[27]

The major liberal response came in 1987 with William Julius Wilson's *The Truly Disadvantaged*, which tried to incorporate family and culture into a social-democratic analysis of inner-city poverty and the underclass. *The Truly Disadvantaged* quickly became the most influential scholarly book on contemporary American poverty.[28]

Despite his concern with African American family structure, Wilson located the origins of the underclass in African American male joblessness. He asserted that neutral terms, such as "lower class" or "working class," did not evoke the recent transformations in America's cities that resulted in increased concentrations of poverty. African American middle- and working-class families, he argued, had abandoned inner-city ghettos to a "heterogeneous grouping of families and individuals who are outside the mainstream of the American occupational system." They were the underclass: "individuals who lack training and skills and either experience long-term unemployment or are not members of the labor force, individuals who are engaged in street crime and other forms of aberrant behavior, and families that experience long-term spells of poverty and/or welfare dependency." For him, "underclass" signified "the groups. . . . left behind," who were "collectively different from those that lived in these neighborhoods in earlier years."[29]

Wilson presented *The Truly Disadvantaged* as a series of hypotheses based on the best evidence available at the time, and he mounted a large research project to test his ideas. As other social scientists followed his lead, *The Truly Disadvantaged* also set the agenda for the first round of research on the urban underclass.

Even before the book's publication, a few social scientists had initiated research on the underclass. This early research attempted to identify underclass areas and to count the group. Because definitions of the underclass varied among researchers, size estimates ranged from 500,000 to 4.1 million.[30] Research intensified after 1987, when the Rockefeller Foundation asked the Social Science Research Council (SSRC) to consider creating a Committee on the Urban Underclass. The new committee tried to stimulate research through a program of fellowships and scholarships (undergraduate, graduate, and postdoctoral) and a set of research planning activities. The activities of the SSRC Committee on the Urban Underclass helped stimulate interest in underclass issues among social scientists and revive research on urban poverty, which had languished since the mid-1970s. The key issues generated by Wilson's work largely, though not wholly, dominated the committee's early deliberations.[31]

Despite its title, the SSRC Committee on the Urban Underclass did not adopt an official definition of "underclass." Rather, it defined its working focus as "persistent and concentrated urban poverty." Nor did other urban researchers adopt a standard definition. Indeed, many, including some members of the committee, objected to the term. In his August 1990 presidential address to the American Sociological Association,

Wilson, who had advocated the usefulness and objective foundation of "underclass," recommended its abandonment by researchers.[32] In January 1991, recounts historian Alice O'Connor, the Rockefeller Foundation "expressed its dissatisfaction" by telling the SSRC's Underclass Committee "that funding would be terminated sooner than expected—after a five-year, rather than what had earlier been held out as a possible ten-year, span of annual grants.[33] In effect, the underclass era had ended.

At the same time that it was funding the Social Science Research Council Underclass Committee, the Rockefeller Foundation was supporting six Community Action and Planning Programs (CPAPs) in major cities. All the CPAPS, reports O'Connor, "rejected 'underclass' as a label." They wanted to mobilize inner-city residents, not stigmatize them with an invidious label. The Rockefeller program staff wanted the two programs—research and community action—to fertilize each other, but they met resistance from each side. When the foundation finally forced a meeting, it turned into a near disaster, with neither camp able to communicate with or influence the other. It was not long after this meeting that the Rockefeller Foundation pulled the plug on the SSRC committee.[34] Together, the six CPAPs made up one of several foundation- and community-sponsored comprehensive community initiatives launched at about the same time.[35] Their goal was "to address the interrelated issues" affecting inner cities "with comprehensive, long-term strategies."[36] By and large, these initiatives did not meet the hopes of their founders. As they wound down, their mixed track records cast doubt on the possibility of comprehensive, long-term strategies of urban revitalization. With the failure of the comprehensive community initiatives and the gap between social science poverty researchers and on-the-ground antipoverty programs, the underclass era concluded without much to show by way of concrete accomplishments.

One weakness of "underclass" as idea was intellectual, for it updated old, moralistic concepts which never had proved helpful in addressing the ubiquitous poverty in the land of plenty. As a modern euphemism for the undeserving poor, "underclass" reinforced the tradition of blaming the victim. It also reinforced emerging political divisions between the working class and the poor, who needed each other as allies, and, through its concentration on the behavior of a relatively small number of people clustered in inner cities, deflected attention from the problem of poverty and minimized its extent. The word "underclass," its critics asserted, had little intellectual substance. It lacked a consistent, defensible theoretical basis. It was not a "class" in any of the usual senses. Most definitions, in fact, substituted varieties of bad behavior for the criteria customary in stratification theories. Nor could the social scientists who used it, let alone the media, agree on a definition.

Whatever its weaknesses, however it was defined, "underclass" was a metaphor of social transformation, a first attempt by social scientists, caught without adequate concepts between what urban America was and what it had become, to construct the intellectual scaffolding from which to survey and map the mysterious new terrain of the nation's inner cities. Their efforts were, at best, only partially successful because they found it hard to shake free of the predispositions and preoccupations that had dogged American discourse about poverty for decades. Was it possible to think and write about poor people without echoing the trope of the deserving and undeserving poor? Without making poverty more a matter of culture and individual behavior than of political economy?

Were other technologies of poverty work available or imaginable? By "poverty work," I mean research on the history, size, demography, behavior, and geographic distribution of the poverty population, as well the formulation, implementation, and evaluation of antipoverty programs and policies. I use "technologies" to signify clusters of ideas and actions: conceptions of the etiology and morphology of poverty linked to mechanisms for its reduction.

Urban ethnographers offered the first theoretical alternative to mainstream poverty work. In anthropology, ethnographers had to buck the tradition of studying pre-modern societies. In sociology, they faced skepticism from practitioners of quantitative methods who dominated the discipline. Only a few ethnographies on inner-city Americans appeared before the 1990s—the most famous was Eliot Liebow's *Tally's Corner*, an insightful reconstruction of the world of street-corner men in Chicago. In the 1990s and early years of the twenty-first century, a number of young scholars—Philippe Bourgois, Elijah Anderson, Loïc Wacquant, Mitch Duneier, and Sudhir Venkatesh—to name some of the most well known—wrote important books showing the complexity and social order within inner-city neighborhoods and the agency of their residents who developed life strategies appropriate for their situations. For the most part, this ethnographic work was virtually ignored by scholars in the mainstream of their disciplines, who made obeisance to "qualitative" methods only as techniques for illustrating what quantitative analyses already had shown. Only a few scholars successfully combined qualitative and quantitative methods in pioneering work. Nor did the ethnographers have any substantial impact on policy.[37]

Market-based proposals for alleviating poverty and reviving inner cities are also alternatives to pathological images of poor people. The values associated with markets have never drifted far from the center of American public policy. What marks the post-1980 period is their hegemony—their replacement of alternative templates in both public and private sectors. Markets are systems of exchange guided, for the most part, by a set of underlying assumptions, including rationality. Rational individuals act in ways that serve their self-interest. Their collective and unimpeded interactions yield the greatest public good. Because markets enhance both individual freedom of choice and the optimal allocation of scarce resources, they are the ultimate source of liberty and prosperity. Governments, therefore, should interfere with markets as little as possible. Everywhere, this language of the market dominated public policy. Poverty and inner cities were no exception.

In the years after 1980, poverty work did not escape the market template stamped on all areas of public policy. To market theorists, poor people were rational actors—consumers, savers, and entrepreneurs. Four distinct, if overlapping, market-based strands were braided through poverty work: place-based initiatives that intended to unleash poor people as consumers by rebuilding markets in inner cities; microfinance programs that turned poor people into entrepreneurs; asset-building strategies that helped poor people accumulate capital; and conditional cash transfers that focused on deploying monetary incentives to change behavior. In the new market-based technologies of poverty work, the underclass had become entrepreneurs.

Prospecting for Wealth in Inner Cities

Consider, first, markets, or their absence. The zones of concentrated poverty at the heart of older American cities lay outside legitimate markets—drug markets and an informal economy substituted for the institutions of commerce and manufacturing that had fled. Prices had dropped so low, supply so outstripped demand, that no housing market existed. Supermarkets and banks exited, leaving residents dependent on small, low-quality, overpriced local grocers and exploitive check-cashing services. Industries had decamped to suburbs, Latin America, or Asia. With public assistance, food stamps, SSI, and a few other transfer programs, governments kept poor people alive, but not much more. Most of the community development and empowerment programs optimistically launched in the heady days of the War on Poverty and Great Society had folded.

What remained was the institutional cluster that the great urban photographer Camilo José Vergara labels the institutional ghetto—the prisons, halfway houses, clinics, and homeless shelters that constitute the institutions of punishment, social control, and welfare.[38] Faced with this situation, it was reasonable for urban planners to think that the way to jump start inner-city revitalization and to attack poverty lay in the re-creation of markets. The first plan, launched during Ronald Reagan's presidency, was Enterprise Zones, which proved a disappointment. The Clinton administration revived the idea with a new twist and a new name, Empowerment Zones. They also fell short of expectations.

Enterprise zones were a British import, first advocated in 1977 by British urban planner Peter Hall and implemented by Margaret Thatcher's chancellor of the Exchequer, Geoffrey Howe. Their American champion, Congressman Jack Kemp, failed to persuade Congress to pass a comprehensive Enterprise Zone bill, but a number of states acted on their own, designating zones in which they offered firms a miscellaneous assortment of incentives. The idea, pointed out urbanists Philip Kasinitz and Jan Rosenberg, sounded "like simple common sense: use tax breaks and other incentives to encourage private employers to locate in poor areas, bringing job opportunities to local residents." The appeal of Enterprise Zones extended across the political spectrum. "Conservatives like them because they promise reduced government and a private-sector answer to poverty. Liberals are attracted by the promise of 'empowerment' for the local community. And enterprise zones have a strong nonideological selling point: they are cheap." After all, they were paid for largely by "uncollected taxes on as yet unmade profits." Alas, the incentives proved too weak to attract many businesses, and many of the firms that relocated to them failed to employ local workers.[39]

The Clinton administration tried to improve on the Enterprise Zone idea with the Empowerment Act of 1993, which called for nine "empowerment zones" and ninety-five "enterprise communities" in both rural and urban areas. Both would be eligible for a bundle of tax breaks and other incentives, such as accelerated depreciation for investments in the zone, tax credits for employment and training, and small inducements to hire local residents. Unlike the earlier plans, Clinton's added eligibility for social services and community-based programs in education, housing, and crime prevention. Nonetheless, incentives again failed to attract large numbers of employers to the zones or open large numbers of jobs for local residents, while the zones' resources, to be managed by local boards, often ended up embroiled in local politics, tinged with nepotism and petty corruption. Zone advocates, Kasinitz and Rosenberg claimed, incorrectly believed that inner-city residents lacked jobs because jobs had migrated to suburbs, while the true reason was that they lacked the social networks—the personal connections—that linked people to work. Neither Enterprise nor Empowerment Zone tried to build networks or find creative substitutes.[40]

For all their emphasis on re-creating markets, Enterprise and Empowerment Zones still began with a deficit model. The point of policy was to supply poor inner-city neighborhoods with the assets they lacked. Harvard Business School professor Michael Porter, on the other hand, wanted to capitalize on the unused assets already there. His famous 1995 *Harvard Business Review* article "The Competitive Advantage of the Inner City" (reprinted in his book *On Competition*), portrayed inner cities as bursting with unharnessed strengths that capitalism, unimpeded by the clumsy, bureaucratic hand of government, could use to revitalize cities and reduce poverty.[41]

"The sad reality," wrote Porter, "is that the efforts of the past few decades to revitalize inner cities have failed." Despite large investments, inner cities still lacked a "sustainable economic base," including "employment opportunities, wealth creation, role models, and improved local infrastructure." Most economic development programs, "fragmented and ineffective," had taken "the form of subsidies, preference programs, or expensive efforts to stimulate economic activity in tangential fields such as housing, real estate, and neighborhood development." They had "treated the inner city as an island isolated from the surrounding economy and subject to its own unique laws of competition." Policies had "fallen into the trap of redistributing wealth" when the "real need—and the real opportunity" was "to create wealth." Policies should reverse the process of starting with "social investment" in the hope that "economic activity" would follow. "Instead, an economic model must begin with the premise that inner city businesses should be profitable and positioned to compete on a regional, national, and even international scale." They should not only serve their local community but also export "goods and services to the surrounding economy."

In short, inner cities needed to exchange their apologetic diffidence for a bold assertion of their competitive advantages. These were four in number, and Porter provided concrete examples of each. First was their "strategic location" near "congested high-rent areas, major business centers, and transportation and communication nodes." Second was the often overlooked "local market demand." While other markets had become "saturated," inner-city markets remained "poorly served—especially in retailing financial services, and personal services." In fact, the market was huge. Incomes might be low, but population density was high. In Boston, for instance, despite a 21 percent lower household income, "spending power per acre" was comparable to the rest of the city. The third advantage was the potential for integration with regional economic clusters. "The most exciting prospects for the future of inner city economic development [lay] in capitalizing on nearby regional clusters: those unique-to-a-region collections of related companies that are competitive nationally and even globally."

Most surprising was the fourth advantage: human resources. Porter dispelled a "number of deeply entrenched myths" about the nature of inner-city residents: they did not want to work and opted "for welfare over gainful employment"; the "only entrepreneurs were drug dealers"; "skilled minorities" had abandoned their roots in inner cities. In fact, "most inner city residents" were "eager to work." There was "a real capacity for legitimate entrepreneurship among inner city residents, most of which . . . [had] been channeled into the provision of social services." A "large and growing pool of talented minority managers" represented "a new generation of potential inner city entrepreneurs [many] . . . trained at the nation's leading business schools and . . . [with] experience in the nation's leading companies."

What had to be done to unleash the inner city's competitive advantages? Porter listed a number of obstacles, including the problem of land assembly, building costs, and higher costs for "water, other utilities, workers' compensation, health care, insurance, permitting and other fees, real estate and other taxes, OSHA compliance, and neighborhood hiring requirements." Other barriers included security, infrastructure, employee skills, management skills, and access to "debt and equity capital." The private sector, government, and community-based organizations all needed to assume new roles, which, for the latter, included creating "a hospitable environment for business by working to change community and workforce attitudes and acting as a liaison with residents to quell unfounded opposition to new businesses." Governments also should realign their activities to serve the needs of business. "These changes," Porter admitted, would be "difficult ones for both individuals and institutions. . . . Businesspeople, entrepreneurs, and investors must assume a lead role; and community activists, social service providers, and government bureaucrats must support them."

In its next issue, *Harvard Business Review* ran ten responses to Porter by professionals and researchers whose work focused on one or another aspect of inner-city economic development. The least critical, and least substantive, was from Robert Rubin, the secretary of the treasury in the Clinton administration. Most critical was James Johnson's response. Johnson, a distinguished scholar of cities, race, and poverty, was E. Maynard Adams Professor of Business, Geography, and Sociology, Kenan Institute of Private Enterprise, University of North Carolina, as well as director of the Urban Enterprise Corps located in Chapel Hill. Porter's proposals, Johnson claimed, echoed the failed efforts of the Reagan and Bush administrations to "facilitate the competitiveness of U.S. companies in the global marketplace" by deregulating business, gutting environmental agencies, and slashing the staff of "governmental agencies charged with enforcing laws governing workplace health, safety, and compensation, as well as hiring, retention, and promotion practices." The major beneficiaries were "hospitality services and craft specialty industries" that Porter presented "as examples of competitive inner-city business enterprises." What was the result? These businesses, which remained profitable and remained in the inner city because they hired "newly arrived illegal immigrants rather than native workers," created "work environments reminiscent of nineteenth century sweatshops." Their profits, moreover, "did little to improve the quality of life of inner city workers and their communities." In light of these outcomes, Johnson doubted that the private sector should "take the lead role in revitalization." Instead, revitalization demanded an "equality of status across" the institutions of government, community-based organizations, and the private sector. "Otherwise, we run the risk of advancing the notion that a knight in shining armor from the outside can initiate an economic turnaround without the support of inner city residents." The failure of Rebuild LA, launched "in the aftermath of the 1992 civil unrest in Los Angeles, cautions us against such an approach."[42] Other critics pounced on Porter's neglect of housing, denigration of community-based organizations, hostility to government, and failure to lay out a strategy for accomplishing his goals.[43]

Porter answered critics with the success of the Initiative for a Competitive Inner City (ICIC), a national not-for-profit that he founded in 1994. Its "mission is to promote economic prosperity in America's inner cities through private sector engagement that leads to job, income and wealth creation for local residents."[44] Its partners and supporters included leading businesses and the federal government's Small Business Administration. ICIC claimed many successes. By 2009, it included more than $2 billion in equity funds channeled "to domestic emerging markets using ICIC's theories and data," while "companies that participated in [its] Inner City Capital Connections program [had] received more than $140 million in funding from investors." Each year, ICIC and Bloomberg Business Week released the "Inner City 100, a list of the fastest-growing inner city companies in the U.S." By 2010, the 607 different companies that had appeared on the list had collectively generated "more than $27.2 billion in revenues" while "creating nearly 72,000 new jobs." In a 2005 report funded by major foundations and posted on the U.S. Federal Government Small Business Administration Web site, ICIC shows that most inner-city jobs were created in small businesses.[45] These are impressive statistics, and ICIC is a hive of applied research, network-building, technical advising, and promotional activities. Yet, nowhere on its Web site does it assess the real bottom line: poverty and employment rates in inner cities and joblessness among African American men. Are the examples of ICIC sites isolated instances of success, or are they representative of major trends? Exemplary or transformative? These questions await answers.

Michael Porter's work catapulted him to the front ranks of strategic thinkers on business; he is one of the few theorists respected in both the academic and business communities. And he has been influential. He played golf with President Clinton and attended Clinton's 1992 economic summit. He is one of the three advisory board co-chairs of Goldman Sachs's 10,000 Small Businesses Initiative, launched in 2009. The other two are Goldman Sachs CEO Lloyd Blankfein and financial wizard Warren Buffett.[46] His ideas have influenced federal government policy, especially through their link with the Small Business Administration, and they were reflected in one of President Clinton's signature programs—the New Markets Initiative.

Clinton's urban strategy focused on the revitalization of places through the re-creation of markets. His New Markets Initiative relied on tax incentives and the mobilization of private capital rather than federal funds or services. To be much more precise, the federal government acted as catalyst and impresario. When Clinton visited several poor rural and urban communities in July, he called them "untapped areas for potential investment." HUD's reference to inner-city neighborhoods as "undiscovered territories for many businesses" echoed Clinton, who hoped that federal tax credit and loan guarantees would "inspire private companies to build plants and stores" in the places "that the economic boom" had "largely passed by." During his second poverty tour in November, Clinton alerted a high school audience in Newark, New Jersey, "Now is the time to say the rest of America should be part of our prosperity, and they're our next great economic opportunity—the new markets of the 21st century."[47]

On December 21, 2000, two weeks before he left office, Clinton signed the bipartisan Community Relief Tax Act, which turned his New Markets Initiative into law. He called it "the most significant effort ever" to help distressed communities by leveraging private investment. The vehicle was a new set of tax credits. The New Markets Tax Credit (NMTC) program was supposed to combine private and public resources to pump $15 billion in new investments over seven years into poor urban and rural districts. Congress extended the program through the end of 2009 and then again through 2010. What had it accomplished? In 2005, two analysts, Julia Sass Rubin and Gregory M. Stankiewicz, offered a midcourse assessment. "Our analysis of the New Markets Tax Credit program," they wrote, "is based on the assumption that the program's intent is one of poverty alleviation—to better the lives of residents of distressed communities—rather than general economic development." The Bush administration, however, had redirected the program. It was "less interested in using community economic development as an avenue to address poverty alleviation, preferring instead to rely on faith-based organizations to take the lead on such issues while emphasizing overall economic growth objectives." Given its original purpose, argued Rubin and Stankiewicz, the program should not be used to "subsidize activities that have a limited community economic development impact." Whether its goal was poverty alleviation or economic growth, the "program should not fund activities that would have occurred without the subsidy." Yet, this was precisely what was happening. The authors, however, did not "want to lose sight" of the NMTC's "many benefits." Case studies and reports from practitioners "consistently demonstrate . . . the program has attracted new investors, and many of the NMTC transactions" were "being used to bolster the economies of "distressed communities."[48] As with the ICIC, supporters once again fell back on anecdotal evidence to imply that market-based urban policies were reviving inner cities and reducing poverty. Others remained skeptical. New Markets was one more place-based antipoverty program, and placed-based programs such as Urban Renewal, Comprehensive Community Initiatives, and Enterprise and Empowerment Zones had a poor track record.

Community development corporations (CDCs) grew up around and within place-based programs. CDCs targeted their work more narrowly than Enterprise or Empowerment Zones, focusing mainly on housing. They became the nation's primary builders of affordable housing, substituting for the federal government, which had withdrawn from the field. CDCs succeeded at producing affordable housing; they did not succeed at reducing poverty. Reflecting on a decade of investing millions of dollars in metropolitan Philadelphia's low-income neighborhoods, Jeremy Nowak, executive director of The Reinvestment Fund, wrote that he and colleagues making similar efforts in other cities had assumed that investing in areas outside the mainstream economy would reverse "the outflow of jobs, capital, and people from the inner city." However, "the persistence and acceleration of poverty" characterized the "very areas where so much community development activity" had taken place. Nowak concluded that CDCs remained too small to "restore the ordinary mechanisms of the market place" to inner cities or to transform them into places where "anyone with choice" would want to live. Community development, he argued, had paid too little attention to "the requirements of social mobility . . . to household poverty defined by access to good jobs and the accumulations of wealth." Understanding urban poverty as a problem of place confounded neighborhood revitalization and "poverty alleviation." Nowak wanted instead to alleviate poverty by linking inner cities to regional economies, which would happen by opening up opportunities for residents and helping families accumulate assets.[49] Despite their limitations as tools for poverty alleviation, community development corporations became catalysts for a housing policy revolution.

"CDCs, new government entities at the state and local levels, capacity-building intermediaries, new private sector participants, and other institutions such as foundations and the government-sponsored enterprises, Fannie Mae and Freddie Mac," according to housing expert David J. Erickson, compose a new "decentralized housing network." In recent decades, this new network produced affordable rental housing of unprecedented quality and quantity. Even more, its flexible, opportunistic, public/private structure exemplified a new model "providing an inspiration for policy areas as diverse as economic development, education, health, and the environment."[50]

In contrast to place-based antipoverty strategies, another Clinton-era signature program—Moving to Opportunity (MTO)—represented a people-based assault on poverty. "MTO set out to test the idea that where you can live in America matters for your well-being and life prospects—and also to test *how* it might matter. . . . If 'bad' neighborhoods are truly bad for children and families, especially the minority poor, can moving to better neighborhoods lead to better lives? Might these families have a better quality of life if they continued to be poor?" In 1994, HUD funded MTO to answer these questions. MTO was an $80 million social experiment that "enrolled nearly 5,000 very low-income, mostly black and Hispanic families, many of them on welfare, who were living in public housing in the inner-city ghettos of Baltimore, Boston, Los Angeles, and New York."[51] Participants were given housing vouchers with which to locate subsidized housing in low-poverty areas. Researchers compared their experiences with security, education, jobs, and community to those of a control group that did not receive financial assistance to leave inner cities.

In *Moving to Opportunity: The Story of an American Experiment to Fight Ghetto Poverty*, Xavier de Souza Briggs, Susan J. Popkin, and John Goering analyze the program's first fifteen years. They tell a nuanced, complicated story of successes and failures, and everything in between, and of a "strong-idea-weakly implemented."[52] They point to improvements in program design—for example, counseling families on education, jobs, and other issues after they had moved—that would overcome some of MTO's weaknesses. They make a persuasive case that without a massive increase in the supply of affordable rental housing, programs such as MTO will not realize their potential, and the lives of the inner-city poor will not improve. But assisted mobility programs are only half the story: "initiatives to expand housing opportunity for the inner-city poor should not be substituted for investing in the revitalization of distressed neighborhoods. Both place-based and people-based policies should be pursued in smart ways; both are central to creating a more equitable geography of opportunity."[53]

Where Briggs and his coauthors implicitly differ from Porter is in Porter's unqualified reliance on markets. The tendency of social policy to adopt market models that emphasize choice in schooling and other areas, including housing, overlooks the information deficit that severely limits the capacity of poor people to make informed choices. The "notion that choice-driven programs tap the efficiency of the market and empower the poor at the same time . . . has always been in the 'DNA' of the federal government's housing voucher program, enacted in 1974. . . . It is a central idea in education and health care reform, too." The problem with this assumption is that "poor people who have lived segregated lives in dangerous, high poverty neighborhoods" have only a "limited choice set." Their "information poverty" allows them to make only limited comparisons, not knowing "what they are missing, just around the bend, because they have never had it, and no one they know or trust has ever had it."[54]

Of the four major market-based technologies of poverty work—rebuilding markets in inner cities, microfinance, asset accumulation, and conditional cash transfers—only the first (rebuilding markets in inner cities) focused on regenerating places. The other three, like MTO, focused squarely on individuals. The most prominent—microfinance—started in Bangladesh and propagated itself around the world—in developed as well as developing countries—with astonishing speed.

Microfinance from the Villages of Bangladesh to the Streets of American Cities

In January 1977, Muhammad Yunus, an economics professor in Bangladesh, began to lend poor women small amounts of money with which to start their own businesses, and in 1983 he founded the Grameen Bank (*Grameen* means "village").[55] The bank "pioneered a simple model of credit" that gave loans at reasonable interest rates to small groups of women. The Grameen program provided poor women with an alternative to the formal banking system with its demand for collateral and the informal loan sharks and moneylenders who exploited poor people. "Premised on the idea that the poor are inherently entrepreneurial, the Grameen Bank bets on the generation of income and the smooth repayment of such loans."[56] Yunus preferred to loan to women because they were more likely than men to use the money for the well-being of their families and because he hoped the program would empower women. Women repaid their loans in weekly installments for one year; the interest rate was 20 percent. Yunus claimed a repayment rate of 98 percent.

The success of the Grameen program, Yunus explained, depended on its requirement that women borrowers belong to groups:

> when we discovered that support groups were crucial to the success of our operations, we required that each applicant join a group of like-minded people living in similar economic and social conditions. . . . Group membership not only creates support and protection but also smoothes out the erratic behavior patterns of individual members, making each borrower more reliable in the process. Subtle, and at times not so subtle peer pressure keeps each group member in line with the broader objectives of the credit program.[57]

Microfinance stood most antipoverty programs on their heads. "Microfinance is the rare antipoverty approach," claims Alex Counts, head of the Grameen Foundation, "based on the poor's strengths rather than their deficiencies."[58] Conventional programs assumed poor people lacked the skills with which to support themselves through paid work or self-employment, and they began with a period of training. Yunus began with cash. He had an abiding belief in the "unexplored potential of the destitute."[59] Poor people, he assumed, were just like anyone else; the source of their poverty lay in their lack of opportunities, including access to credit. The "poor are poor not because they are untrained or illiterate," wrote Yunus, "but because they cannot retain the returns of their labor."[60] Lurking within them were latent entrepreneurs. "To me," he emphasized, "an entrepreneur is not an especially gifted person. I rather take the reverse view. I believe that all human beings are potential entrepreneurs." Yunus believed that self-employment was a more effective route out of poverty than wage employment. In this, he rejected microeconomic theory, which mistakenly divided "human beings" into "consumers or laborers" ignoring "their potential as self-employed individuals." Disregarding "the creativity and ingenuity of each human being," microeconomic theory mistakenly considered "widespread self-employment in Third World countries as a symptom of underdevelopment." The key to self-employment was credit—and credit, Yunus proclaimed, was a fundamental human right. But it was a fundamental right denied to most of the world's poor, who, lacking other alternatives, turned to private money lenders who exploited them.

Yunus's politics do not conform to conventional divisions between right and left. He is a harsh critic of capitalism as it is usually practiced, and he is acutely aware of exploitation and the contextual roots of poverty. At the same time, he "argues against the provision of free health and education for the poor. He suggests that the most important thing is that people be given the means to earn an income so they can pay for health, education, and other essentials. Until such time as they can pay with money, education and health should be provided in exchange for a *social payment*, such as a person agreeing to organize a sanitation program in his or her village."[61]

Yunus believed that capitalist activity that focused solely on maximum profits was one-dimensional. "Our economic theory has created a one-dimensional world peopled by those who devote themselves to the game of free-market competition, in which victory is measured purely by profit. . . . Yet the reality is very different from the theory. People are not one-dimensional entities; they are excitingly multidimensional . . . which is why tycoons from Andrew Carnegie and the Rockefellers to Bill Gates have ultimately turned away from the game of profit to focus on higher objectives."[62] Despite his criticism of capitalism as it is currently practiced, Yunus was not antibusiness, but he believed that business could be profitable and serve a social purpose at the same time. Social business, Yunus argued, should have a double bottom line, making a profit while also doing good—a belief sparked by a joint project between Danone, the French yogurt company, and Grameen. Grameen itself started several for-profit businesses designed to run on "social business" principles.

As the Grameen Bank opened more and more branches, its fame—and Yunus's renown—spread around the world. Inspired by Grameen, many other organizations developed microcredit programs in Bangladesh and elsewhere. In Bangladesh, the largest was BRAC, which grew from a "small-scale relief rehabilitation project" started in 1972 into one of the largest NGOs in the world. A number of organizations affiliated with Grameen tried to replicate its model in other countries. In 1998, the Grameen Trust reached 6.18 million borrowers in thirty-eight countries. Founded in Washington, D.C., in 1998, the Grameen Foundation built a network in twenty-eight countries, with fifty-five local microfinance organizations serving 6.8 million borrowers.[63] In 2008, throughout the world, 112 million people participated in microcredit programs, making it, according to Counts, "the most successful effort to organize the poor in human history."[64] In 2005, the International Year of Microcredit, the first worldwide microcredit summit took place in Washington. In October 2006, Muhammad Yunus received word that he had won the Nobel Peace Prize.

Grameen was the first antipoverty program to spread from a poor East Asian country to the developed West—including the United States. Microfinance, observes Ananya Roy in *Poverty Capital*, her brilliant study of the movement, "is one of those rare development ideas that originated in the global South and was taken up by powerful development institutions in the global North."[65] With Grameen America, opened in January 2008 in New York City in Queens, microfinance came to the United States. A second branch opened in Omaha, Nebraska, in 2009, and two additional branches opened in Manhattan and Brooklyn, New York, in 2010. Experienced managers from Bangladesh were brought to the United States to manage the Queens and Omaha branches. Developmental efforts were underway in other states as well. "Grameen America," reported its Web site, "believes that the system that has succeeded with remarkable results in the villages of Bangladesh could work in urban America. Professor Yunus believes that for the world to really take notice of the power of microfinance, it has to work in the capital of international finance, New York City," where, despite the glamour of Wall Street, there exists a "huge population of underserved people who do not have access to banks and mainstream financial institutions."[66] Remarkably, Grameen America opened, flourished, and grew during the worst financial recession since the Great Depression of the 1930s. The Great Recession that began in 2008 proved good for microlending. "Before the economic collapse," reported the *New York Times*, "microfinance—the granting of very small loans, most to poor people—was a concept most closely associated with the developing world." But "tight credit" and recession boosted "demand for small loans in the United States, giving microlending a higher profile and broadening its appeal." The 2009 economic stimulus bill "granted $54 million to the Small Business Administration for lending and assistance to microlenders." Applications for loans from the 362 microfinance organizations in the United States "more than doubled."[67] As of June 2010, Grameen America counted about 3,500 borrowers, with a repayment rate consistently around 99 percent.[68]

His apparent success in alleviating poverty by providing the means for individuals to help themselves won Yunus a warm reception in the United States across the political spectrum. "Many of the arguments" Yunus "had heard against the possibility of adapting Grameen in the United States," Counts reported, "had a familiar ring, since he had heard them in Bangladesh—that the poor can't invest, that they can't save, that they need training and social services before they can start a business, and so on." These arguments, Yunus believed, had no more validity in the United States than in Bangladesh, where his work had proved them wrong. Bill and Hillary Clinton first met Yunus in 1986; deeply impressed by his ideas and accomplishments, Clinton declared his intention, if elected, to "start a thousand Grameen-style microenterprise programs." At the same time, "members of Congress from liberal Democrat Tony Hill to conservative Fred Grandy were talking about the need to encourage self-employment as a path out of poverty."[69]

Microcredit, microenterprise, and microfinance institutions (MFIs) took a variety of forms in the United States, some quite far from the Grameen ideal. "Since the mid-1990s," reported Counts, "dozens of nonprofit organizations in the United States were operating lending programs based (if only loosely) on the Grameen methodology, and many others had incorporated the approach in some form." In the United States, the method was most often called "peer lending."[70] In Chicago in 1986, Mary Houghton, one of the founders of South Shore Bank, who had visited Bangladesh, founded the Women's Self-Employment Project (WSEP). In 1988, it introduced the Full Circle Fund (FCF), an adaptation of Grameen's group membership practice. "On the whole," reports Counts, "Grameen's group structure and lending methodology translated surprisingly well to Chicago."[71]

The FCF had "the distinction of being an effort to solve poverty in the industrialized world by using a strategy developed in the Third World."[72] One of its "most important accomplishments" was "to show that poor black women from distressed neighborhoods can benefit from its approach."[73] Quite different was the approach of the Women's Initiative in San Francisco, founded in 1988. Its purpose was to assist "high-potential low-income women who dream of business ownership. Through an intensive 20-session program—in English or Spanish—women are enabled to start, or expand their business." The Women's Initiative also maintains a "revolving loan fund, disbursing loans ranging from $1000 to $25,000, and links women with asset building opportunities." In 2010, it claimed its graduates had "started and expanded over 1,600 businesses from photography studios to catering companies to mechanic shops."[74]

In the federal government, the Microloan Program in the Small Business Administration (SBA) "provides small loans to start-up, newly established, and growing small businesses." The SBA made its loans through community-based lenders acting as intermediaries. The definition of a microloan was not the same in the SBA program as on Chicago's South Side, let alone Bangladesh. In fiscal year 2010, the maximum loan was $35,000—the Obama administration wanted to fund $25 million worth of loans and proposed to raise the ceiling to $50,000.[75]

Microlending, in fact, had become an industry with its own national organization, the Association for Enterprise Opportunity (AEO), "dedicated to advancing microenterprise as a means of job creation and economic development in the United States." AEO collaborated with "State Microenterprise Associations, national policy coalition partners, local agencies and other policymakers to advance the awareness and utilization of microenterprise as an effective job creation and economic development tool."[76] Its direct grants, ranging in 2008 from $6,000 to $43,000, went to public and private agencies, not directly to individuals. New York City operated its own microenterprise programs as part of Mayor Michael Bloomberg's Opportunity NYC, his city antipoverty program. New York's program placed banking and other financial services in poor districts of the city. San Francisco also has it own microlending program.

Both the Charles Stewart Mott Foundation and Aspen Institute traced the growth of MDPs—microenterprise development programs—in the United States. The Aspen Institute reported a growth from 108 to 472 from 1992 to 2002.[77] The U.S. programs emphasize training more than loans and, according to Professor of Social Justice and Inquiry Nancy Jurik, have "transformed" the southern hemisphere practice in five ways. They provide more up-front training; encounter more problems with peer lending; experience higher operating costs; serve a lower percentage of poor clients; and rely on a narrower approach. "The northern programs are focused on the scientific-like transfer of peer lending as a technology for self-employment. The programmatic focus shifts from poverty alleviation and collective empowerment strategies to the narrower goal of self-employment advocacy."[78]

The terrible 1998 flood that devastated Bangladesh—two-thirds of the country was under water for eleven weeks—accentuated problems with the Grameen model of microfinance. "The flood affected 71% of the branches . . . and 52% of the members. With their houses under water or otherwise damaged by the flood, borrowers had to halt all economic activities. . . . One hundred and fifty-four of the bank's members died as a result of the flood. In addition, many members lost family members while still others suffered damage or loss to their homes."[79] In the face of this disaster, the carefully scripted microcredit process crumbled. In 2002, as a response to the mounting criticism of the program's rigidity, reinforced by the consequences of the flood, Yunus launched Grameen II. Grameen II eased repayment schedules, initiated individual borrowing without group membership, opened accounts to nonborrowers, offered an array of financial services, and introduced other changes to increase the program's flexibility. "The most innovative aspect of Grameen II," wrote Asif Dowla and Dipal Barua in *The Poor Always Pay Back: The Grameen II Story*, "is the introduction of numerous savings products and a major emphasis on collective savings from members and the general public."[80] Yunus, observed Stuart Rutherford in *The Poor and Their Money*, "had long believed that savings were of limited value to the poor. With Grameen II he changed his mind, and Grameen became a leader in pro-poor savings."[81]

One of the surprising discoveries of the early microcredit movement was the realization that poor people were savers. In fact, they saved astonishing amounts of money given their meager incomes. But they had no place to put it and no way to earn interest. Poor people, explains Rutherford,

Get by on incomes that are small and irregular. But they often need sums of money larger than they have immediately to hand, to pay for life-cycle events such as birth, education, marriage, and death, for emergencies, and to seize opportunities to invest in assets or businesses. The only reliable and sustainable way to obtain these funds is to build them, somehow or other, from savings. Poor people have to save; and financial services for the poor are there to help them find ways to do so.[82]

By the early years of the twenty-first century, participants in the microcredit industry generally agreed that providing poor people with financial services, including savings facilities, was as important—even more important—as giving them credit. As a result, the term of choice became MFI—microfinance institutions—rather than microcredit.

Despite this agreement on the importance of saving, sharp philosophical differences divided microfinance organizations into competing camps. To Yunus, the purpose of microcredit was poverty alleviation. The Consultative Group to Assist the Poor (CGAP), a donor forum located at the World Bank, gave priority to economic development. In practice, this meant that for-profit businesses developed microcredit and microfinance programs with an eye to the bottom line; they intended to make money. "Over the years," wrote Yunus, "I have been watching the difference between the business styles of the World Bank and Grameen. Theoretically, we are in the same business—helping people get out of poverty. But the ways in which we pursue this goal are very different."[83]

"Drawn by the prospect of hefty profits from even the smallest of loans," reported the *New York Times* in April 2010, "a raft of banks and financial institutions now dominate the field, with some charging interest rates of 100 percent or more." "We created microcredit to fight the loan sharks," Yunus reminded his listeners at the United Nations, "we didn't create microcredit to encourage new loan sharks. . . . Microcredit should be seen as an opportunity to help people get out of poverty in a business way, but not as an opportunity to make money out of poor people."[84] Within the microfinance community, Counts explains, "two world views" conflicted. "One belief was that the core business of microfinance was poverty reduction; the other that microfinance was simply a variation on commercial banking" whose first responsibility was to make enough of a profit to "attract mainstream financiers who might not have as much, if any, of a social impact agenda."[85] In the Grameen model, the poor were entrepreneurs; in the World Bank model, they were consumers.

Even so, Roy reports that Grameen, BRAC, and ASA, another major microfinance network that originated in Bangladesh, "sought to insert themselves in the circuits of capital. This is evident in the striking trend of microfinance securitizations."[86] BRAC, aided by major international banks, launched the first of these funds in 2006 and received about

$180 million in financing. The securitizations, Roy points out, "are meant to create access to cheap capital for microfinance institutions, thereby, as BRAC argues, 'reducing dependency on volatile donor financing.'" Securitization embodied the "double promise of microfinance: that it can extend opportunity to the 'non-banked poor' and that it can yield profits for investors."[87] Microfinance is, in fact, a variant of subprime lending, which "offers high-risk borrowers access to credit at interest rates that exceed those made available to 'prime' borrowers."[88] With its global reach, benevolent objectives, and record of growth and resilience in the face of major recession, microfinance has become the "subprime frontier." The question is whether its insertion into the world of global finance will undercut its animating purpose. "If microfinance is now a resilient subprime market, then it must be asked whether such markets work or fail for the poor."[89]

Microcredit and microfinance do not lack for critics. There is, first, the often repeated criticism that Grameen does not reach the poorest of the poor, even though in Bangladesh and elsewhere in the developing world virtually all the program participants are poor. Yunus responded to the criticism in 2004 by starting a program for rural beggars whom he and his colleagues referred to as "struggling members." For this program, the Grameen Bank suspended its usual rules and offered the loans, most around fifteen dollars, interest-free. Within a few years, the program was helping about one hundred thousand members, of whom over ten thousand had "already stopped begging and become full-time salespeople."[90] BRAC's Income Generation for Vulnerable Group Development and Challenging the Frontiers of Poverty Reduction/Targeting the Ultra Poor were the "most complex experiments. . . . targeting the poorest of the poor, mainly female-headed, landless households, this program combines safety nets . . . with skills training and compulsory savings, and, ultimately, with microfinance . . . 'opportunity ladders.'"[91] Unlike other programs, Targeting the Ultra Poor requires subsidies that amount to about $135 per woman—a bargain in the development world.

Another criticism results from studies showing that a significant fraction of borrowers use the money for household consumption rather than for business activity. This criticism, argues Roy, is "misplaced, for it is in fact proof of the social protection effects of microfinance that the poor use microfinance loans to smooth dips in consumption and manage vulnerability. This is an effective anti-poverty strategy, not a failure of development."[92] Others criticize loans as an antipoverty strategy, arguing that debt is a "slippery slope" leading to increased dependency. "Most lending," asserts Thomas Dichter, "is used for consumption purposes; the few entrepreneurial loans are in easy-entry microbusinesses with little potential. Although defended with a development rhetoric, most support for microfinance seems to be based on simple but superficial poverty relief; it gets some resources to the poor."[93] Others find microlending a ruse for imposing neoliberal practices. In a scorching attack on the impact of microfinance in Bosnia, Milford Bateman complains that "the commercial microfinance model seems to have worked against most of the core triggers that lie behind sustainable local economic and social development" and is unlikely to relieve poverty. Microfinance's popularity, he claims, derives from "its political and ideological serviceability in terms of underpinning key neoliberal imperatives, principally the desire to discredit state and collective intervention strategies and to increasingly recast community development and survival solely in terms of individual entrepreneurship."[94]

Others offer more qualified assessments. In his study of microcredit in Bangladesh, development economist Tazul Islam granted the program's ability "to help reduce the vulnerability of the poor to downward mobility pressures, to develop their microenterprises, and to increase their net wealth." Nonetheless, the Grameen Bank's efforts to "alleviate overall poverty" were "very marginal. . . . the assumption that credit alone can automatically translate into successful microenterprises is fatal."[95] Islam, however, was modestly optimistic that the wider array of financial services introduced by Grameen II would improve the program's outcomes.[96] As matters stood, however, his research found that 23 percent of members had reasonably improved their position, 50 percent had experienced only "marginal improvements," 17 percent did not experience any change, and 10 percent ended up worse off.[97]

Examining U.S. programs, Nancy Jurik concluded that most of them were "Low-growth, labor-intensive businesses . . . most closely associated with women, minority, and economically disadvantaged clients. Yet assistance to such clients often meant assisting businesses that were structurally doomed to remain at the economic margins." To satisfy its sponsors, the program she studied acted on a "perceived need to produce client business successes" and to show a "high rate of loan repayment." These demands pulled it away from serving the neediest and reinforced a shift from peer lending to an individualized model.[98] "Rhetorical claims of poverty alleviation and empowerment sound good," she observed, "but without more comprehensive agendas" the microfinance "movement merely attempts to absorb poor and low-income people into the market in ways that neither fundamentally improve their situation nor challenge the logic of the market."[99]

Critics' case against microcredit was reinforced by the startling events in fall 2010 in Andhra Pradesh, on India's eastern coast, where competing microcredit entrepreneurs enticed poor people to take out high-interest loans they could not afford. High-pressure collection tactics resulted in the suicides of seventy-five borrowers in the six months prior to November 23, 2010.[100] Local politicians urged borrowers not to repay their loans. As a result, reported the *New York Times*, "repayments on nearly $2 billion in loans in the state have virtually ceased. . . . If the trend continues, the industry faces collapse in a state where more than a third of its borrowers live." Microlenders also found difficulty "making new loans in other states, because banks have slowed lending to them as fears about defaults have grown."[101] A clampdown by the state government on lending practices led to a sharp drop in the stock price of SKS, the leading for-profit microcredit corporation, which had jumped in value in the months following its issue. One day after the announcement of new Andhra Pradesh regulations, SKS's shares dropped 20 percent in value before regaining 7.5 percent on news that banks had not withdrawn their money.[102] Although the stock regained some of its earlier value, the whole microcredit industry trembled as shock waves spread outward, reminding observers of the collapse of the subprime mortgage market that had triggered the Great Recession a few years earlier. Microfinance was, indeed, as Roy had observed, the new "subprime frontier."

Not long before SKS's share prices collapsed, its founder, Vinod Khosla, a billionaire venture capitalist and cofounder of Sun Microsystems, bragged about the "roaring success of SKS's recent initial public stock offering in Mumbai," which had earned him a profit of $117 million, which he intended to reinvest in projects to help the poor. Khosla hoped to show the world that "commercial entities can better help people in poverty than most nonprofit charitable organizations."[103] SKS, which started lending in 2006, was also backed by George Soros and had 6.8 million clients and a loan portfolio worth 43 billion rupees or $940 million. Khosla contrasted the success of SKS to the much slower growth of CashPor, a nonprofit started in 1996, which had 417,000 borrowers and a portfolio of 2.7 billion rupees or $58 million.

India was not alone in its microcredit crisis. "Already in the past two years," pointed out the *Financial Times*, "Morocco, Bosnia, Nicaragua, and Pakistan have all been hit by microloan repayment crises." The World Bank–linked group Consultative Group to Assist the Poor blamed the crisis on a failure to focus on borrowers' ability to repay their loans. "In Nicaragua and Pakistan, the problems were compounded when political and religious leaders—like Andhra Pradesh politicians now—urged non-repayment."[104] While Khosla gamely defended SKS's practices, attacks by his critics grew sharper, exposing the differences between the not-for-profit Grameen model and the Washington Consensus.[105]

The heightened controversy that emerged in late 2010 did nothing to clarify the bottom line. The answer to the question "Does microfinance work?" remains elusive. Partly, the problem is defining a measure of success. Is a program successful if it boosts the income of 40 percent of its members? Fifty percent? Sixty percent? What if it boosts individual income but makes little impact on the overall poverty rate? Or fails to give women more power in their families? The questions go on. There is no standard metric. Context and program design also pose tough problems. How can researchers compare programs whose designs differ or are located in different places? And what methodology should be used? Economist Katherine Odell, who analyzed the first batch of random controlled trials of microfinance, was unable to reach definitive assessments.[106] Are statistical comparisons the best way to find out if the programs are working? Perhaps ethnographic studies would penetrate more deeply into the texture of individual experiences over time. The lack of conclusive or consistent evidence about results aside, the microcredit tsunami unleashed by Muhammad Yunus and Grameen has transformed the landscape of poverty policy and displaced pathological stereotypes of the poor with images of competent entrepreneurs intent on accumulating assets. In the history of ideas about poverty, this is a signal achievement.

Assets Against Poverty

"The question," assert Mark Schreiner and Michael Sherraden in *Can the Poor Save?* "is no longer whether the poor should save and build assets; instead, the question is how to help them do it."[107] Muhammad Yunus and the other leaders of the microfinance movement, proponents of both the Bangladesh and Washington consensus, would agree. Microfinance's tilt toward financial services recognized the surprising importance of saving to poor people, even the poor in rural Bangladesh. Reframed as asset building, saving composed the core of the asset-building movement that started in the United States in the early 1990s and quickly became an antipoverty technology of choice throughout the social policy world. As interpreted in the United States, asset building generally took on a different role than it did in the villages of Bangladesh.

As it originated in the Grameen program, savings—as Roy observed—were intended to "smooth dips in consumption and manage vulnerability."[108] The irregularity of employment and income made them essential. In the United States, saving formed part of a strategy to build wealth, not to cover day-to-day expenses and discrete emergencies. Combined with matching funds from government or private sources, savings became asset accumulation targeted at specific purposes, primarily postsecondary education, home purchase, or the capitalization of a small business. Participants in experimental asset accumulation programs were discouraged from withdrawing their money early.[109]

In one of his influential books, Michael Sherraden, professor of social development and social welfare at Washington University, and his colleagues observed that, "Broadly, conceived, assets can refer to anything that has a potential for positive returns."[110] This expansive definition included both tangible and intangible assets. None of the items listed as tangible assets were surprising: money savings, stocks, bonds, and other financial securities; real property; hard assets other than real estate; machines, equipment, tools, and other tangible components of production; durable household goods; natural resources; and copyrights, patents, and other intellectual property. Their list of intangibles, however, included as assets access to credit; human capital; cultural capital; informal social capital; formal social or organizational capital; and political capital—items we might not immediately include in an asset inventory.[111] As the authors of "The Assets Report 2010"—a report of the New America Foundation—put it, "We typically think of education, homeownership, entrepreneurship, savings, and thrift as the fruits of [the] pursuit" of the American dream, "but they are just as much the assets upon which opportunity for upward economic and social mobility are built."[112] Assets, in this view, are both the products and the drivers of upward mobility. A footnote put it more simply: "Asset building refers to public policy and private sector efforts to enable individuals to accumulate and preserve long-term, productive assets—savings, investments, a home, post-secondary education and training, a small business, and a nest-egg for retirement."[113]

Sherraden introduced the concept of "asset effects" to emphasize that the "economic, social, and psychological effects of asset ownership . . . go beyond mere consumption." People, he argued, "think and behave differently when they are accumulating assets, and the world responds to them differently as well." Influenced by behavioral economics, a prominent new movement in the discipline, he asserted that the noneconomic or social and psychological effects of assets are equivalent to their economic effects. Assets "spark hope and change how people think and act."[114]

Sherraden rejects pathological, moral, and cultural theories about the sources of poverty. He promises to explain "without recourse to concepts of weakness or moral sloth . . . how the poor might come to believe that the world and their chances in it are worse than they really are. The theory also suggests," he argues optimistically, "how assets might help to align views more closely with the real world." He contrasts his "psychological model" to an "economic model." In the economic model, only the actual use of assets matters. But the psychological model understands that "people look ahead and enjoy contemplating the possible economic effects of the use of their savings."[115] Outcomes in life, Sherraden believes, "depend on three factors: choices, effort, and luck." By improving the information available to people when they make choices, the ownership of assets "reduces the psychological cost of making effort, and helps people to 'make their own luck' by improving their social relationships."[116]

In the United States, the federal government and state governments have both recognized the importance of individual assets. The federal government helps individuals build assets in many ways. Interest on home mortgages, for instance, has been tax deductible since 1913, the earliest days of the modern income tax. In the Great Depression of the 1930s, the federal government promoted homeownership by guaranteeing and changing the terms of mortgages and insuring individual bank accounts. It encourages the accumulation of savings for retirement by allowing businesses to deduct the cost of savings from their income taxes and by allowing individuals to participate in various forms of tax-deferred investment accounts, such as IRAs. Free public education and highly subsidized higher education have facilitated asset building through the provision of human capital. The GI Bill, by paying for college and professional school education and offering veterans low-interest, long-term loans, jump-started the asset accumulation that built the post–World War II middle class.

Most of this government facilitation of asset building is delivered either through the tax code or as employment benefits. And almost all of it goes to steadily employed homeowners, not to the poor. There is the rub. The poor do not pay income taxes; nor do they enjoy work-related benefits. For 2011, President Obama's budget proposed to spend $701.1 billion to promote asset building, the authors of "The Assets Report 2010" calculate. Of this, $549.1 billion would be tax subsidies, overwhelmingly benefiting "middle- and upper-income Americans," and $152 billion would be direct expenditures. The government proposed to allocate $200.4 billion of these asset-building expenses to subsidizing homeownership, $142.3 billion to retirement security, $56.4 billion to postsecondary education, $0.7 billion to entrepreneurship, and $149.5 billion "to savings and investment activities."[117] More than 70 percent of the tax expenditures go to the 20 percent of households with the highest incomes, while 80 percent of tax expenditures for retirement go to the same group.[118] The only substantial subsidies delivered through tax refunds are the Earned Income Tax Credit, the Child Care Tax Credit, and the Making Work Pay Tax Credit. Together, the credits total $151.8 billion, of which $112.8 billion is delivered as tax refunds. In their "fact sheet" on asset building, McKernan and Sherraden state:

Federal tax breaks, in dollars, subsidizing assets (fiscal 2008 estimate): 407 billion

Percentage of subsidies going to top-fifth families (fiscal 2005): nearly 90

Percentage of subsidies going to bottom three-fifth families (fiscal 2005): less than 3[119]

This combination—the proven effectiveness of asset-building policies that serve the well-to-do and the disproportionately small number and size of asset-building policies directed to helping people leave poverty—helped spark interest in using assets as a technology for fighting poverty.

Two streams nourished the asset-building movement that accelerated in the 1990s. One originated when researchers drew public attention to the distinction between income and wealth and to the racial inequality in wealth, described in Chapter 2. In 1995, Melvin Oliver and Thomas Shapiro published *White Wealth/Black Wealth: A New Perspective on Racial Inequality*, which showed that reductions in the gap separating white and African American incomes masked an enormous inequality in wealth. Most of this inequality resulted from homeownership. For among both blacks and whites, homeownership was the principal source of wealth. However, blacks owned homes less frequently than whites, and the homes they did own often were worth less—a residue of racial segregation. Sharp wealth differences existed even among blacks and whites with similar incomes.[120] Other researchers, notably Dalton Conley, have found similar patterns of wealth inequality.[121]

Individual Development Accounts (IDAs) formed the second strand in the asset-building movement. "The year 1988," write two leading researchers, "saw the start of the birth of a movement in industrial countries to include the poor in policies that promote asset accumulation." In that year, two books—*The Safety Net as Ladder* by Robert Friedman and *Starting Even* by Robert Haveman—and one article, "Rethinking Social Welfare: Toward Assets" by Michael Sherraden—sparked the movement.[122] In his 1991 book, *Assets and the Poor: A New American Welfare Policy*, Michael Sherraden published the first major theoretical and policy justification for IDAs. In the years since then, he has continued to champion them vigorously in articles and books and to design research to test the idea.[123]

IDAs are subsidized savings accounts. Unlike other subsidized accounts, such as Individual Retirement Accounts or 401(k) plans, IDAs are targeted to the poor, provide subsidies through matches rather than through tax breaks, and require participants to attend financial education classes. Participants accrue matches as they save for assets that increase long-term well-being and financial self-sufficiency.[124]

To Sherraden, IDAs represent more than one additional technology for reducing poverty. They are, he argues, the cutting edge of a revolution in welfare policy that will shift its emphasis from income support to asset accumulation. "Indeed, it seems likely," predict Schreiner and Sherraden, "that we are in the midst of a major transformation in social policy, moving from a welfare state based almost exclusively on income support to something else. . . . a major pillar of the new social policy will probably be asset building in the form of individual accounts. This trend has already started in the United States and other countries."[125] They want to be clear that IDAs "are not a cure-all." Supporting saving and asset accumulation by poor people is an important objective, but there are others as well. "Support for subsistence (and medical care, and education, and other dimensions of well-being) is also important."[126] Nonetheless, they emphasize, the "shift to asset-based policy is perhaps the greatest social-policy transformation of our time, yet it is little discussed." In fact, it remains "an uphill struggle" to convince legislators and policy makers "to enact a new, large-scale, and inclusive asset based policy." Why? "At best," policy makers do not recognize that "the poor—like everyone else—require assets for long-term development," while "at worst, there is a suspicion that the poor are unworthy or incapable of acquiring assets and using them for development."[127]

Midway through the first decade of the twenty-first century, hundreds of IDA programs existed throughout the country. Most states had "some type of IDA-enabling policy, and federal legislation . . . provided a legal structure and a funding mechanism for IDAs."[128] Federal support came from the Assets for Independence Act, passed by Congress in 1998 and amended in 2000, which enabled "community-based nonprofits and government agencies to implement and demonstrate an assets-based approach for giving low-income families a hand up out of poverty." In his 2011 budget, President Obama proposed maintaining funding for the act at $24 million, the same as in the previous two years. His budget also proposed a new program, the Bank on USA Initiative, which would direct $50 million "to help increase access to safe and affordable financial services for unbanked and under-banked households by seeking local initiatives"—something crucial to both the microfinance and asset-building movements. In Congress, members from both political parties sponsored the America Saving for Personal Investment, Retirement, and Education Act (the ASPIRE Act), which would "set up a special account at birth for every child in America. The 'Lifetime Savings Account' (LSA) can later be used to pursue post-secondary education, buy a first home, or build up a nest-egg for retirement. The ASPIRE Act calls for each child's LSA to be endowed with a one-time $500 contribution at birth." Children from families with incomes below the national median income would qualify "for both a supplemental contribution of up to $500 at birth as well as the opportunity to earn up to $500 per year in matching funds for amounts saved in the account." Participants also would be offered financial education.[129]

Many community-based organizations implemented IDAs in the 1990s, usually with foundation funds—the Ford Foundation, the New American Foundation, and several others supported asset-building programs. In November 2010, the Bill and Melinda Gates Foundation energized the asset-building movement by hosting a "Global Savings Forum. . . . the first event to join leaders from around the world to discuss how to provide the world's poor with access to financial services, especially savings. . . . [Melinda] Gates urged leaders in government, banking, mobile communications, and international development to work together to build a new kind of financial infrastructure to bring savings to the poor." The foundation backed up its exhortation with its enormous prestige and influence as well as a pledge of $500 million.[130] According to the *Wall Street Journal*, the Gates foundation took its financial services advice from the World Bank's Consultative Group. Not surprisingly, in the debate within the microfinance movement "over two opposing philosophies"—whether "financial services for the poor should direct any profits back into services for the needy" or whether "banks and other profit-seeking businesses . . . can best serve the broadest swath of people by using tools such as capital markets to fund expansion"—the "Gates plan is a nod" to the latter. A 2006 study by the Consultative Group, which found "that demand for savings accounts outstripped demand for loans by a six-to-one ratio," reinforced the foundation's earlier experimentation with microfinance and convinced it to put its money on savings and financial services rather than on loans. "The strategy," observed the *Wall Street Journal*, "comes as the microcredit movement is attracting questions about whether the small loans actually help alleviate policy."[131]

There are three metrics for identifying the transformation of an advocacy group into a social movement: legislative support in state houses and Congress; support from major foundations; and a national infrastructure of not-for-profit organizations dedicated to lobbying, fundraising, and knitting scattered programs into a powerful and coherent national movement. The CFED (Corporation for Enterprise Development), founded in 1980 as a national voice for both microenterprise and asset building, erected an infrastructure that complemented legislative and foundation support. A "multifaceted organization at the local, state, and federal level to create economic opportunity that alleviates poverty," CFED mounted the first national IDA conference in 1995. With headquarters in Washington, D.C, and other offices in Durham,

North Carolina, and San Francisco, CFED runs conferences, advocates for legislation, operates demonstration programs, conducts research, publishes reports, and tries to educate public opinion about the promise of microenterprise, asset building, and related activities. For 2010, it planned a large "assets learning conference" titled "The Assets Movement at Its Moment: Creating the Save and Invest Economy." Its four priorities, listed on its impressive Web site, are savings and financial security, affordable housing, entrepreneurship, and economic development. The primary financial sponsor of the 2008 conference was Wal-Mart.[132]

Two major research projects have tested asset building as policy. Sherraden helped develop the comprehensive and sophisticated research design for the first, the American Dream Demonstration (ADD), which was "a demonstration of IDAs in fourteen programs across the United States." The first opened in 1997, and in all but one, only deposits made through the end of 2003 could be matched.[133] There were 2,350 participants in the program.[134] The program's "multiple findings and policy lessons," observe Schreiner and Sherraden, can "be boiled down into two observations." The first is about people. The "results of this study do not indicate that the very poor, the unemployed, or those on welfare cannot save and build assets in IDAs."

Second, "the structure, rules, and the implementation of the savings program . . . were associated with savings outcome." The combination of the modest impact of personal characteristics with the robust impact of institutional practice "suggest that attempts to include all Americans—even the poor—in asset-building would most fruitfully focus not on changing people but rather on changing policies."[135] In other words, the results of the ADD called for turning the centuries-old emphasis in poverty policy—what I have called "improving poor people"—on its head.[136]

The other major demonstration program, the Savings for Education, Entrepreneurship, and Downpayment (SEED) Initiative yielded similar results. SEED, initiated in 2003, "was a 10-year national policy, practice and research endeavor whose goal was to find out what would happen if low-income children received savings accounts, 'seeded' with modest financial incentives and paired with age-appropriate financial education." SEED chose twelve community partners from across the United States. Participants in the program established more than 1,300 accounts. "Each of the partners," reported SEED's Web site, "established matched savings accounts for children or youth, and each engaged a different age cohort, utilized slightly different savings incentives, delivered financial education and worked with financial institutions to deliver accounts." The four "overarching lessons" that emerged from the research were consistent with the results of ADD. "Children's Saving Accounts appeal broadly to Americans across political and geographic lines." "Families of all income levels can save." "Saving is not easy, especially for lower-income families." "Program and account design can have important effects on saving."[137]

Research on IDA demonstration programs raises as many questions as it answers, as the researchers themselves admit. Some of these are practical: What are the most effective ways to design programs? To what degree can they promote social mobility and alleviate poverty, and how should they be integrated with the income support programs that Sherraden recognizes need to remain in place? The Great Recession that began in 2008 showed the limits of home equity as a source of increasing wealth. In an asset-based welfare state, what happens to families who lose their only substantial asset? Do the drop in home equity and rise in foreclosure undercut incentives to save for the down payment on a house? When African Americans and other minorities find themselves disproportionately the subjects of foreclosure, what are the implications for asset-based policy? Has homeownership hurt more than helped them? Other issues are more normative or philosophical. The reorientation of the welfare state around asset building would facilitate its redesign on market principles, a reversal of the "subordination of market price to social value," which the great British theorist T. H. Marshall located at the heart of the welfare state.[138] It should never be forgotten that political and moral values and priorities underlie all technical choices. Is "asset building" an anodyne term for "capital accumulation"? Is it a way of substituting individual responsibility for redistribution and government support? Is it part of what some would call the neoliberal re-engineering of the welfare state?[139]

From Mexico to Manhattan: Conditional Cash Transfers Move North

In New York City, two antipoverty initiatives drew national attention. One was the Harlem Children's Zone, the other was Mayor Michael Bloomberg's ambitious antipoverty program. Complementary rather than competitive, both reflected the new social policy paradigm—the decentralized, flexible, opportunistic, public/private network—identified by David J. Erickson in his analysis of the "housing policy revolution." They also represented the fashionable idea of "social innovation," which elevated private initiative over the diminished role of the state.

The Harlem Children's Zone (HCZ), a hybrid of Comprehensive Community Initiative and CDC, offers an example of the new social policy model in an area other than housing. The HCZ is the creation of

Geoffrey Canada. Canada grew up one of four brothers in a single-parent family in the Bronx. His ability won him a scholarship to Bowdoin College in Maine. He later earned a graduate degree from the Harvard Graduate School of Education. In 1983, he became director of the Rheedlen Foundation, dedicated to reducing truancy in Harlem. At the foundation, he conceived the idea for a web of cradle-to-college social services, which became the HCZ. In 1997, he expanded the zone to include two new charter schools, called Promise Academies. The HCZ now embraces ninety-seven square blocks of Harlem, an area home to about seventeen thousand people; its budget grew from approximately $6 million in 1994 to $75 million in 2009–2010. The zone's revenue derives from a variety of sources, including foundations, wealthy donors, and the city government. CEOs of major national corporations play a prominent role on its board.[140]

Canada uses two concepts to explain the HCZ: first, the "pipeline," a metaphor for the integrated social and educational programs that move young people from cradle to college. Indeed, children enter the pipeline when their expectant parents enroll in the "Baby College," a prenatal education program. The "tipping point" is the other concept. Canada predicts that when the HCZ succeeds with 65 percent of the zone's residents, the rest will be pulled upward by osmosis. No theory or data supports this prediction; it is an article of faith,[141] and Canada does not expect to reach full success for several years—twenty years was the time he projected for the HCZ to fully attain its goals.

It is hard to know just how well the HCZ is succeeding. The HCZ Web site points to the stunning success of high school students who attend its after-school program and the 100 percent of third graders in the Promise Academies who met or exceeded state standards in math. However, after New York State revised the proficiency standard, test results in many schools, including the Promise Academies, plummeted. In August 2010 the *New York Times* reported, "At the main campus of the Harlem Promise Academy, one of the city's top-ranked charter schools, proficiency in third-grade math dropped from 100 percent to 56 percent." Canada responded calmly: "There are two reactions those of us in this business can have. . . . One is to complain, and it's human nature to do that. The other is to say we need to do something dramatically more intensive and powerful to prepare our kids. We are going to look at the mirror and say we have got to do better."[142] At best, then, test results from the Promise Academies are mixed; other schools do better, despite the Promise Academies' relentless focus on test-taking.[143] As of 2011, no measures of success are available for the social services, while employment data for the zone shows little change.[144] However, enthusiasm in the zone remains high, and Canada exudes optimism. "This is a science we're creating," he told an audience in another city as he enumerated a litany of urban problems. "All of these problems are solvable. We had a plan at the Harlem Children's Zone, and it worked."[145]

The Harlem Children's Zone might have remained an inspiring local New York story, even after it was discovered and canonized by the national media, including the feature film *Waiting for Superman*. But its promise attracted presidential candidate Barack Obama, who made its replication part of his campaign platform. As president, Obama and his education secretary Arne Duncan adopted the Harlem Children's Zone as their key strategy for fighting poverty among children. They proposed taking the HCZ national by creating twenty Promise Neighborhoods based on its model. At the same time, other cities, notably Newark and Camden, New Jersey, announced that they would use the HCZ template to revitalize their schools and neighborhoods. Whether the HCZ model can be replicated successfully, whether it can flourish without Geoffrey Canada's charisma, whether Congress will appropriate enough money, remains unknown. Certainly, Newark and Camden, which in November 2010 announced they would lay off huge percentages of police and firefighters, could not afford to mount the program on their own.[146] Whatever difficulties stand in the way of its replication, the HCZ model, with its high expectations and optimism, stands as a powerful alternative to the pathological image of inner-city poverty reinforced by the culture of poverty and underclass ideas.

New York City Mayor Michael Bloomberg's poverty program also rejected pathological images of the urban poor. Nowhere was this more evident than in Conditional Cash Transfers, the fourth new technology of poverty work, imported by Bloomberg from Mexico. Conditional Cash Transfers were not the most important part of his ambitious antipoverty agenda. But they were the most controversial and the focus of most publicity. And, after eighteen months, they proved the most visible failure.

In March 2006, Bloomberg appointed a thirty-six-member Commission for Economic Opportunity to advise him on an antipoverty strategy. The co-chairs of the commission were Geoffrey Canada, founder of the famous Harlem Children's Zone, and Richard D. Parsons, chairman and CEO of Time Warner. Its other members included prominent academics, heads of major civic agencies, leading businessmen, trade union officials, and foundation officers, including Judith Rodin, president of the Rockefeller Foundation. The commission reported in September 2006. Bloomberg incorporated virtually all its recommendations into the antipoverty program he announced in December. Both microfinance and asset building were important components of the commission's report and Bloomberg's program. But a program of Conditional

Cash Transfers—a program neither recommended nor discussed by the commission—was added to the plans by Bloomberg.

The commission prefaced its recommendations with an impressive, hard-hitting analysis of poverty in New York City and a criticism of the official poverty line, which, it argued, severely understated the amount of poverty in the city.[147] It recommended focusing antipoverty work on three demographic groups—the working poor, young adults age sixteen to twenty-four, and young children age zero to five—which, it believed, were the groups particularly at risk. Each required a distinct, carefully targeted array of programs.[148]

Although its recommendations did not include relief or income maintenance, the commission urged the city to continue its generous support to individuals incapable of supporting themselves. *"Our recommendations . . . in no way reflect a reduction in or retreat from New York City's historic commitment to helping those unable, whether temporarily or permanently, to care for themselves. We uphold and affirm that commitment, though we recognize it is distinct from that which we recommend here."* The commission itself was less concerned with relieving poverty than with equipping individuals with the human capital to escape poverty through their own efforts.[149]

The commission emphasized that all programs should be evaluated rigorously and held accountable for reaching their goals. "Evidence-based practice is the hallmark of any accountability structure," the commission stressed. "Developing an evaluation strategy must be an integral part of the design process itself, as it also aids in clarifying underlying assumptions. When evaluating initiatives New York City must strive for the highest standards and most rigorous methods feasible."[150] The commission underscored that evaluation requires a standard against which to measure results, including a defensible poverty line. For many years, the commission explained, researchers and policy experts had demonstrated the inadequacies of the official poverty line used in federal statistics. The commission proposed replacing the existing poverty standard and monitoring the program's progress with in-house as well as contracted research. Recognizing that its proposals called for action throughout city government, the commission recommended a new agency to coordinate the program's many arms.[151]

Mayor Bloomberg's official plan, announced in December 2006, followed the commission's recommendations closely. He lodged oversight and authority in a new Center for Economic Opportunity (CEO), but the programs themselves were located in departments throughout city government. The CEO, observed *The Economist*, "bypassed" the city's service delivery system by investing "a mixture of public and philanthropic money in social entrepreneurs' ideas to help lift people out of poverty, particularly by emphasizing personal responsibility." Projects were chosen by competition, and "the CEO . . . received one of the first grants awarded" by the Obama administration's Social Innovation Fund.[152]

Social innovation has become "the increasingly common shorthand" for an "approach to public-private partnerships," pointed out *The Economist*. Social innovation departs from the contracting out of public services fashionable in the 1990s and early 2000s, a practice meant to cut costs. Rather, social innovation "aims to do more than save a few dollars or pounds—although that is part of its attraction. The idea is to transform the way public services are provided, by tapping the ingenuity of people in the private sector," particularly a new breed of actor referred to as "social entrepreneur." Social entrepreneurs are individuals who develop "an innovative answer to a social problem (for instance, a business model for helping to tackle poverty)." Hardly used a decade ago, "today everyone from Lagos to London wants to be one." Propelling the diffusion of social innovation is a new generation of rich philanthropists. "These people take a businesslike approach to giving that *The Economist* christened 'philanthrocapitalism' in 2006." Enamored with the model, the Obama administration created the Social Innovation Fund (SIF). On July 22, 2010, it announced its first eleven investments, about $50 million matched by $74 million from foundations to be "given to some of America's most successful non-profit organizations in order to expand their work." Although the SIF is small, it is important because "the fund embodies an approach that the administration plans to spread throughout government." It is one of a number of attempts "to promote new partnerships of government, private capital, social entrepreneurs and the public." In Britain, Prime Minister David Cameron instituted a similar project to achieve his vision of a "Big Society."[153] Both the HCZ and Bloomberg's antipoverty program also exemplified social innovation. With the HCZ, innovation lodged primarily in one charismatic and entrepreneurial person, Geoffrey Canada; with Bloomberg's antipoverty program, it was diffused through many unrelated programs.

Within the Department of Consumer Affairs, Mayor Bloomberg created the Office of Financial Empowerment, "whose mission is to educate, empower, and protect New Yorkers with low incomes to help them make the best uses of their financial resources to move forward economically."[154] He also adopted the new poverty line recommended by the commission. To the commission's recommendations, he added an experimental new program, Opportunity NYC, which featured Conditional Cash Transfers (CCTs).

According to a 2009 worldwide program review by the World Bank, Conditional Cash Transfers are programs that transfer cash, generally to poor households, on the condition that those households make pre-specified investments in the human capital of their children. Health and nutrition conditions generally require periodic checkups, growth monitoring, and vaccinations for children under five years of age; perinatal care for mothers; and mothers' attendance at periodic health information talks. Education conditions usually include school enroll-ment, attendance on 80 to 85 percent of school days, and occasionally some measure of performance. Most CCT programs transfer the money to the mother of the household or, in some circumstances, the student.[155]

The details of individual country-based programs varied, but for the most part they shared these characteristics. CCT programs, points out Laura B. Rawlings, Senior Monitoring and Evaluation Specialist in Human Development at the World Bank, represent "an innovative ap-proach to the delivery of social services." They provide poor families with cash "on the condition that they make investments in human capi-tal such as sending children to school or bringing them to health cen-tres on a regular basis." CCT programs thus aim not only for "short-term social assistance" but for longer-term "human capital investment." As one of a "new generation of social programmes" that rely "on market principles," they represent "a marked departure from traditional . . . mechanisms" for targeting assistance to the poor, "such as general sub-sidies or investments in schools, health centres and other providers of social services."[156] In CCT programs, as in the other new technologies of poverty work—rebuilding markets in inner cities, microfinance, and asset accumulation—poor people are rational actors, capable of re-sponding to incentives and opportunities. Their children are potential assets, bundles of human resources, targets of investment on whose full development the future of the economy and national strength depend.

Conditional Cash Transfers and other new technologies of poverty work embodied the rehabilitation of cash in programs for the poor. Despite an early twentieth-century preference for cash relief, suspicion of money as the medium of assistance remained a strong current in American poverty work. Nineteenth-century charity workers preferred fuel, clothing, food, health care, and housing to straight cash. To the traditional forms of in-kind assistance, the latter part of the twentieth-century added social services and educational or job training while in-troducing massive forms of federal in-kind assistance with food stamps and housing programs. Distrust of the poor—at least the dependent as contrasted to the working poor—remains an undercurrent in social thought and policy. The hallmark of the War on Poverty was service provision, not cash assistance or job creation. These recent market-based technologies of poverty work reject the idea that the poor lack the competence to manage their own affairs and, instead, view poor people as customers, entrepreneurs, or rational actors. In this, they represent a notable a break with the history of American charity and welfare.

CCTs originated in Latin America, with Mexico and Brazil running huge programs. According to the World Bank, the number of countries with CCT programs exploded from three in 1997 to approximately twenty-eight in 2008. Mexico's PROGRESA (subsequently renamed Oportunidas in 2001) grew from three hundred thousand beneficiary households in 1997 to five million in 2008.[157]

Bloomberg, along with senior staff, visited Mexico to observe first-hand its gigantic Oportunidas program. Despite his enthusiasm for what he saw, Bloomberg did not try to persuade the New York City Council to pay for a New York–based CCT program. Instead, he formed a public-private partnership, Opportunity NYC, to implement the first full CCT program in the United States. A cross section of the elite of American philanthropy, the program's funders—the Rockefeller Foundation, the Starr Foundation, the Robin Hood Foundation, the Open Society Institute, AIG, the Broad Foundation, the Tiger Foundation, the Annie E. Casey Foundation, the John D. and Catherine T. MacArthur Foundation, and Bloomberg Philanthropies—together put up $50 million to fund a trial implementation of the program. The program targeted five thousand families, half as a control group. From the start, the experiment aroused wide national and international attention. "Opportunity NYC," reported MDRC, the national research and evaluation firm that helped design and assess the program, "includes three separate demonstration projects, each of which takes a somewhat different approach to the idea of linking cash transfers to actions and achievements." The Family Rewards program was "a comprehensive two-generation strategy" focused on "children's education, family preventative health care, and parents' workforce efforts." Work Rewards, the second program, targeted "the workforce efforts of low-income adults living in subsidized housing." The Spark program, the third, concentrated "solely on children and their school performance." MDRC helped design the first two programs and led a random assignment evaluation. Roland Fryer from Harvard University, together with the New York City Department of Education, "designed and evaluated" the Spark program.[158]

After eighteen months, MDRC conducted an overall evaluation of Opportunity New York's accomplishments. James Riccio and his colleagues, authors of the report, summarized their findings:

Despite initial challenges in understanding the program's large number of incentives and related payment requirements, nearly all families eventually earned rewards—more than $6,000, on average, over the first two years. In addition, effects from Family Rewards varied across a wide range of outcome measures—for example, the program

- Reduced current poverty and hardship, including hunger and some housing and health care hardships
- Increased savings and the likelihood that parents would have bank accounts, and reduced the use of alternative banking institutions (such as check cashers)
- Did not improve school outcomes overall for elementary or middle school students, but *did* increase school attendance, course credits, grade advancement, and standardized test results among better-prepared high school students
- Somewhat increased families' continuous use of health insurance coverage, reduced their reliance on hospital emergency rooms for routine care, and increased their receipt of medical care
- Substantially increased families' receipt of preventive dental care
- Increased employment in jobs that are not covered by the unemployment insurance (UI) system but reduced employment in UI-covered jobs

Because only the first twelve to twenty-four months of the program are covered—including a "start-up" phase during which operational "kinks" were being worked out—it is too soon to draw firm conclusions about the full potential of Family Rewards. Future reports will present longer-term findings, eventually covering all three years of program operations plus two additional years after the cash incentives are no longer offered.[159]

The authors clearly believed they were writing an interim report; they expected the program to continue. As their last paragraph made clear, eighteen months was too soon to know whether the program ultimately would improve school achievement or boost employment. Nonetheless, on March 31, 2010, Mayor Bloomberg announced that the program would terminate at the end of August, although evaluation would continue for another three years. "If you never fail, I can tell you, you've never tried new, innovative things," Bloomberg said. "And I don't know that this is a failure. I think it is, some things worked, and some things didn't, and some things the jury's still out on. And anything new you're going to have that diversity of results." Foundation and city officials pointed to the program's rocky start. Margot Brandenburn, an associate director of the Rockefeller Foundation, highlighted the difficulty of recruiting the initial families. "I think people were confused, and there was some amount of distrust," Brandenburg said. "For some people it sounded too good to be true. It took a while to explain to people what the offer was." Linda Gibbs, Deputy Mayor for Health and Human Services, reported that "many families had been perplexed by the guidelines that were laid out for them. Cash payments were eventually eliminated for actions like getting a library card and follow-up visits with a doctor. 'Too many things, too many details, more to manage in the lives of burdened, busy households' Ms. Gibbs said. 'Big lesson for the future? Got to make it a lot more simple.' "[160]

Why Bloomberg decided to pull the plug on Opportunity NYC remains unclear. The MDRC report could have been read as cautious encouragement to continue with some midcourse corrections. MDRC found that the program had worked most effectively in reducing poverty by boosting incomes. Bloomberg, though, was not interested in the program's demonstrated capacity to relieve poverty in the short run or in direct redistribution of income. His goal was reducing poverty and dependence in the long run by improving human capital. He objected, for instance, to a "living-wage" proposal that programs subsidized by the city pay at least ten dollars per hour plus benefits.[161]

In fact, Bloomberg was in the midst of a fight over the living-wage proposal. In the spring, Democratic Council members introduced the Fair Wages for New Yorkers Act. "It would require developers of any project that receives more than $100,000 in city subsidies—such as bond financing, tax abatements or infrastructure improvements—to guarantee a minimum wage of $10 an hour plus benefits, or $11.50 without benefits." The wage was to be indexed to inflation.[162] Bloomberg stalled by appointing a commission to report in 2011 on the likely impact of the law. Writing in the *Huffington Post*, Reverend Peter Goodwin Heltzel observed icily: "There is an ironic injustice in it all: a billionaire commissions a million-dollar study to consider the life chances of the poor. At a moment when our city sits at the center of the foreclosure and unemployment crisis, Mayor Bloomberg has chosen to spend a million dollars of the city's money to commission a study on how paying a living wage to the poor might affect the non-poor."[163] New York's living-wage campaign echoed similar initiatives around the country. The modern living-wage movement began in Baltimore in 1994 and spread quickly to other cities. Within a few years, 122 cities had passed living-wage ordinances, and more than 75 living-wage campaigns were under way. Their content varied. In general, according to ACORN (the Association of Community Organizations for Reform), their goal was "to pass local ordinances, requiring private businesses that benefit from public money to pay their workers a living wage." Public funds, they emphasized, should not subsidize employers who paid a poverty wage. To the contrary, public funds should be "reserved for those private sector employers who demonstrate a commitment to providing decent, family-supporting jobs in our local communities."[164]

To Bloomberg, clearly, the living wage and Conditional Cash Transfers represented two poles of antipoverty strategy, and he was interested in only one of them. His decision to end the CCT trial did not represent a rejection of incentive-based programs. Rather, it probably resulted from political considerations as much as, or more than, from data. Neither the political right nor left liked Opportunity NYC. The right claimed it rewarded the undeserving poor—why reward those parents who had not been sending their children to school regularly or taking them for medical checkups? The political left found Opportunity NYC paternalistic and offensive. Without a solid constituency behind it, Bloomberg would not be able to scale up the program with city funds. Perhaps pulling the plug was less of an embarrassment than a defeat in a battle with city council.

The brief, conflicted life of Opportunity NYC did not cast doubts over the other programs in Bloomberg's antipoverty initiative. A 2009 report from the Center for Economic Opportunity (CEO) gave an upbeat assessment. "CEO's great strength," reported Executive Director Veronica White, "is our ability to seek out new, innovative ideas, break down silos that inhibit results, and carefully measure the impacts of our programs. We tackle issues that matter: disconnected youth, unemployment and low wages, intergenerational poverty, and measuring poverty in a more accurate way that can better shape public policy. Our programs help people put food on their tables and build skills and earning potential." In a little more than two years, CEO had "implemented more than 40 initiatives which represent new ideas, best practices, and expansions of successful program models," explained the report. For its first two years, CEO focused primarily "on program development, implementation, and early evaluation. Throughout 2009, with strong evidence in hand, CEO advocated for, and witnessed, the replication of its successful initiatives throughout New York City and beyond."[165]

Bloomberg had created the perfect antipoverty program for a twenty-first-century American city. His boldness should be appreciated. Not only was poverty off political agendas, virtually banned from political discourse; no other mayor of an American city within memory—perhaps within history—had mounted an independent assault on poverty. Bloomberg built on the example of mayors like Ed Rendell of Philadelphia, who realized in the 1990s that the federal government had withdrawn from the business of pumping large amounts of money directly into American cities and that, as a result, they would need to find creative means to solve their problems themselves. Like these mayors, Bloomberg turned to market-based principles and funded an ambitious program—more comprehensive and ambitious than any other mayor's—with a combination of city and private sector money. Could it be replicated outside of New York City with its vast resources of talent and wealth, including resident foundations and major corporations? The federal government's Social Innovation Fund granted the city $5.7 million to find out by attempting to replicate the program in seven other cities.[166]

The program fit the twenty-first century perfectly because it did not rest on federal initiatives or funding, it combined public and private resources, it reflected market-based principles, and it was resolutely pragmatic and nonideological. (Market-based principles, it might be argued, were an ideology, but they had so permeated public life that for the most part they were noncontroversial.) It also fit the twenty-first century well because it focused on the deserving poor, eschewed redistribution, and paid no attention to the dependent poor. In this way, it was like national policy, which since the 1990s had developed a successful array of programs to help the working poor, while the situation of the nonworking poor, largely neglected by new public policies, stagnated or deteriorated.[167] At the same time, the program's diffuse, opportunistic, commonsense quality was a limitation. How were programs to be prioritized and coordinated? Was it possible to find a single set of measures with which to evaluate the program's success?

In a preface to the CEO 2009 annual report, Sheldon Danziger and Marie Cancian, widely respected poverty researchers and editors of *Changing Poverty, Changing Policies*, tried to rein in the programmatic diversity of Bloomberg's poverty program by assimilating it to the agenda of mainstream poverty research. In light of their assumptions "about trends in work, family structure, and the anti-poverty effects of economic growth," Danziger and Cancian concluded that "an anti-poverty policy agenda for the twenty-first century should pursue three fundamental goals. The first is 'to make work pay.' The second is to support parents so that those in both one-parent and two-parent families can work not only steadily, but also flexibly, with sufficient time for parenting and care-giving. Finally, we need to increase investments in education and training over the life course to raise employment and earnings for this generation and the next." These, they reported, were precisely the goals targeted by CEO. "Policymakers," they advised, "would do well to emulate the efforts underway in New York City."[168]

Changing Poverty, Changing Policies is the fifth volume "in a series of edited volumes sponsored by the Institute for Research on Poverty (IRP) that evaluate the nature of poverty and the scope of antipoverty policies." Sheldon Danziger has been coeditor of the second through fifth volumes. The Institute for Research on Poverty, founded in 1968 to be the Office of Economic Opportunity's "think tank," has been the major center of poverty research in the United States.[169] Each of the IRP volumes, meticulously edited, combines social accounting—statistics on poverty, demographic portraits of poor populations, and discussions of measures of poverty—with definitive overviews of current research on major poverty-related topics and judicious explications of poverty issues. Together, they showcase what might be called the best in mainstream poverty research.

Similar concerns run through each volume: for instance, the impact of family structure on poverty; the effectiveness of social programs on lifting individuals over the poverty line; the role of education; the implications of labor market changes. New concerns emerge as well—in the 2009 volume, notably, global and comparative questions and the impact of the recession in full swing at the time of the book's production.[170] There is, remarkably, virtually no mention of the new technologies of poverty work discussed in this chapter, with the exception of a brief reference to the literature on asset poverty and a short reference to Bloomberg's antipoverty program in New York City, or (except for a passing mention) to the Harlem Children's Zone. Geoffrey Canada, Michael Porter, Muhammad Yunus, the Grameen Bank, microfinance, microenterprise: these persons and programs do not appear. The focus of the IRP volumes is national. Their implicit goal, it would seem, is to inform and influence policy professionals and legislators as much as researchers. They remain, therefore, relentlessly in the mainstream.

Conversely, promoters of the new technologies of poverty work pay relatively little attention to the mainstream world of poverty research and policy. Nor do either say much about or interact with grassroots antipoverty initiatives, such as the living-wage movement, which is very much alive and active throughout the country. The universe of poverty research and policy is like a Venn diagram of spheres that overlap only slightly.

The uncomfortable questions about New York City's antipoverty initiative that remain unanswered parallel questions that might be asked about mainstream poverty policy. Would the energetic array of programs recommended by poverty researchers obscure the needs of the dependent poor and block initiatives, like the living wage, which could make a dent in working poverty faster than just about anything else? Is it possible to shrink poverty in America without economic redistribution? Would the programs have helped Herbert Manes and Shorty, who fell outside all three of the groups targeted by Bloomberg's plan? In the end, neither Bloomberg's antipoverty program, the Harlem Children's Zone, the market-based technologies of poverty work, nor mainstream poverty policies assault the rigidities of social structure or the citadels of power. They propose to solve poverty on the cheap, with relatively little public money and without growing the size of government very much.

Rather than create and manage programs, governments are impresarios organizing and coordinating the new show. To be sure, mainstream policies and new technologies together contain the potential to improve the prospects of a great many people while smoothing the rough edges of capitalism. Maybe that is the most for which we can hope.

Epilogue: The Existential Problem of Urban Studies

When I became director of the undergraduate Urban Studies Program at the University of Pennsylvania in 1983, I was surprised to find that the program lacked a multidisciplinary course that synthesized writing about cities into a coherent interpretation of contemporary urban America. What accounted for deindustrialized, segregated, financially strapped, often violent cities with their failed public institutions and surrounding white suburbs that this book has described? I wanted to give the students a single book that explained it all and to take off from there with in-depth explorations of the issues. The problem was that no such book existed. Under the circumstances, I felt compelled to undertake the task of synthesis myself in a single introductory-level course.

Urban Studies 104/History 153 entered the Urban Studies curriculum in the spring semester of 1984 and has been taught every year since then. I called the course "Urban Crisis: American Cities Since World War II." I often have taught it myself; in other years various colleagues have replaced me. The years since 1984 have witnessed extraordinary changes in cities—so great, in fact, that the first part of the course title, "Urban Crisis," is probably an anachronism. But maybe not. There is, as the chapters of this book make clear, a continuity to the issues that has made it possible to retain the course's intellectual framework while updating the reading list and modifying components, including, for instance, the surge in immigration and the recent decline in crime.

This book has emerged from teaching the course. Like the course, it has explored the consequences of the economic, demographic, and spatial transformations that have resulted in urban forms unlike any others in history. Both the course and the book are about the collision between urban transformation and rightward-moving social politics—the withdrawal of federal aid to cities, the fraying safety net, individualization of risk, and application of market fundamentalism to public policy.

Shorty's death illustrated one of the worst consequences of this collision: its devastating impact on African American men. Urban transformations left huge numbers of black men excluded from the regular labor market; social politics left them with their own special welfare state—prison. The consequences not only foreclosed the future prospects of huge numbers of black men; they also undermined families and turned growing up into an obstacle course where failure to find the right path around successive barriers had permanent, devastating, and sometimes fatal consequences.

A widespread interpretation holds deindustrialization responsible for the economic marginality of black men. But deindustrialization by itself, as this book shows, is not the only culprit in the story. Manufacturing industries never provided jobs for more than a relatively small minority of African American men. Of equal importance is the revolution in southern agriculture, the major employer of black men for most of American history before World War II. Agricultural mechanization left millions redundant, unable to scratch out a living from tiny sharecropper plots. African American men left the South for northern and midwestern cities just as jobs for poorly educated, semiskilled workers grew increasingly scarce. In the cities to which they travelled, racism closed the most promising doors. In the same years, even greater numbers of poor, semiskilled white southerners moved north. To be sure, they encountered hostility and some discrimination, but never on a scale that matched the racial discrimination and violence that confronted African Americans. White southerners melded into the urban fabric, living where they wanted, sometimes being given jobs over African Americans with more work experience.

Exploitative work, bad pay, racism, and foreclosed opportunities amounted to a formula for poverty. In 1940, about three of every four African Americans lived below the poverty line; twenty years later, on the eve of the War on Poverty, the number had only declined to about three of five. Income figures for Mexicans were only a tiny bit better. Public officials and major media remained reluctant to notice poverty or admit its extent, which is why the publication of Michael Harrington's *The Other America* in 1962 caused such a sensation—a sensation that lasted for only a little more than a decade, the life span of the War on Poverty and Great Society. Popular explanations displaced responsibility for poverty from politics, economics, and racism onto individuals. The culture of poverty, as we have seen, coated the old trope of the undeserving poor with a varnish of bad anthropology. In the 1980s and 1990s, the discovery of the "urban underclass" revived the spectre of the dangerous classes, a recurring urban fear since the nineteenth century. The epithet "welfare mother" joined sex and race into a euphemism for the undeserving poor, with powerful implications for public policy.[1]

Since 1973, income inequality has widened; wealth inequality has exploded. Real wages have stagnated or declined. The minimum wage is worth less than it was decades ago; for those who can get them, TANF benefits (federal "welfare") are worth less than AFDC was in the early 1970s. Poverty went down a little in the 1990s, but, fueled by the Great Recession, moved sharply upward. Fewer unemployed workers receive unemployment insurance; workers' compensation benefits have been made more restrictive. A smaller proportion of Americans are covered by medical or retirement benefits. Unemployment rates refuse to drop. Hunger is rampant, and food stamp (known as SNAP—Supplemental Nutrition Program—as of October 2008) use is soaring while food banks run out of food. In 2009, more than one in five young people under the age of eighteen lived in poverty—an increase of about one-third since the low point in 1974. What has been the response of public authorities?

In the 1990s, public policy did not ignore poverty. President Bill Clinton greatly expanded the Earned Income Tax Credit, a benefit that boosted large numbers of working poor families above the poverty line. A combination of work and benefits lifted the income of working single mothers more than 25 percent. In both of these examples, the important word is "working." Policy initiatives sharpened divisions between the working and nonworking poor, improving conditions for the former, while benefits for the others stagnated or went down.

Looked at in the long run, however, there is good news to tell about poverty. With 1960 the reference point, poverty rates have plummeted. African American poverty, high as it is, remains less than half of what it was a century ago. With the indexing of Social Security benefits in 1972, the elderly became the big winners in poverty reduction. Where they once had been three times as likely as any other age group to be poor, they began the twenty-first century with the lowest poverty rate of any group. In the half century from 1959 to 2009, poverty rates for people age sixty-five or older had dropped from about 27 percent to 8.9 percent. These were real improvements, and painting with a broad brush that obscures them distorts recent history.

By the late 1990s, as Chapter 4 described, market-based theories, ubiquitous throughout the policy world, had begun to invade ideas about poverty. Poor people became rational actors—budding entrepreneurs, savers, and consumers—served best not by conventional welfare state programs but by rebuilding markets in inner cities, providing start-up loans and financial services, and offering cash incentives for good behavior. This new image of poor people eschewed pathological and cultural

conceptions of poverty, replacing them with an optimistic, can-do atti-
tude reflecting the idea that poor people, like anyone else, need only a
little help to act in their own self-interest. This was a revolution in American ideas about poverty—but not a total revolution. Like the older pathological concepts of poverty, it located the source of material improvement
within individuals. The journey out of poverty remained a solo trip, or,
as in the Grameen model of microcredit, an individual journey moni-
tored by a community of women. The role of outside agencies—NGOs,
public authorities, or profit-making social entrepreneurs—was to provide
modest initial capital and to clear roadblocks. From that point, finding
the way out of poverty remained an individual responsibility. The obverse
was a diminished role for the state.

One of the paradoxes of recent American history is how little most
people appear to care about poverty and inequality, even when their
own wages stagnate and their security becomes precarious. Among recent presidential candidates, only John Edwards talked about poverty,
which turned out to have no political traction as an issue, even before
his candidacy imploded. Poverty talk is clearly a third rail in American
politics, and conservatives have succeeded in transmuting discussion of
inequality into class warfare. Among major politicians, only New York
Mayor Michael Bloomberg wore a concern with poverty on his sleeve
and implemented a major antipoverty program. Most other politicians,
including President Obama, focused their attention on an amorphous
middle class, carefully avoided the word "poverty," and talked of opportunity, not inequality.

The poverty story points to the difficulty of striking a balance between
the bad news and the good news and brings me back to the challenge of
writing and teaching recent urban history—and to my course. After
teaching the course a couple of times, I observed a problem. The course
tells a depressing story of deindustrialization, population decline, racial
segregation, failed public housing, and so on—the story repeated in
this book. All of it is true and inescapable. But it leaves students
depressed—indeed, it leaves me depressed as well. Wonderful young
people, eager to help change the world, confront a tale of powerful
structural forces abetted by ambitious politicians, every level of government, racism, greedy real estate and corporate interests, and academic
researchers impotent to suggest realistic avenues for change. Is this the
vision with which my colleagues and I really want to leave our students
or readers?

The answer, of course, is no. So I have searched for rays of hope, examples of progressive change, and found many. Useful, even energizing, as they are, they do not add up to a coherent response to the narrative of failure that dominates writing about recent urban history. In

this, my experience teaching the course parallels a wider dilemma confronting urban studies as a field. The dilemma facing urban studies, in turn, encapsulates the failure of the American left to reclaim the narrative of recent American history.

In the summer of 2009, I was asked to write a short article for a special issue of a journal in which urbanists would offer policy advice to the new administration in Washington. I lacked the hubris to offer advice to an administration that was taking cities seriously enough to hire talented, well-informed staff who knew more about policy issues than I did. But I did think it might be useful, or at least interesting, to consider what historians had to say about federal urban policy. I found something puzzling. Writers on both the political left and right told essentially the same story about the history of American cities since World War II. Although their explanations of trends and the morals they drew differed, they agreed that recent urban history was an account of failure. There are innumerable examples. From the left, take as one example Colin Gordon's extraordinary 2008 book *Mapping Urban Decline: St. Louis and the Fate of the American City.* "A half century of urban renewal and redevelopment programs," Gordon observes, "not only failed to stem the decline of central St. Louis but pointedly avoided the very neighborhoods in which that decline was most palpable. . . . Most American cities emerged from the heyday of urban renewal in similar shape—central city decay punctuated by the occasional stadium or convention center; urban problems (segregation, poverty, unemployment, fiscal crisis) spilling into the inner suburbs; employment and the tax base continuing to sprawl to the outer suburbs."[2]

Locating politically conservative, card-carrying historians of recent urban America is difficult. There don't seem to be any. But myriad conservative commentators have framed a narrative about post–World War II cities that is remarkably similar to the one offered by the political left. To take only one example, in *City of the Right*, Gerald Houseman's review of recent conservative thought on cities. Houseman points out that the late Milton Friedman concluded, "The record of government in dealing with urban problems is one of miserable failure . . . a failure so complete that it is impossible to name a single governmental program developed over recent decades and aimed at poverty, or urban problems, or social welfare, or 'reform,' that has achieved its objectives."[3]

Writers on both the political left and the right used the same trope, "urban crisis," to sum up the results of postwar urban history. In the 1980s and 1990s, they even began to use the same metaphor, "urban underclass," to describe the stigmatized women and men who embodied the urban crisis and the failures of public policy. What accounts for this uncharacteristic consensus across ideological lines? There were, to begin with, the "facts on the ground." The physical deterioration of American cities; the increase in concentrated poverty; the rise in crime; the flight of industry and jobs; the loss of white population; the spread of segregation; and the failure of urban schools—all exacerbated by a shrinking tax base and inadequate revenues—could not be missed or minimized by any honest reporter of urban conditions. Nor was it possible to elide the coincidence of urban crisis with both the major successes of the Civil Rights Movement and unmatched federal spending on cities and urban-related programs.

Despite general consensus on the facts on the ground, writers on the political left and right told partially different stories about the origins of urban decline. The political left linked urban crisis to a number of factors: deindustrialization and job loss; the impact of the Vietnam War's voracious appetite for money on federal urban and social spending; the institutionalized racism that still tainted public policies and institutions; greedy state and local politicians unwilling to relinquish power or resources; narrowly self-interested homeowners who resisted racial integration; Americans' historic distrust of cities and contempt for their disadvantaged residents; and federal policies that fueled the growth of suburbs. Conservatives tended to blame the urban crisis on the inherent inefficiency and wastefulness of government; moral hazards introduced by generous public programs; obstacles that inhibited market processes; selfish labor unions that drove up costs without corresponding increases in productivity; and disastrous, if politically correct, policies like affirmative action and busing.

Despite their different ontologies, in the 1960s and 1970s progressive and conservative versions of urban crisis shared a common enemy: bureaucracy. To critics on both the left and the right, the growth of large, rigid, unresponsive bureaucracies shielded public officials from the people they served and the consequences of their actions. Concerned mainly with self-protection and institutional aggrandizement, public bureaucracies were citadels guarding the status quo. Attacks on public bureaucracy from the political left, together with the left's withering criticisms of public institutions and programs, helped legitimate and fuel the right's drive to shrink government, unleash markets, and privatize public programs and institutions. The left found itself trapped in an ideological box from which it could not easily escape. Did left-leaning historians really believe that government was the problem, not the solution? If they did not, how should they incorporate their radical criticism of social policy into a narrative that, unlike conservatives', subordinated "market price to social value," to borrow a phrase from T. H. Marshall?[4]

In the 1960s and 1970s, when historians finally began to rip away the veil that obscured uncomfortable images of America's past, they discovered jarring contradictions between the theory and practice of major institutions, such as public schools, mental asylums, reformatories, social welfare, and public housing. What, historians now asked, had been the actual purpose and results of state-led institution building? Their answers focused on the reproduction of class, race, and gender inequalities and on the dysfunctions of bureaucracy. In these new histories, government was as much the problem as the solution. (In the interest of full disclosure, I was one of the historians coming of age professionally in the late 1960s and early 1970s who contributed to this interpretation.)[5]

As leftist historians composed a narrative of failure, they unwittingly gave the right a gift—an interpretation that could be appropriated in the campaign to reduce the size and influence of government and privatize public functions. Urbanists' relentless emphasis on government complicity in the failures of public housing and the growth of urban ghettos opened doors through which other writers with different agendas happily passed. Similar stories could be told about interpretations of public education, social welfare, mental hospitals, reform schools, and criminal justice by historians on the political left. One result was a shared narrative of decline that cut across institutional domains. The political left lost control of the emerging narrative of failure, which was appropriated by the political right to buttress its goals with historical evidence.

The left was trapped by its own historical interpretations because it lacked a viable counter-narrative. As urban historians piled on accounts of failed urban policies and programs, they naturalized public failure as the master narrative of urban history. Researchers unearthed ever more instances of publicly sanctioned racial discrimination, badly flawed public housing, venal politicians and realtors, government-encouraged suburban sprawl, and on and on. None of what they said or wrote (and I include myself among them) was untrue or unimportant. But they virtually stopped looking for a counter-narrative that would support a different politics.

Was the narrative of failure the only game in town? Or had urban scholars grown lazy and unimaginative? The history of public housing provides an interesting case. Most historians have told more or less the same story about the failures of public housing in different cities. The story begins with the idealistic hopes of the 1930s dashed by a deadly mix of racism, mean-spirited public officials, and an overdose of modernist, high-rise architecture that climaxed with the demolition of high-rise public housing projects in city after city, starting with the Pruitt-Igoe complex in St. Louis in 1972–1974. All this is true. But it is not complete. Success stories fill the early history of public housing. In *Public Housing That Worked: New York in the Twentieth Century*, Nicolas Dagen Bloom shows that some cities managed high-rise public housing well.[6] But most public housing never consisted primarily of high-rise towers, and whatever the critics think, public housing developments usually have long waiting lists. In the Web-based Talking Points Memo, housing expert Peter Dreier observes:

> the best-kept secret about public housing is that it actually provides decent, affordable housing for many people. . . . There are probably 500,000 families on the waiting lists of the nation's 3,060 local housing authorities. In many cities, it takes between two and five years—and sometimes longer—to get off the waiting list and into public housing. Public housing developments are often better—and certainly more affordable—than apartments available to the poor in the private housing market. Despite the popular stereotypes, a decade ago high-rises accounted for only one-quarter of public housing buildings. Many of those high-rise projects have been demolished in the last two decades. . . . most public housing developments today are garden apartments, low-rise walk ups, and single family homes or townhouses. But the high-rise projects, most of them in the largest cities, accounted for many of the most problematic developments and cast a giant shadow on the whole program.[7]

The giant shadow cast over public housing by high-rise projects in large cities has obscured not only low-rise developments but also the "housing policy revolution" identified by housing scholar David James Erickson in his 2009 book *The Housing Policy Revolution: Networks and Neighborhoods*. Erickson argues that decentralized networks of CDCs, public agencies, private partners, fiscal intermediaries, and others have replaced top-down, centralized housing authorities as builders of affordable housing.[8] As it applies to affordable housing, the narrative of failure, if Erickson is correct, has become an anachronism.

The bits and pieces of a new narrative of recent urban history illustrating the constructive role of government lie scattered, waiting to be assembled into a coherent story. They include the results of federal urban policies, notably the Community Reinvestment Act and Hope VI, and the indirect consequences of other public programs that pour money into cities—for instance, jobs created through Great Society programs; Social Security, Medicare, and Medicaid; the state- and federally funded expansion of "anchor institutions" (hospitals and universities); and even the 1965 repeal of nationality-based immigration quotas that opened the national gates to the newcomers who have revived stagnating cities. They also include the surprising identification of a local urban liberalism that moderated the impact of deindustrialization—a story told by Guian McKee in his extraordinary 2009 book *The Problem of Jobs*—and the signs of neighborhood revival reported by Paul S. Grogan and Tony Proscio in *Comeback Cities: A Blueprint for Urban Neighborhood Revival*. Grogan and Proscio find the "American inner city rebounding—not just here and there, not just cosmetically, but fundamentally." More material for a new narrative also derives from urban politics revived by grass-roots social movements like those described by Annelise Orleck and Lisa Levenstein; new forms of public/private partnerships; and, some-times—as in Los Angeles, in the account by Robert Gottlieb and his colleagues—from multiethnic coalitions.[9]

There is also good news embedded in the African American story. In the recent history of African Americans, the main thread is not immis-eration but, as Chapter 3 showed, differentiation. African American men and women broke into occupations previously restricted mainly to whites. Herbert Manes and Shorty fought on the streets; Barack Obama was elected president of the United States. Differentiation served to boost the fortunate fraction of African Americans onto the higher rungs of the social ladder, not to alter the distance between them. Individual experience proved fluid while social structures remained rigid. Differ-entiation was at once a sign of improvement and the method by which the structure of inequality reproduced itself. For African Americans, as we have seen, even the story of economic mobility needs qualification, because their distinctive niche in public and publicly financed employ-ment left them vulnerable to government retrenchment and because about one in four of them still lives below the poverty line. But a look back only as far as the mid-twentieth century reveals a profound shift in the opportunities open to African Americans and the success of many women and men in taking advantage of them.

The temptation to jettison the narrative of urban failure in favor of a story based on progress and hope must be resisted. A narrative that sub-ordinates urban decline and failed urban polices—that substitutes Pol-lyanna for Cassandra—would be no more complete or helpful than its opposite. Cities face huge unsolved problems; as *MetroNation: How U.S. Metropolitan Areas Fuel American Prosperity*, a 2010 Brookings Institution report, makes clear, many recent metropolitan trends point in troubling directions. The Great Recession has decimated city budgets, increased homelessness and hunger, and pushed up poverty rates in suburbs as well as cities.[10]

One of the central tasks of a new narrative is to rehabilitate the role of government. At one level, it is not a very difficult job. A close look at any realm of public life—from poverty reduction to health—will iden-tify many examples of constructive action that are not only taken by government but that are impossible for any institution other than gov-ernment. Take health, for instance. Through Medicare, government vastly increased the availability of quality medical care to the elderly, who by and large have taken full advantage of the program. It is hard, if not impossible, to imagine any agent other than the federal government quickly and efficiently bringing national health care to the elderly. Indirectly, government funding of research and medical training has resulted in revolutionary new medications and therapies. Government, not cowboy pioneers in Silicon Valley working out of their garages, provided the incentives and funding for digital computing and the Internet.[11]

At another level, the problem is more difficult. Government initiatives did not always succeed or work as intended. The prevailing master narrative is a litany of such failures. The issue is not assessing praise and blame, arriving at grades for a government report card. Rather, the challenge is figuring out why some initiatives worked better than others, and why, in other cases, perverse unintended outcomes outweighed benefits. Meeting the challenge is important for at least three reasons: countering the myth of government ineptitude, undermining the disabling myth of inevitability, and balancing the focus on structure with an appreciation of agency. Replacing the canard of ubiquitous government failure is, as we have seen, the easiest and most obvious task. But the others are equally important, if less immediately apparent. The myth of inevitability—what the late journalist Daniel Singer called "TINA" (There Is No Alternative)—remains one of the oldest and most disabling rhetorical defenses of the status quo.[12] We may deplore the outcome, laments TINA with crocodile tears, but the forces of modernization or globalization, the imperatives of national security, the implacable laws of economics—take your pick or add your own—mean that no other result was possible; to think otherwise is idle, utopian, romantic speculation. Here history is the antidote. Close analysis of any moment, of any decision, reveals options, alternatives recognized by sane, intelligent people.

Balancing structure and agency in a new narrative is the trickiest task of all. For the most part, this book has taken a structural tack, concentrating on limning the contours of urban transformation and examining its consequences for inequality, race, and civil violence. To bring the story down from the clouds of abstraction, it has turned repeatedly to the encounter between Herbert Manes and Shorty, which encapsulates its major themes. But the book has not foregrounded agency, the action of individuals and groups on their own behalf. By contrast, ethnographers such as Philippe Bourgois and Robert Fairbanks II have brought marginalized people to life as real human beings full of contradictions—flawed, but with dignity and talent, at once appealing and maddening. Historians, too, have looked for agency among subaltern people and found it everywhere. Especially by chronicling social movements and community organizing, historians have shown how, time and again throughout American history, the mobilization of ordinary people has challenged power. In fact, the most important movements for social and political change in American history have taken shape outside of government: think of abolition, temperance, women's suffrage, trade unions, civil rights, feminism, and, on a local level, the living-wage movement. None of them, however, believed they could prevail on their own. They made claims on government, and they succeeded when the state incorporated their demands into law. They appreciated the balance between collective agency and state power. How to capture the balance poses a huge, crucial challenge for a new narrative of urban history and twenty-first-century urban studies.

Urbanists who want to replace the narrative of failure have three tasks: rehabilitating the role of the state, undermining the myth of inevitability, and locating a balance between the roles of individuals acting together and the power of organized interests and government. These tasks are not confined to urbanists; they constitute, in fact, a project for the American left, which has lost control of the narrative of recent American history. How the narrative of failure permeates American life—how it is being pushed back from the Great Society to the New Deal—is a topic for another book. But its consequences are all around us, from the hegemony of market models in public policy to public opinion polls showing that huge majorities of Americans distrust government and lack faith in its capacity to solve public problems.

So we are back where we started. The problem of writing recent urban history is the same as the problem of teaching it. How do we construct a coherent and realistic narrative that does not leave our students either cynical or depressed? In her brilliant book *Poverty Capital: Microfinance and the Making of Development*, Ananya Roy puts the dilemma this way:

> In teaching my course [Global Poverty] at Berkeley I am struck by a contrast. On the one hand, I have students who are brimming with enthusiasm to do good; they want to save the world. They believe they can. On the other hand, I have students who are cynical, those who are able to level sharp critiques of structures of injustice but not believe that change is possible. I teach in the impossible space between the hubris of benevolence and the paralysis of cynicism.[13]

Locating and occupying this impossible space is the existential dilemma of urban studies. And of the American left as well.

Notes

Prologue: The Death of Shorty

1. I have changed all personal names and, with the exception of three major streets, the names of all streets. The nickname Shorty, however, is real, and for reasons that the Prologue makes clear, could not be changed without destroying part of the meaning. This Prologue is based on my observations as a juror, documents from the police file and Social Security Administration, conversations with defense attorney and defendant, criminal records, and various census, tax, and Home Owners Loan Corporation documents compiled by Chris Rupe. Special thanks during the research go to Alice Goffman, Scott Flander, and Wendell Pritchett; for perceptive and constructive readings to Daniel Amsterdam, Michael Frisch, and Vivian Zelizer; and for sharing his editorial wisdom, Mike Rose.

2. Craig R. McCoy, Nancy Phillips, and Dylan Purcell, "Justice: Delayed, Dismissed, Denied," *Philadelphia Inquirer*, December 13, 2009. In fairness, readers should know that the newspaper articles aroused public anger that led to significant reforms.

3. These data come from the criminal statistics compiled by the *Philadelphia Inquirer* and accessed by a link on the newspaper's Web site: http://www.philly.com/Inquirer/multimedia/15818502.html.

4. Steve Bogira, *Courthouse 302: A Year Behind the Scenes in an American Courthouse* (New York: Vintage, 2006).

5. Jacob A. Riis, *How the Other Half Lives: Studies Among the Tenements of New York* (New York: Charles Scribner's Sons, 1890); Michael Harrington, *The Other America: Poverty in the United States* (New York: Macmillan, 1962); Elliot Liebow, *Tally's Corner: A Study of Negro Streetcorner Men* (Boston: Little Brown, 1967); Robert P. Fairbanks, II, *How It Works: Recovering Citizens in Post-welfare Philadelphia* (Chicago: University of Chicago Press, 2009); Philippe Bourgois and Jeff Schonberg, *Righteous Dopefiend* (Berkeley: University of California Press, 2009).

6. I have published case studies of the early twentieth-century urban poor in various places. See, for example, chapter 4, "Surviving Poverty," in Michael B. Katz, *Improving Poor People: The Welfare State, the "Underclass," and Urban Schools as History* (Princeton, N.J.: Princeton University Press, 1995), 144–72.

7. Mike Davis, *Planet of Slums* (New York: Verso, 2007).

8. Sudhir Alladi Venkatesh, *Off the Books: The Underground Economy of the Urban Poor* (Cambridge, Mass.: Harvard University Press, 2009).

Chapter 1. What Is an American City?

A shorter version of this chapter, without endnotes, appeared in *Dissent* magazine (Summer 2009), and a longer version appeared in Merlin Chowkwanyun and Rand Serhan, eds., *Democracy, Inequality, and Political Participation in American Life* (Boulder, Colo.: Paradigm Publishers, 2011). For producing the maps, my thanks to Mark J. Stern. For his background research on Philadelphia and Los Angeles, thanks to Domenic Vitiello. And thanks to Michael Frisch for his suggestions.

1. Jane Jacobs, *The Death and Life of Great American Cities* (New York: Random House, 1961).

2. NewUrbanism.org, "Charter of the New Urbanism," www.newurbanism.org/charter.html.

3. Robert Bruegmann, *Sprawl: A Compact History* (Chicago: University of Chicago Press, 2005), 151–53, 259nn38–40, quote from n40.

4. Michael B. Katz and Mark J. Stern, *One Nation Divisible: What America Was and What It Is Becoming* (New York: Russell Sage, 2006).

5. Charles Richmond Henderson, "Are Modern Industry and City Life Unfavorable to the Family?" *American Journal of Sociology* 14, 5 (1909): 668–80.

6. A fine collection of attempts to come to grips with the new industrial city can be found in Richard Sennett, ed., *Classic Essays on the Culture of Cities* (New York: Appleton-Century Crofts, 1969).

7. Peirce Lewis, "The Urban Invasion of Rural America: The Emergence of the Galactic City," in *The Changing American Countryside: Rural People and Places*, ed. Emery N. Castle (Lawrence: University of Kansas Press, 1995), 40–42.

8. Lewis Mumford, *The City in History: Its Origins, Its Transformations, and Its Prospects* (New York: Harcourt, Brace, Jovanovich, 1961), 543.

9. Jean Gottman, *Megalopolis: The Urbanized Northeastern Seaboard of the United States* (New York: Twentieth Century Fund, 1961), 3, 5, 776–77.

10. Bruegmann, *Sprawl*, 51.

11. This comparison of Philadelphia and Los Angeles summarizes the work of Domenic Vitiello, "Urban America: What It Was and What It Is Becoming" (2004). The text of the paper, which includes full bibliographic citations, is available on the America at the Millennium project Web site as Working Paper 15, www.sp2.upenn.edu/america2000/wp15all.pdf.

12. Robert Gottlieb, Mark Vallianatos, Regina M. Freer, and Peter Dreier, *The Next Los Angeles: The Struggle for a Livable City* (Berkeley: University of California Press, 2005), 2.

13. Migrant agricultural labor was also important on the East Coast, but not as extensive as in the Southwest. On East Coast migrant labor, see Cindy Hahamovitch, *Fruits of Their Labor: Atlantic Coast Farmworkers and the Making of Migrant Poverty, 1870–1945* (Chapel Hill: University of North Carolina Press, 1997).

14. Immigration to Philadelphia is the subject of research by the Philadelphia Immigration Project at the University of Pennsylvania. See Audrey Singer, Domenic Vitiello, Michael Katz, and David Park, "Recent Immigration to Philadelphia: Regional Change in a Re-emerging Gateway" (report from the Brookings Institution, Metropolitan Policy Program, November 2008).

15. In *Sprawl* (65), Bruegmann points out, "The density of the Los Angeles urbanized area, as calculated in the 2000 census, was just over 7,000 people per square mile, nearly twice that of the Chicago urbanized area and significantly denser than the New York area." This points to a difference in urban growth patterns. With just city boundaries considered, New York and Chicago are much denser than Los Angeles, a pattern that underscores the differential models of urbanism represented by the older and newer cities.

16. Gottlieb et al., *Next Los Angeles*, 33.

17. This discussion of economic, demographic, and spatial transformation is based on Michael B. Katz, *The Price of Citizenship: Redefining the American Welfare State* (New York: Metropolitan Books, 2001), chap. 2.

18. Guian A. McKee, "Hospital Cities: Health Care Institutions as Post-industrial Anchors" (unpublished paper, Urban History Association Biennial Conference, Las Vegas, Nev., October 2010).

19. Penn Institute for Urban Research, *Retooling HUD for a Catalytic Federal Government: A Report to Secretary Shaun Donovan* (Philadelphia: Penn Institute for Urban Research, 2009), chap. 8, "Anchor Institutions as Partners in Building Successful Communities and Local Economies," 148; Ira Harkavy and Harmon Zuckerman, "Eds and Meds: Cities' Hidden Assets" (report from the Brookings Institution Survey Series, August 1999).

20. James N. Gregory, *The Southern Diaspora: How the Great Migrations of Black and White Southerners Transformed America* (Chapel Hill: University of North Carolina Press, 2005).

21. Herbert J. Gans, *The Levittowners: Ways of Life and Politics in a New Suburban Community* (New York: Pantheon, 1967).

22. Kevin Fox Gotham, *Race, Real Estate, and Uneven Development: The Kansas City Experience, 1900–2000* (Albany: State University of New York Press, 2002), provides a vivid account of how realtors promoted racial segregation.

23. Camilo J. Vergara, *The New American Ghetto* (New Brunswick, N.J.: Rutgers University Press, 1995). Laura J. Lawson, *CityBountiful: A Century of Community Gardening in America* (Berkeley: University of California Press, 2005) and Dominic Vitiello, "Growing Edible Cities," in Eugenie L. Birch and Susan J. Wachter, *Growing Greener Cities: Urban Sustainability in the Twenty-First Century* (Philadelphia: University of Pennsylvania Press, 2008), pp. 259–78.

24. Stephen Castles and Mark J. Miller, *The Age of Migration: International Population Movement in the Modern World*, 3d edition (New York and London: Guildford Press, 2003).

25. Edward L. Glaeser and Jesse M. Shapiro, "City Growth: Which Places Grew and Why," in *Redefining Urban and Suburban America: Evidence from Census 2000*, ed. Bruce Katz and Robert E. Lang (Washington, D.C.: Brookings Institution, 2003), 13–32.

26. Roberto Suro and Audrey Singer, "Changing Patterns of Latino Growth in Metropolitan America," in *Redefining Urban and Suburban America*, ed. Katz and Lang, 181–210, 182; Singer et al., "Recent Immigration."

27. Testimony of Jonathan Bowles, Director, Center for an Urban Future, Before City Council Committees on Small Business and Immigration, "Creating Greater Opportunities for Immigrant Entrepreneurs," December 14, 2007. See nycfuture.org.

28. Mamie Marcuss with Ricardo Borgos, Federal Reserve Bank of Boston, "Who Are New England's Immigrants?" http://www.bostonfed.org/commdev/c&b/2004/fall/Immigrants.pdf.

29. Allan Mallach, Amanda Frazier, and Diane Sterner, "Cities in Transition: New Jersey's Urban Paradox" (report from the Housing and Community Development Network of New Jersey, the New Jersey Urban Revitalization Research Project, September 2006), 6 (emphasis original).

30. Singer et al., "Recent Immigration."

31. Mike Davis, *Magical Urbanism: Latinos Reinvent the U.S. City*, rev. and expanded ed. (London: Verso, 2000), 49–54.

32. Andrew Wiese, *Places of Their Own: African American Suburbanization in the Twentieth Century* (Chicago: University of Chicago Press, 2004).

33. Michael B. Katz, Mathew Creighton, Daniel Amsterdam, and Merlin Chowkwanyun, "Immigration and the New Metropolitan Geography," *Journal of Urban Affairs* 32, 5 (2010): 523–47.

34. Katz and Stern, *One Nation Divisible*, 153–70.

35. Gans, *The Levittowners*.

36. Figures here are based on a sample of fourteen exemplary metropolitan areas.

37. Douglas Massey and Nancy Denton, *American Apartheid: Segregation and the Making of the Underclass* (Cambridge, Mass.: Harvard University Press, 1993), 46–48, 64, 74, 85–87, 332–33.

38. Edward L. Glaeser and Jacob L. Vigdor, "Racial Segregation: Promising News," in *Redefining Urban and Suburban America*, ed. Katz and Lang, 211–33, 217.

39. Douglas Massey, Jonathan Rothwell, and Thurston Domina, "The Changing Bases of Segregation in the United States," *Annals AAPSS* 626 (November 2009): 74–90.

40. Peter Dreier, John Mollenkopf, and Todd Swanstrom, *Place Matters: Metropolitics for the Twenty-First Century*, rev. 2nd ed. (Lawrence: University Press of Kansas, 2004), 18, 48.

41. Ibid., 130–32.

42. Bureau of Justice Statistics, "Reported Crime in United States—Total," http://bjs.ojp.usdoj.gov/dataonline/Search/Crime/State/statebystaterun.cfm ?stateid=52.

43. Mike Davis, *City of Quartz: Excavating the Future in Los Angeles* (New York: Vintage, 1992), 225–26.

44. Stephen Graham, *Cities Under Siege: The New Military Urbanism* (London: Verso, 2010), xiii, xxi, xxiii.

45. Myron Orfield, *Metropolitics: A Regional Agenda for Community and Stability* (Washington, D.C. and Cambridge, Mass.: Brookings Institution and Lincoln Institute of Land Policy, 1997), 22.

46. "The Urban Beat," *Maclean's*, July 19, 1999, 2.

47. John H. Mollenkopf, *The Contested City* (Princeton, N.J.: Princeton University Press, 1983), 12–13.

48. John Hull Mollenkopf and Manuel Castells, eds., *Dual City: Restructuring New York* (New York: Russell Sage, 1991), 16–17; Mike Davis, *Planet of Slums* (London: Verso, 2006), 119.

49. Davis, *Planet of Slums*, 120–50.

50. Paul Krugman, "The New York Paradox," *New York Times*, July 10, 2006.

51. Robert Geddes, "Metropolis Unbound: The Sprawling American City and the Search for Alternatives," *American Prospect* 35 (1997): 40–47.

52. Todd Gardner, "Settlement Type Areas in the United States" (U.S. Census Bureau, n.d., unpublished paper in author's possession).

53. Robert Fishman, *Bourgeois Utopias: The Rise and Fall of Suburbia* (New York: Basic Books, 1987). For a criticism of the concept that the traditional suburb had been replaced by a new urban form, see the stimulating, if not wholly convincing, William Sharpe and Leonard Wallock, "Bold New City or Built-Up 'Burb? Redefining Contemporary Suburbia," *American Quarterly* 46, 1 (1994): 1–30.

54. Orfield, *Metropolitics*.

55. Dolores Hayden, *Building Suburbia: Green Fields and Urban Growth, 1820–2000* (New York: Pantheon, 2003), 14.

56. Joel Garreau, *Edge City: Life on the New Frontier* (New York: Doubleday, 1991), 414, 425. Useful discussions of Garreau are Kenneth T. Jackson, "The View From the Periphery," *New York Times*, September 22, 1991, BR11; Jane Holz Kay, "Edge City: Life on the New Frontier" (book review), *The Nation*, 454, 2 (October 14, 1991); and Ross Miller, "Edge City: Life on the New Frontier" (book review), *Journal of the Society of Architectural Historians* 52, 3 (1993): 349–51.

57. Robert E. Lang and Patrick A. Simmons, eds. "'*Boomburbs*': The Emergence of Large, Fast-Growing Suburban Cities," in *Redefining Urban and Suburban America*, ed. Katz and Lang, 101.

58. Wei Li, *Ethnoburb: The New Ethnic Community in Urban America* (Honolulu: University of Hawaii Press, 2009), 1.

59. Lewis, "Urban Invasion," 46, 50.

60. Davis, *Magical Urbanism*, 96.

61. Saskia Sassen, *Cities in a World Economy* (Thousand Oaks, Calif.: Pine Forge Press, 1994), xiv. See also Saskia Sassen, *Global City: New York, London, and Tokyo* (Princeton, N.J.: Princeton University Press, 1991).

62. Sassen, *Cities in a World Economy*, 65.

63. Patrick McGeehan, "Top Executives Return Offices to Manhattan," *New York Times*, July 3, 2006. The article is based on U.S. Bureau of Labor Statistics data.

64. Karen G. Mills, Elisabeth B. Reynolds, and Andrew Reamer, "Clusters and Competitiveness: A New Federal Role for Stimulating Regional Economies" (report from Blueprint for American Prosperity, Brookings Institution, Metropolitan Policy Program, April 2008).

65. Manuel Castells, *The Rise of the Network Society*, 2nd ed., vol. 1, *The Information Age: Economy, Society, and Culture* (Malden, Mass.: Blackwell, 2000), 16–17.

66. Ibid., 430–31.

67. Ibid., 434.

68. Margaret Pugh O'Mara, *Cities of Knowledge: Cold War Science and the Search for the Next Silicon Valley* (Princeton, N.J.: Princeton University Press, 2005).

69. See, for instance, Edward Ewing Pratt, *Industrial Causes of Congestion of Population in New York City* (New York: Columbia University, Longmans, Green, 1911).

70. Peter Dreier, Regina Freer, Robert Gottlieb, and Mark Vallianatos, "Movement Mayor: Can Antonio Villaraigosa Change Los Angeles? *Dissent* (Summer 2006): 52.

71. Katz and Stern, *One Nation Divisible*, 46.

Chapter 2. The New African American Inequality

This chapter is an adaptation of Michael B. Katz, Mark J. Stern, and Jamie J. Fader, "The New African American Inequality," *Journal of American History* 92 (June 2005): 75–108. I want to thank my remarkable co-authors for agreeing to allow me to use the article in this book.

1. Thomas J. Sugrue, *Not Even Past: Barack Obama and the Burden of Race* (Princeton, N.J.: Princeton University Press, 2010), 1.

2. Faulkner's quotation from *Requiem for a Nun* is the inspiration for the title of Sugrue, *Not Even Past*.

3. Sugrue, *Not Even Past*, 4.

4. Frances Fox Piven and Richard Cloward, *Poor People's Movements: Why They Succeed, How They Fail* (New York: Pantheon, 1977); Mary L. Dudziak, *Cold War*

Civil Rights: Race and the Image of American Democracy (Princeton, N.J.: Princeton University Press, 2000).

5. Martha F. Davis, *Brutal Need: Lawyers and the Welfare Rights Movement* (New Haven, Conn.: Yale University Press, 1993); John David Skrentny, *The Ironies of Affirmative Action: Politics, Culture, and Justice in America* (Chicago: University of Chicago Press, 1996).

6. For an account of black wage growth by 1940, see Robert Higgs, "Black Progress and the Persistence of Racial Economic Inequalities," in *The Question of Discrimination: Racial Inequality in the U.S. Labor Market*, ed. Steven Shulman and William Darity (Middletown, Conn.: Wesleyan University Press, 1989), 9–31.

7. Michael K. Brown et al., *Whitewashing Race: The Myth of a Color-Blind Society* (Berkeley: University of California Press, 2003) provides an extended criticism of the Thernstroms as well as others they term "racial realists."

8. Andrew Hacker, *Two Nations: Black and White, Separate, Hostile, Unequal* (New York: Scribner's, 1992); Stephan Thernstrom and Abigail Thernstrom, *America in Black and White: One Nation, Indivisible* (New York: Simon and Schuster, 1997).

9. An excellent assessment of the question of black progress as of 1990 is Reynolds Farley, *The New American Reality: Who We Are, How We Got Here, Where We Are Going* (New York: Russell Sage, 1996). A sober examination of this question from various viewpoints is found in the essays in Steven Shulman and William Darity, eds., *The Question of Discrimination: Racial Inequality in the U.S. Labor Market* (Middletown, Conn.: Wesleyan University Press, 1989). See also James Smith and Finis Welch, "Black Economic Progress After Myrdal," *Journal of Economic Literature* 27, 2 (1989): 519–64.

10. For another discussion that stresses the cumulative nature of racial inequality, see Brown et al., *Whitewashing Race*. Brown and his coauthors also draw on Charles Tilly's notion of durable inequality. Their work is the best modern book-length account of current-day racial inequality.

11. African American women's economic experience has received surprisingly little analysis, a point made by Mary Corcoran in "The Economic Progress of African American Women," in *Latinas and African American Women at Work: Race, Gender, and Economic Inequality*, ed. Irene Browne (New York: Russell Sage, 1999), 35–60.

12. Most of the data are from the remarkable census samples developed by Steven Ruggles and Matthew Sobek et al., *Integrated Public Use Microdata Series: Version 3.0* (Minneapolis: Historical Census Projects, University of Minnesota, 2003), www.ipums.org. Here we present only a sample of the data on which the analysis is based in order to highlight major trends. Full tables are available on the project website, www.ssw.upenn.edu/america2000/.

13. Frank Hobbs and Nicole Stoops, "Demographic Trends in the Twentieth Century," in *Census 2000 Special Reports*, Ser. CENSR-4, ed. U.S. Census Bureau (Washington, D.C.: U.S. Government Printing Office, 2002), 206, table 16.

14. Douglas S. Massey and Nancy A. Denton, *American Apartheid: Segregation and the Making of the Underclass* (Cambridge, Mass.: Harvard University Press, 1993). On the origins of black ghettos, see James Grossman, *Land of Hope: Chicago, Black Southerners, and the Great Migration* (Chicago: University of Chicago Press, 1989); Arnold R. Hirsch, *Making the Second Ghetto: Race and Housing in Chicago, 1940–1960* (New York: Cambridge University Press, 1983).

15. Lewis Mumford Center for Comparative Urban and Regional Research, "Ethnic Diversity Grows, Neighborhood Integration Lags Behind" (report by

the Lewis Mumford Center for Comparative Urban and Regional Research, Albany, N.Y., 2001); Massey and Denton, *American Apartheid.*

16. John Logan, "The New Ethnic Enclaves in America's Suburbs" (report by the Lewis Mumford Center for Comparative Urban and Regional Research, Albany, N.Y., n.d.), 2, 6, 10.

17. John F. Bauman, *Public Housing, Race, and Renewal: Urban Planning in Philadelphia, 1920–1974* (Philadelphia: Temple University Press, 1987); Hirsch, *Making the Second Ghetto*; Raymond A. Mohl, "Race and Space in the Modern City: Interstate-95 and the Black Community in Miami," in *Urban Policy in Twentieth-Century America,* ed. Arnold R. Hirsch and Raymond A. Mohl (New Brunswick, N.J.: Rutgers University Press, 1993), 100–158; Thomas J. Sugrue, *The Origins of the Urban Crisis: Race and Inequality in Postwar Detroit* (Princeton, N.J.: Princeton University Press, 1996).

18. It is true that some blacks in the nineteenth and twentieth centuries lived near the factories that offered decent working-class jobs. In Philadelphia, for instance, blacks lived closer to manufacturing jobs than any other ethnic group, even though they held the fewest jobs. Theodore Hershberg, *Philadelphia: Work, Space, Family, and Group Experience in the Nineteenth Century: Toward an Interdisciplinary History of the City* (New York: Oxford University Press, 1981). It is possible that concentration is itself a source of inequality. On this, see John J. Beggs, Wayne J. Villemez, and Ruth Arnold, "Black Population Concentration and Black-White Inequality: Expanding the Consideration of Place and Space Effects," *Social Forces* 76, 1 (1997): 65–91. On the impact of concentration on inequality, see Samuel Cohn and Mark Fossett, "Why Racial Employment Inequality Is Greater in Northern Labor Markets: Regional Differences in White-Black Employment Differentials," *Social Forces* 74, 2 (1995): 511–42.

19. Massey and Denton, *American Apartheid.*

20. A useful review of the issue of labor force attachment, including its measurement, is found in Monica D. Castillo, "Persons Outside the Labor Force Who Want a Job," *Monthly Labor Review* 121, 7 (1998): 34–42. See also John Blair and Rudy H. Fichtenbaum, "Changing Black Employment Patterns," in *The Metropolis in Black and White: Place, Power, and Polarization,* ed. George Galster and Edward Hill Galster (New Brunswick, N.J.: Center for Urban Policy Research, 1992).

21. On the history of black women's work, see Jacqueline Jones, *Labor of Love, Labor of Sorrow: Black Women, Work and the Family from Slavery to the Present* (New York: Basic Books, 1985). On the history of women's work, see also Alice Kessler-Harris, *Out to Work: A History of Wage-Earning Women in the United States* (New York: Oxford University Press, 1982).

22. We discuss trends in women's work and income in Michael B. Katz and Mark J. Stern, "Women and the Paradox of Economic Inequality in Twentieth Century America," *Journal of Social History,* Fall 2005: 65–88; and Michael B. Katz and Mark J. Stern, *One Nation Divisible: What America Was and What It Was Becoming* (New York: Russell Sage, 2006), chap. 4.

23. The question of public assistance raises the issue of the impact of changes in family structure on the economic situation of black women. We deal with family structure in Katz and Stern, *One Nation Divisible,* chaps. 7 and 8.

24. Lawrence M. Mead, *The New Politics of Poverty: The Nonworking Poor in America* (New York: Basic Books, 1992); William Julius Wilson, *The Truly Disadvantaged: The Inner City, the Underclass, and Public Policy* (Chicago: University of Chicago Press, 1987); William Julius Wilson, *When Work Disappears: The World of the New Urban Poor* (New York: Knopf, 1996).

25. For the most part, a little less than half of black women engaged in market work. White women were not only less likely to work; unlike blacks, their labor force participation declined with age. (The 1910 figures, which seem to show greater labor force participation, should not be taken to indicate an actual increase. In that year only, the census counted work on a family farm as a formal occupation. With most blacks working in agriculture, this method of recording occupation boosted labor force participation among them even more than among whites.)

26. The difference between blacks and whites notable among the twenty-six- to thirty-year-olds reflected the greater prevalence of family work in agriculture among blacks, not differences in market labor.

27. On the relative decline in black women's labor force participation, see Karen Christopher, "Explaining the Recent Employment Gap Between Black and White Women," *Sociological Focus* 29, 3 (1996): 263–80.

28. Many writers have commented on this trend. A good discussion is found in Daphne Spain and Suzanne M. Bianchi, *Balancing Act: Motherhood, Marriage, and Employment Among American Women* (New York: Russell Sage, 1996).

29. Edna Bonacich, "Advanced Capitalism and Black/White Race Relations in the United States: A Split Labor Market Interpretation," *American Sociological Review* 41, 1 (1976): 34–51, discusses the emergence of an unemployment gap between black and white men. Our interpretation differs from hers, both because unemployment is quite different from labor force nonparticipation and because we have reservations about her interpretive framework.

30. For a discussion of black men's nonparticipation in the labor force, see James J. Heckman, "The Impact of Government on the Economic Status of Black Americans," in Shulman and Darity, *The Question of Discrimination*, 50–80.

31. Chinhui Juhn, "Black-White Employment Differential in a Tight Labor Market," in *Prosperity for All? The Economic Boom and African Americans*, ed. Robert D. Cherry and William M. Rodgers (New York: Russell Sage, 2000), 88–109.

32. William E. Spriggs and Rhonda M. Williams, "What Do We Need to Explain About African American Unemployment?" in Rodgers and Cherry, *Prosperity for All?* 188–207. They write, "The fact that African American unemployment rates are consistently twice as high as white rates should be one of the greatest mysteries in labor economics, yet is among the least-researched dimensions of racial economic inequality" (203).

33. A trenchant look at the rise in incarceration is found in Christian Parenti, *Lockdown America: Police and Prisons in an Age of Crisis* (New York: Verso, 1999). In the argument suggested here, labor force nonparticipation should not be confounded with official unemployment. There appears to have been little relation between unemployment rates and incarceration. In other words, the economic boom of the 1990s did not reduce the imprisonment of black men, which had other sources, particularly state policy. William A. Darity and Samuel L. Myers, Jr., "The Impact of Labor Market Prospects on Incarceration Rates," in Rodgers and Cherry, *Prosperity for All?* 279–307. On the labor market impact of incarceration, see Bruce Western, Jeffrey R. Kling, and David F. Weiman, "The Labor Market Consequences of Incarceration," *Crime & Delinquency* 47, 3 (2001): 410–27; Devah Pager, "The Mark of a Criminal Record," *American Journal of Sociology* 108, 5 (2003): 937–75.

34. Loïq Wacquant, *Punishing the Poor: The Neoliberal Government of Social Insecurity* (Durham and London: Duke University Press, 2009), vol. 2.

35. Randal C. Archibold, "California, in Financial Crisis, Opens Prison Doors," *New York Times*, March 23, 2010; "Bill Designed to Cut Prison Costs," *Philadelphia Daily News*, June 9, 2010; Jeremy W. Peters, "Albany Reaches Deal to Repeal '70s Drug Laws," *New York Times*, May 3, 2010. Ian Urbina, "Citing Cost, States Consider End to Death Penalty," *New York Times*, February 25, 2009.

36. "U.S. Prison Populations—Trends and Implications" (paper prepared for the Sentencing Project, Washington, D.C., May 2003); Marc Mauer, "The Crisis of the Young African American Male and the Criminal Justice System" (paper prepared for the U.S. Commission on Civil Rights, Washington, D.C., April 15–16, 1999); Pager, "The Mark of a Criminal Record." Another consequence of incarceration for inequality is the reduction in the number of marriageable men—a topic treated in Katz and Stern, *One Nation Divisible*, chaps. 7 and 8.

37. Jacqueline Jones, "Southern Diaspora: Origins of the Northern 'Underclass,'" in *The "Underclass" Debate: Views from History*, ed. Michael B. Katz (Princeton, N.J.: Princeton University Press, 1993).

38. David Gerald Jaynes and Robin M. Williams, Jr., eds., *A Common Destiny: Blacks and American Society* (Washington, D.C.: National Academy Press, 1989), 169.

39. Throughout the century, 5 to 6 percent of black men worked in construction; in 1910, railroads employed 6 percent; and later, other forms of transportation provided many jobs as well. Michael B. Katz, Mark J. Stern, and Jamie J. Fader, "Women and the Paradox of Inequality in the Twentieth-Century," *Journal of Social History*, Fall 2005, 65–88.

40. The percentages in manufacturing are calculated from the individual occupational categories for all men in manufacturing industries. The numerator is the number in blue-collar occupations in manufacturing industries. The denominator is all employed black men.

41. Robert Self, *American Babylon: Race and the Struggle for Postwar Oakland* (Princeton, N.J.: Princeton University Press, 1996), 173.

42. Gunnar Myrdal describes the tenuous presence of blacks in public employment before World War II. The contrast with the post-1960 years is striking. See Gunnar Myrdal, *An American Dilemma: The Negro Problem and Modern Democracy*, 2 vols. (New Brunswick, NJ: Transaction Books, 2002); Brown et al., *Whitewashing Race*, also emphasizes the crucial role of public employment (73).

43. The role of public employment in African American history deserves much more attention from historians. Some useful social science works on the subject are: Peter K. Eisinger, "The Economic Conditions of Black Employment in Municipal Bureaucracies," *American Journal of Political Science* 26, 4 (1982): 754–71; Kevin M. O'Brien, "The Determinants of Minority Employment in Police and Fire Departments," *Journal of Socio-Economics* 32, 2 (2003): 183–95; Joshua G. Behr, "Black and Female Municipal Employment: A Substantive Benefit of Minority Political Incorporation?" *Journal of Urban Affairs* 22, 3 (2000): 243–64; Marlese Durr and John R. Logan, "Racial Submarkets in Government Employment: African American Managers in New York State," *Sociological Forum* 12, 3 (1997): 353–70; Philip Harvey, *Securing the Right to Employment: Social Welfare Policy and the Unemployed in the United States* (Princeton, N.J.: Princeton University Press, 1989); Margaret Weir, *Politics and Jobs: The Boundaries of Employment Policy in the United States* (Princeton, N.J.: Princeton University Press, 1992); Eisinger, "The Economic Conditions." On the role and characteristics of black public employment in a large city in 1940, see St. Clair Drake and Horace Cayton, *Black Metropolis: A Study of Negro Life in a Northern City*, revised and enlarged

ed. (Chicago: University of Chicago Press, 1993), 254–57; R. L. Boyd, "Differences in the Earnings of Black Workers in the Private and Public Sectors," *Social Science Journal* 30, 2 (1993): 133–42; Martin Carnoy, *Faded Dreams: The Politics and Economics of Race in America* (New York: Cambridge University Press, 1994), 161–65.

44. Jaynes and Williams, eds., *A Common Destiny: Blacks and American Society*, 169.

45. Suzanne Model, "The Ethnic Niche and the Structure of Opportunity: Immigrants and Minorities in New York City," in *The "Underclass" Debate: Views from History*, ed. Michael B. Katz (Princeton, N.J.: Princeton University Press, 1993), 161–93; Roger Waldinger, *Still the Promised City? African Americans and New Immigrants in Post-Industrial New York* (Cambridge, Mass.: Harvard University Press, 1996).

46. Skrentny, *The Ironies of Affirmative Action*; Robert Weisbrot, *Freedom Bound: A History of America's Civil Rights Movement* (New York: Norton, 1990).

47. Self, *American Babylon*, 57.

48. Michael B. Katz, *In the Shadow of the Poorhouse: A Social History of Welfare in America*, 10th anniv. ed. (New York: Basic Books, 1996).

49. On the history of federal labor market policy, see Weir, *Politics and Jobs*; and Philip Harvey, *Securing the Right to Employment: Social Welfare Policy and the Unemployed in the United States* (Princeton, N.J.: Princeton University Press, 1989).

50. Gretchen Aguiar, "The Roots of Headstart," Ph.D. dissertation, chapter 3.

51. An important issue not discussed in this chapter is black self-employment, which has remained relatively low. Good discussions of trends and reasons are found in Robert L. Boyd, "A Contextual Analysis of Black Self-Employment in Large Metropolitan Areas, 1970–1980," *Social Forces* 70, 2 (1991): 409–29; Robert W. Fairlie and Bruce D. Meyer, "Trends in Self-Employment Among White and Black Men During the Twentieth Century," *Journal of Human Resources* 35, 4 (2000): 643–69.

52. Manual working class," which is used synonymously with "blue collar" here, is a category considerably broader than manufacturing.

53. In 1960, for instance, 21 percent of white men, compared to 10 percent of blacks, worked in crafts, while 28 percent of blacks and 19 percent of whites were employed as semiskilled operatives, and 20 percent of blacks and only 4 percent of whites worked as laborers.

54. White women did not often work in crafts either. But many more of them worked as operatives earlier in the century—accounting for 28 percent of employed women in 1900. By 1940, as women moved into clerical jobs, the number working as operatives had declined to 15 percent. By 2000, it was 6 percent, lower than the number among black women. In Figure 11, the denominator is employed women.

55. Ellis Cose and Allison Samuels, "The Black Gender Gap," *Newsweek*, March 3, 2003, 46.

56. John F. Zipp, "Government Employment and Black-White Earnings Inequality, 1980–1990," *Social Problems* 41, 3 (1994): 363–82.

57. Among black women, technician jobs became important. In 1940, technicians represented 1.8 percent of white women employed in professional and technical work and 0.0 percent of black women; in 2000, they represented 9.9 percent of white women and 13.4 percent of black women. What is most striking, though, about the comparison between black and white women is their convergence within professional and technical occupations. By 2000, the differences among them were minor.

58. The increasing sex differentiation within municipal employment is shown for New Orleans in Behr, "Black and Female Municipal Employment."

59. Eisinger, "The Economic Conditions." A study based on 1980 data found that African Americans in the public sector were more protected and earned higher incomes. See Boyd, "Differences in the Earnings." Declining black incomes in the 1980s resulted in part from reductions in government employment. See Carnoy, *Faded Dreams*, 161–65. Carnoy also points to higher wages for blacks in public employment. Also see Peter Eisinger, "Local Civil Service Employment and Black Socio-economic Mobility," *Social Science Quarterly* 67, 2 (1986): 171–75; M. V. Lee Badgett, "The Impact of Affirmative Action on Public-Sector Employment in California, 1970–1990," in *Impacts of Affirmative Action: Policies and Consequences in California*, ed. Paul Ong (Walnut Creek, Calif.: Sage, 1999), 83–102.

60. The literature on employer preferences is summarized in Philip Moss and Chris Tilly, "How Labor-Market Tightness Affects Employer Attitudes and Actions Toward Black Job Applicants: Evidence from Employer Surveys," in Cherry and Rodgers, *Prosperity for All?* (New York: Russell Sage, 2000), 129–59.

61. On African Americans' commitment to education in the early twentieth century, see Grossman, *Land of Hope*; Timothy L. Smith, "Native Blacks and Foreign Whites: Varying Responses to Educational Opportunity in America, 1880–1950," *Perspectives in American History* 6 (1972): 309–35. An excellent discussion of educational attainment trends among African Americans from 1940 to 1990 is found in Farley, *The New American Reality*, 228–38.

62. Louis Harlan, *Separate and Unequal: Public School Campaigns and Racism in the Southern Seaboard States, 1901–1915* (Chapel Hill: University of North Carolina Press, 1958). An excellent study of education in the South after the Civil War is James L. Leloudis, *Schooling the New South: Pedagogy, Self, and Society in North Carolina, 1880–1920* (Chapel Hill: University of North Carolina Press, 1996). On the education of blacks in the South, the best overview is James D. Anderson, *The Education of Blacks in the South, 1860–1935* (Chapel Hill: University of North Carolina Press, 1988).

63. Mary Frances Berry and John W. Blassingame, *Long Memory: The Black Experience in America* (New York: Oxford University Press, 1982), 265.

64. We used twelve years of schooling as a proxy for high school graduation.

65. "Telling the Whole Truth (or Not) About High School Graduation Rates: New State Data," *Education Trust* (December 2003); "Trends in the Well-Being of America's Children and Youth, 1997 Edition" (report from the Office of the Assistant Secretary for Planning and Development, U.S. Department of Health and Human Services), EA1.5; David Boesel, Nabeel Alsalam, and Thomas M. Smith, "Educational and Labor Market Performance of GED Recipients" (report from the U.S. Department of Education Office of Educational Research and Improvement, February 1998), www.ed.gov/pubs/GED/apendb5a.html; Jay Greene, "The GED Myth."

66. Race and gender trends for individuals with one to three years of college differed from those for college graduates. In 2000, little difference separated blacks and whites or men and women with less than four years of higher education. In fact, adult black women had attended college for one to three years slightly more often than white women.

67. For a superb exposition of the declining economic prospects of young white men, see Annette Bernhardt et al., *Divergent Paths: Economic Mobility in the New American Labor Market* (New York: Russell Sage, 2001).

68. Karen W. Aronson, "Colleges Struggle to Help Black Men Stay Enrolled," *New York Times*, December 30, 2003, A1.

69. An interesting analysis of how socialization and peer group influence work in the case of Mexican American young people in New York City—a case that has parallels to the black experience—is found in Robert C. Smith, "Mexicans: Social, Educational, Economic, and Political Problems and Prospects in New York," in *New Immigrants in New York*, ed. Nancy Foner (New York: Columbia University Press, 2001). See also John U. Ogbu, *Minority Education and Caste: The American System in Cross-Cultural Perspective* (New York: Academic Press, 1978).

70. Aronson, "Colleges Struggle to Help Black Men Stay Enrolled."

71. The best source on the expansion of high school enrollment is Claudia Goldin and Lawrence F. Katz, "Human and Social Capital: The Rise of Secondary Schooling in the United States, 1890 to 1940," *Journal of Economic Perspectives* 13 (Winter 1999): 37–62; Robert L. Church, *Education in the United States: An Interpretive History* (New York: Free Press, 1976).

72. Coincidence in timing, of course, does not prove causation. There is much research to be done on the links between civil rights measures, affirmative action, and the increase of African Americans in higher education. The hypothesis here is that the link works in two ways: first, through improving access and making facilities more appealing, or less threatening; second, through the job market, by opening access for African Americans to jobs that require advanced education—that is, by increasing the economic payoff of higher education. The proposition here is not that the reasons for the increase in higher education among white Americans were not operative among blacks, but that African Americans needed something more than occupational change and increasing returns to human capital. The impact of government antidiscrimination and affirmative action programs on African Americans is assessed, and the literature reviewed, in Heckman, "The Impact of Government." Government, Heckman points out, can have both a negative and positive impact. An example of the former is the woeful underfunding of black public education in the South for many decades.

73. The concept of durable inequality is borrowed from the work of Charles Tilly, *Durable Inequality* (Berkeley: University of California Press, 1998).

74. For a discussion of African American income trends, see Farley, *The New American Reality*.

75. The first year in which income was reported on the census is 1940.

76. "Earnings" is used here rather than "income" because it is the variable on which the analysis is based. "Income" includes items other than wages or salary, such as investment results, rent, or public transfers. Thus, it is a less exact measure of earning capacity, which is what is at issue here.

77. A useful, concise description of income trends by gender is found in Mary Bowler, "Women's Earnings: An Overview," *Monthly Labor Review* 122, 12 (1999): 13–21.

78. Farley, *The New American Reality*.

79. For detail on poverty and its measurement, see Katz and Stern, *One Nation Divisible*, chap. 8; Farley, *The New American Reality*, gives an overview of black poverty.

80. Elise Gould and Heidi Shierholz, "A Lost Decade: Poverty and Income Trends Paint a Bleak Picture for Working Families," *Economic Policy Institute*, September 16, 2010.

81. For more detail on these points, see Michael B. Katz and Mark J. Stern, "Poverty Since 1940," in Alice O'Connor and Gwendolyn Mink, *Poverty in the United States: An Encyclopedia of History, Politics, and Policy* (Santa Barbara: ABC-CLIO, 2004), v.1, pp. 33–46, and Katz and Stern, *One Nation Divisible*, chap. 8. Mark Stern conceived of the analysis between poverty rates, industrial employment, public service work, and welfare generosity.

82. The earliest cohort identifiable in the data is the one born between 1876 and 1885, and the youngest cohort is the one born between 1976 and 1985. In practice, however, the income of the latter is not a very good measure of their achievement, because many of them had only recently entered the labor market. Therefore, they will not be used as the standard against which to measure black income gains. The denominator here is all individuals who report some income. In 1940, income includes only wages and salaries.

83. John Bound and Laura Dresser, "Losing Ground: The Erosion of the Relative Earnings of African American Women During the 1980s," in *Latinas and African American Women at Work: Race, Gender, and Economic Inequality*, ed. Irene Browne (New York: Russell Sage, 1999), 61–104. Relative incomes of black and white women, it should be noted, differed by region. See Corcoran, "The Economic Progress of African American Women."

84. On the decline in black men's incomes and labor market position in the 1980s, see John Bound and Richard B. Freeman, "What Went Wrong? The Erosion of the Relative Earnings and Employment of Young Black Men in the 1980s," *Quarterly Journal of Economics* 107, 1 (1992): 201–32; Carnoy, *Faded Dreams*; Richard B. Freeman, "Black Economic Progress After 1964: Who Has Gained and Why?" in *Studies in Labor Markets*, ed. Sumner Rosen (Chicago: National Bureau of Economic Research, University of Chicago Press, 1981). In the 1990s boom, black income started to rise once again—the decline in unemployment had more impact on blacks' prospects than on whites. See Cordelia W. Reimers, "The Effect of Tighter Labor Markets on Unemployment of Hispanics and African Americans: The 1990s Experience," in Cherry and Rodgers, *Prosperity for All?* 3–49. For the non–college educated, the impact of the boom was greatest on young men; among older men there were no similar gains. See Richard B. Freeman and William M. Rodgers, "Area Economic Conditions and the Labor Market Outcomes of Young Men in the 1990s Expansion," in Cherry and Rodgers, *Prosperity for All?* 50–87.

85. Bernhardt et al., *Divergent Paths*.

86. Elise Gould and Heidi Shierholz, "A Lost Decade: Poverty and Income Trends Paint a Bleak Picture for Working Families," Economic Policy Institute, September 16, 2010. http://www.epi.org/publications/entry/a_lost_decade_poverty_and_income_trends.

87. Bennett Harrison and Lucy Gorham, "What Happened to African American Wages in the 1980s?" in *The Metropolis in Black and White*, ed. George Galster and Edward Hill (New Brunswick, N.J.: Center for Urban Policy Research, 1992), 56–71.

88. Carmen DeNavas-Walt, Bernadette D. Proctor, and Jessica C. Smith, *Income, Poverty, and Health Insurance Coverage in the United States: 2009*, U.S. Census Bureau, Current Population Reports, P60-238 (Washington, D.C.: U.S. Government Printing Office, 2010), Table 1.

89. The beta coefficients for variables that combined ethnicity and sex by education declined and the amount of variation accounted for by the whole set of variables also went down. Cancio et al. argue that the influence of race on

inequality increased between 1976 and 1985. This does not contradict the argument here, which uses a much longer time frame. See A. Silvia Cancio, T. David Evans, and David J. Maume, Jr., "The Declining Significance of Race Reconsidered: Racial Differences in Early Career Wages," *American Sociological Review* 61, 4 (1997): 541–56.

90. In their case, the beta measuring the relation rose from 0.16 to 0.28; for black men who had graduated from college, it moved only from −0.01 to 0.03.

91. A discussion of the different pathways from marriage and employment to economic security for black and white women is found in Andrea E. Willson, "Race and Women's Income Trajectories: Employment, Marriage, and Income Security over the Life Course," *Social Problems* 50, 1 (2003): 87–110.

92. Melvin L. Oliver and Thomas M. Shapiro, *Black Wealth/White Wealth: A New Perspective on Racial Inequality* (New York: Routledge, 1997); Dalton Conley, *Being Black, Living in the Red: Race, Wealth, and Social Policy in America* (Berkeley: University of California Press, 1999). See also Francine D. Blau and John W. Graham, "Black-White Differences in Wealth and Asset Composition," *Quarterly Journal of Economics* 105, 2 (1990): 321–39.

93. Jennifer Wheary, Tatjana Meschidi, and Thomas M. Shapiro,"Declining Economic Security Among the African and Latino Middle Class, 2000–2006," Institute on Assets and Social Policy Brandeis University and Demos: A Network for Ideas and Action, 2009,5. http://iasp.brandeis.edu/pdfs/batfive.pdf.

94. Thomas M. Shapiro, Tatjana Meschede, and Laura Sullivan, "The Racial Wealth Gap Increases Fourfold," *Research and Policy Brief* (May 2010): 1.

95. Debbie Guenstein Bocian, Wei Li, and Keith S. Ernst, "Foreclosures by Race and Ethnicity: The Demographics of a Crisis" (research report by the Center for Responsible Lending, June 18, 2010), 2, www.Responsiblelending.org/mortgage-lending/research-analysys/foreclosures-by-race-ethnicity.pdf, accessed November 24, 2010.

96. A further "screen" was incarceration, which lowers the subsequent earnings opportunities of black men. See Pager, "The Mark of a Criminal Record." An argument for the cumulative deficits acquired by young black men as a result of job instability is found in Marta Tienda and Haya Stier, "Generating Labor Market Inequality: Employment Opportunities and the Accumulation of Disadvantage," *Social Problems* 43, 2 (1996): 147–65.

97. For a similar argument about the bifurcation of black social structure in Los Angeles, see David M. Grant, Melvin L. Oliver, and Angela D. James, "African Americans: Social and Economic Bifurcation," in *Ethnic Los Angeles*, ed. Roger Waldinger and Mehdi Bozorgmehr (New York: Russell Sage, 1996). Bifurcation is also discussed in Heckman, "The Impact of Government." On the black middle class, see Thomas J. Durant, Jr., and Joyce S. Louden, "The Black Middle Class in America: Historical and Contemporary Perspectives," *Phylon* 47, 4 (1986): 253–63. See also Harrison and Gorham, "What Happened to African American Wages in the 1980s?"; Bart Landry, *The New Black Middle Class* (Berkeley: University of California Press, 1987); William Julius Wilson, *The Declining Significance of Race: Blacks and Changing American Institutions* (Chicago: University of Chicago Press, 1978); William Julius Wilson, *The Truly Disadvantaged: The Inner City, the Underclass, and Public Policy* (Chicago: University of Chicago Press, 1987).

98. Another "screen," hard to see and not visible with just the census, consists of the "glass ceilings" that have remained in occupations. On this, see Heather Boushey and Robert Cherry, "Exclusionary Practices and Glass-Ceiling Effects

Across Regions: What Does the Current Expansion Tell Us?" in Cherry and Rodgers, *Prosperity for All?* 160–87.

Chapter 3. Why Don't American Cities Burn Very Often?

1. Luther Carpenter, "Job Redistribution à la Francaise," *Dissent* (Spring 2006): 28.

2. The Los Angeles violence spilled over into Las Vegas. This chapter is not a history or explanation of past urban riots; its focus is on why they do not occur more often. For studies of the riots, see Janet L. Abu-Lughod, *Race, Space, and Riots in Chicago, New York, and Los Angeles* (New York: Oxford University Press, 2007); Kevin Mumford, *Newark: A History of Race, Rights, and Riots in America* (New York: New York University Press, 2007); Michael W. Flamm, *Law and Order: Street Crime, Civil Unrest, and the Crisis of Liberalism in the 1960's* (New York: Columbia University Press, 2005), chap. 5.

3. In the summer of 2006, an upsurge in this form of violence made headlines in Boston and Philadelphia. See, for instance, Larry Eichel, "In the City, Any Day Can Be a Killing Day," *Philadelphia Inquirer,* July 16, 2006; Barbara Boyer, "An Uphill Fight to Stem Violence," *Philadelphia Inquirer,* July 18, 2006.

4. For a trenchant dissection of the differences between U.S. ghettos and French banlieus, see Loïc Wacquant, *Urban Outcasts: A Comparative Sociology of Advanced Marginality* (Cambridge, Eng. And Malden, Mass.: Polity Press, 1967). Wacquant shows that immigrants in France do not experience residential segregation.

5. Charles Tilly, *The Politics of Collective Violence* (Cambridge: Cambridge University Press, 2003), 3.

6. Tilly labels them "opportunistic violence" (*The Politics*, 130–50).

7. I understand social control as defined by Ira Katznelson—the means "for the fashioning of order in societies faced with the disjunction between the formal legal equality of citizenship and the franchise and the structural inequities produced by the routine operation of the political economy." Although universal, patterns of social control "are of necessity distinctive from society to society. . . . Understood this way, 'social control' refers to a crucible of interaction and struggle that has its own idiom, grammar, and expectations." Ira Katznelson, *City Trenches: Urban Politics and the Patterning of Class in the United States* (New York: Pantheon, 1981), 208–9.

8. *The Kerner Report: The 1968 Report of the National Advisory Commission on Civil Disorders* (New York: Pantheon, 1988), 9.

9. Ibid., 1.

10. Thomas J. Sugrue and Andrew P. Goodman, "Plainfield Burning: Black Rebellion in the Suburban North," *Journal of Urban History*, 33, 4 (May 2007): 558–601.

11. Robert Gottlieb, Mark Vallianatos, Regina M. Freer, and Peter Dreier, *The Next Los Angeles: The Struggle for a Livable City* (Berkeley: University of California Press, 2005), 126.

12. Michael B. Katz and Mark J. Stern, *One Nation Divisible: What America Was and What It Is Becoming* (New York: Russell Sage, 2006), 66.

13. U.S. Congress Joint Economic Committee, "Income Inequality and the Great Recession," Executive Summary, September 2010.

14. Ibid., 88.

15. Ibid., 88–89.

16. Abu-Lughod, *Race, Space, and Riots*, 32.

17. On police professionalization, see Robert Fogelson, *Big City Police* (Cambridge, Mass.: Harvard University Press, 1977), 219–42.

18. Paul Jargowsky, "Stunning Progress, Hidden Problems: The Dramatic Decline of Concentrated Poverty in the 1990s," in *Redefining Urban and Suburban America: Evidence from Census 2000*, ed. Alan Berube, Bruce Katz, and Robert E. Land (Washington, D.C.: Brookings Institution, 2005), vol. 3, 138.

19. Poverty statistics are from the U.S. Census Bureau, "Historical Poverty Tables—People," www.census.gov/hhes/www/poverty/data/historical/people.html, accessed December 1, 2010.

20. Douglas S. Massey and Nancy A. Denton, *American Apartheid: Segregation and the Making of the Underclass* (Cambridge, Mass.: Harvard University Press, 1993), 74, 85–87.

21. Katz and Stern, *One Nation Divisible*, 104. For a good overview of immigration trends in American history, see Mary M. Kritz and Douglas T. Gurak, *Immigration and a Changing America* (New York and Washington, D.C.: Russell Sage and Population Reference Bureau, 2004).

22. Michael B. Katz, *In the Shadow of the Poorhouse: A Social History of Welfare in America*, 10th anniv. ed. (New York: Basic Books, 1986), 106, 297, 318. After 1996, TANF (Temporary Assistance for Needy Families) replaced AFDC, and Congress increased the minimum wage, but not enough to reach its 1955 value in real terms.

23. Sandra Ball-Rokeach and James F. Short, Jr., "Collective Violence: The Redress of Grievance and Public Policy," in *American Violence and Public Policy: An Update of the National Commission on the Causes and Prevention of Violence*, ed. Lynn A. Curtis (New Haven, Conn.: Yale University Press, 1985), 165.

24. Tom Wicker, "Introduction," in *Kerner Report*, xiii.

25. Abu-Lughod, *Race, Space, and Riots*, 269.

26. Charles Tilly, *Identities, Boundaries, and Social Ties* (Boulder, Colo.: Paradigm, 2005), 147. See also Tilly, *Politics of Collective Violence*, 75.

27. Tilly, *Identities*, 8–9.

28. Kevin Boyle, *Arc of Justice: A Saga of Race, Civil Rights, and Murder in the Jazz Age* (New York: Henry Holt, 2004); Arnold R. Hirsch, *Making the Second Ghetto: Race and Housing in Chicago 1940–1960* (New York: Cambridge University Press, 1983).

29. Campbell Gibson and Kay Jung, *Historical Census Statistics on Population Totals by Race, 1790 to 1990, and by Hispanic Origins, 1970 to 1990, for Large Cities and Other Urban Places in the United States* (Working Paper 76, presented by the U.S. Census Bureau, Population Division, February 2005).

30. Josh Sides, *L.A. City Limits: African American Los Angeles from the Great Depression to the Present* (Berkeley: University of California Press, 2003), 2, 44.

31. Hirsch, *Making the Second Ghetto*; Thomas J. Sugrue, *Origins of the Urban Crisis: Race and Inequality in Postwar Detroit* (Princeton, N.J.: Princeton University Press, 1986); Kevin Boyle, *The Arc of Justice: A Saga of Race, Civil Rights, and Murder in the Jazz Age* (New York: Holt, 2004).

32. Gerald Gamm, *Urban Exodus: Why the Jews Left Boston and the Catholics Stayed* (Cambridge, Mass.: Harvard University Press, 1999); J. Anthony Lukas, *Common Ground: A Turbulent Decade in the Lives of Three American Families* (New York: Knopf, 1985); Lillian B. Rubin, *Busing and Backlash: White Against White in a California School District* (Berkeley: University of California Press, 1972); Ronald Formisano, *Boston Against Busing: Race, Class, and Ethnicity in the 1960s and 1970s* (Chapel Hill: University of North Carolina Press, 1991).

33. Ball-Rokeach and Short, "Collective Violence," 161.

34. "Tracking Change: A Look At the Growth of Black Elected Officials in the United States, Based on Reports by the Joint Center for Political and Economic Studies, Chart," *New York Times*, March 29, 2006.

35. Mumford, *Newark*, 199.

36. W. Marvin Dulaney, *Black Police in America* (Bloomington: Indiana University Press, 1996), 121–22.

37. Ball-Rokeach and Short, "Collective Violence," 163.

38. H. Paul Friesema, "Black Control of Central Cities: The Hollow Prize," *Journal of the American Institute of Planners* (March 1969): 75.

39. Mike Davis, *Planet of Slums* (London: Verso, 2006), 37, 111, 114.

40. Ibid., 119.

41. I use *mechanisms* in Charles Tilly's definition as a "form of delimited class of events that change relations among specified sets of elements in identical or closely similar ways over a variety of situations," and *processes* as "frequently occurring combinations or sequences of mechanisms." Tilly, *Identities*, 28.

42. Ball-Rokeach and Short, "Collective Violence," 162. On African American public employment, see also Roger Waldinger, *Still the Promised City? African Americans and New Immigrants in Post-Industrial New York* (Cambridge, Mass.: Harvard University Press, 1996).

43. For the concept of limited ladders of mobility, I am indebted to John Foster, "Nineteenth Century Towns: A Class Dimension," in *The Study of Urban History*, ed. H. J. Dyos (London: St. Martin's, 1968), 281–399.

44. Katz and Stern, *One Nation Divisible*, 92.

45. Sides, *L.A. City Limits*, 88, 91.

46. Ball-Rokeach and Short, "Collective Violence," 160.

47. For the idea of mimetic reform, I am indebted to Katznelson, *City Trenches*, 177, 187.

48. Katznelson, *City Trenches*, 179, 187.

49. Gottlieb et al., *Next Los Angeles*, 178–83.

50. The idea of indirect rule applied to African American ghettos was developed as part of the theory of internal colonialism advanced by black writers in the late 1960s. See, for example, Stokely Carmichael and Charles V. Hamilton, *Black Power: The Politics of Liberation in America* (New York: Random House, 1967).

51. Gerald E. Frug, *City Making: Building Communities Without Building Walls* (Princeton, N.J.: Princeton University Press, 1999).

52. The term is from Lizabeth Cohen, *A Consumers' Republic: The Politics of Mass Consumption in Postwar America* (New York: Knopf, 2003).

53. Robert E. Weems, Jr., *Desegregating the Dollar: African American Consumption in the Twentieth Century* (New York: New York University Press, 1998), 71 table 4.1, 75.

54. Weems, *Desegregating the Dollar*, 107; *The 1993/94 Report on the Buying Power of Black America* (Chicago: Target Market News Group, 1993), 22; *Household Spending: Who Spends How Much on What* (Ithaca, N.Y.: New Strategies and Publications, 2005), 125–26.

55. In his history of youth in postwar West Philadelphia, Carl Nightingale claims that, rather than being disaffected from the American mainstream, in their frustrated aspirations as consumers, young African Americans are the most American of Americans. Carl Husemoller Nightingale, *On the Edge: A History of Poor Black Children and Their American Dreams* (New York: Basic Books, 1993).

56. Alison Isenberg, *Downtown America: A History of the Place and the People Who Made It* (Chicago: University of Chicago Press, 2004), 203–54.

57. Cohen, *Consumers' Republic*, 7, 88–89, 190.

58. Weems, *Desegregating the Dollar*, 90, 100.

59. Elizabeth Chin, *Purchasing Power: Black Kids and American Consumer Culture* (Minneapolis: University of Minnesota Press, 2001), 168–69.

60. José García and Tamara Dracut et al., *The Plastic Safety Net: Findings from a National Survey of Credit Card Debt Among Low- and Middle-Income Households* (New York: Demos and Center for Responsible Lending, 2005), 8; Jennifer Wheary, *The Future of the Middle Class: African Americans, Latinos, and Economic Opportunity* (New York: Demos, 2006), 22.

61. The way inequality structures consumption is a major theme of Chin, *Purchasing Power*.

62. Chin, *Purchasing Power*, 1–26, 88, 115.

63. Alan R. Gordon and Norval Morris, "Presidential Commissions and the Law Enforcement Administration," in *American Violence and Public Policy: An Update of the National Commission on the Causes and Prevention of Violence*, ed. Lynn A. Curtis (New Haven, Conn.: Yale University Press, 1985), 117. On the politics of federal anticrime legislation, see Flamm, *Law and Order*.

64. Kenneth O'Reilly, "The FBI and the Politics of Riots, 1964–1968," *Journal of American History* 75, 1 (June 1988): 91–114. On the politics of federal anticrime legislation, see also Flamm, *Law and Order*, 124–41.

65. O'Reilly, 113.

66. Fogelson, *Big City Police*, 220.

67. Gordon and Morris, "Presidential Commissions," 125.

68. Lynn A. Curtis, "Introduction," in Curtis, *American Violence*, 7–8.

69. Robert A. Diegeleman, "Federal Financial Assistance for Crime Control," *Journal of Criminal Law and Criminology* 73, 3 (Autumn 1982): 1001.

70. Richard Sutch, "Criminal Justice Expenditures, by Level of Government: 1902–1996," in *Historical Statistics of the United States Millennial Edition Online*, ed. S. Carter and S. S. Gartner et al. (New York: Cambridge University Press, 2006), table Ec1159-1178, http://husu/Cambridge.org.

71. Fogelson, *Big City Police*, 220.

72. Elliott Currie, "Crimes of Violence and Public Policy: Changing Directions," in Curtis, *American Violence*, 44.

73. Sutch, "Criminal Justice Expenditures."

74. Congressional Budget Office, *Federal Law Enforcement Assistance: Alternative Approaches, April 1978* (Washington, D.C.: U.S. Government Printing Office), xii. See also Malcolm M. Feeley and Austin D. Surat, *The Policy Dilemma: Federal Crime Policy and the Law Enforcement Assistance Administration, 1968–1978* (Minneapolis: University of Minnesota Press, 1980).

75. Currie, "Crimes of Violence," 45.

76. "Estimated Rates of Crime Known to Police, by Type of Offense, 1960–1997," *Historical Statistics*, Series Ec11-20.

77. Stephen Graham, *Cities Under Siege: The New Military Urbanism* (New York: Verso, 2010), xiii–xiv.

78. Mike Davis, *City of Quartz: Excavating the Future in Los Angeles* (Vintage: New York, 1992), 297–300.

79. Davis, *City of Quartz*, 298.

80. Haya El Nasser and Jonathan T. Lovitt, "Frustration Makes Gang Truce More Tenuous," *USA Today*, August 6, 1992, 9A.

81. Ibid.
82. Gottlieb et al., *Next Los Angeles*, 126.
83. Ibid., 126–27.
84. Nasser and Lovitt, "Frustration."
85. Gottlieb et al., *Next Los Angeles*, 178–83.
86. Don Terry, "Guardian America: Youth Power Hits the Streets," *The Guardian* (London), October 28, 1993, 16.
87. Paul Shepard, "Gang Peace Leaders Need Jackson's Pull, Most Say, Want Policy-Makers to Provide Job Training, Employment," *Cleveland Plain Dealer*, October 25, 1993, 5A. See also Seth Mydans, "Gangs Go Public in New Fight for Respect," *New York Times*, May 2, 1993, section 1, 1; Peter Leyden, "Gang Chiefs End Summit," *Minneapolis Star Tribune*, July 19, 1993, 1A; Don Terry, "Chicago Group, Extends Turf, Turns to Politics," *New York Times*, October 25, 1993, section A, 12; Dennis R. Roddy and Lamont Jones Junior, "Gang Summit: An Invitation to Hope or Disaster?" *Pittsburgh Post-Gazette*, March 6, 1994, A1; and Dennis R. Roddy and Lamont Jones Junior, "Gang Summit Opens Despite Cold Shoulder," *Pittsburgh Post-Gazette*, May 27, 1994, A1.
88. The Sentencing Project, "Felony Disenfranchisement Laws in the United States," www.sentencingproject.org/pdfs/1046.pdf, accessed November 16, 2006.
89. For this point, as well as for directing me toward the impact of felony disenfranchisement, my thanks to Alice Goffman. See Alice Goffman, "On the Run: Wanted Men in a Philadelphia Ghetto," *American Sociological Review* 74, 3 (June 2009): 339–57.
90. Matthew J. Countryman, *Up South: Civil Rights and Black Power in Philadelphia* (Philadelphia: University of Pennsylvania Press, 2006), 328–30.
91. Sudhir Alladi Venkatesh, *Off the Books: The Underground Economy of the Urban Poor* (Cambridge, Mass.: Harvard University Press, 2006), 240–44.
92. See the interesting article by Lisa Y. Sullivan, "The Demise of Black Civil Society: Once Upon a Time When We Were Colored Meets the Hip-Hop Generation," *Social Policy* 27, 2 (Winter 1996): 6–10.
93. This is based on my eyewitness observations.
94. Two good brief overviews of immigration to France are found in Emmanul Peignard, "Immigration in France" (report from the Embassy of France in the United States, July 2001); and Kimberly Hamilton and Patrick Simon, "The Challenge of French Diversity" (report from the Migration Policy Institute, November 2004).
95. J. Huffington, "The May Day Marches: Cities' Immigrants Spoke One Language This Time," *Los Angeles Times*, May 2, 2006, part A, 10; Anna Gorman, Marjorie Miller, and Michelle Landsberg, "The May Day Marches: Marchers Fill L.A. Streets," *Los Angeles Times*, May 2, 2006, part A, 1.
96. Jean Louis Rallu, "Access to Citizenship and Integration of Immigrants: Lessons from the French Case" (paper presented at the Australian Population Association 12th Biennial Conference, September 15–17, 2004, Canberra, Australia).
97. Ira Katznelson and Margaret Weir, *Schooling for All: Class, Race, and the Decline of the Democratic Ideal* (New York: Basic Books, 1985).
98. John R. Bowen, "France's Revolt: Can the Republic Live Up to Its Ideals?" *Boston Review* (January/February 2006), http://bostonreview.net/BR31.1/bowen.html; James R. McDonald, "Labor Migration in France 1946–1965," *Annals of the Association of American Geographers* 59, 1 (1996): 116–34.

99. Mark Leon Goldberg, "Continental Drift," *American Prospect* (May 2006): 16.

100. Among the large literature on the history of immigration policy, two recent outstanding books are Daniel J. Tichenor, *Dividing Lines: The Politics of Immigration Control in America* (Princeton, N.J.: Princeton University Press, 2002); and Mae M. Ngai, *Impossible Subjects: Illegal Aliens and the Making of Modern America* (Princeton, N.J.: Princeton University Press, 2004).

101. For a trenchant discussion of the issues surrounding multiculturalism, see David A. Hollinger, *Postethnic America: Beyond Multiculturalism* (New York: Basic Books, 1995).

102. Víctor Zúñiga and Ruben Hernández-León, eds., *New Destinations: Mexican Immigrants in the United States* (New York: Russell Sage, 2005). As far as I know, there are no data comparing immigrant economic or occupational mobility or the educational and occupational achievement of their children in the United States and Europe.

103. Anti-immigrant spokespeople, not for the first time in American history, have mounted a xenophobic attack on birthright citizenship.

104. Rallu, "Access to Citizenship."

105. Tichenor, *Dividing Lines*, is especially sharp on the contradictory elements in the politics of immigration.

Chapter 4. From Underclass to Entrepreneur

1. This discussion of the underclass is adapted from the introduction to my edited volume, *The "Underclass" Debate: The View from History* (Princeton, N.J.: Princeton University Press, 1995).

2. "The American Underclass," *Time*, August 29, 1977, 1, 15.

3. Ken Auletta, *The Underclass* (New York: Random House, 1982), xvi.

4. Philadelphia Board of Guardians, "Report of the Committee Appointed by the Board of Guardians of the Poor of the City and Districts of Philadelphia, to visit the Cities of Baltimore, New York, Providence, Boston, and Salem [1827]," in *The Almshouse Experience: Collected Reports*, ed. David J. Rothman (New York: Arno Press, 1971).

5. Walter Channing, *An Address on the Prevention of Pauperism* (Boston: Office of the Christian World, 1843), 20.

6. For example, see Robert Hunter, *Poverty* (1904; repr., New York: Harper and Row, 1965), 3, 63.

7. *Second Annual Report of the Children's Aid Society of New York* (New York, 1855), 3.

8. Thomas W. Langfitt and Rebecca W. Rimel, "Suffer the Little Children," and "In Philadelphia There's Suffering Enough," *Philadelphia Inquirer*, June 4, 1989; Charles Rosenberg, "What Is an Epidemic? AIDS in Historical Perspective," *Daedalus*, 118, 2 (1989): 1–17.

9. *Fourth Annual Report of the Central Council of the Charity Organization Society of the City of New York, January 1st 1886* (New York Central Office, 1886), 14; David Ward, *Cities and Immigrants: A Geography of Change in Nineteenth-Century America* (New York: Oxford University Press, 1971); Roy Lubove, *The Progressives and the Slums: Tenement House Reform in New York City, 1890–1917* (Pittsburgh: University of Pittsburgh Press, 1962).

10. I discuss the transformation of the poorhouse and the problems with outdoor relief in *In the Shadow of the Poorhouse: A Social History of Welfare in America*, 10th anniv. ed. (New York: Basic Books, 1996), chaps. 2 and 4, and the criti-

cisms of urban school systems in *Reconstructing American Education* (Cambridge, Mass.: Harvard University Press, 1987), chap. 3.

11. My conclusions here rest on reading case records of nineteenth-century philanthropic agencies. See Michael B. Katz, *Improving Poor People: The Welfare State, the "Underclass," and Urban Schools as History* (Princeton, N.J.: Princeton University Press, 1995), 144–72.

12. Mark H. Haller, *Eugenics: Hereditarian Attitudes in American Thought* (New Brunswick, N.J.: Rutgers University Press, 1963); Donald K. Pickens, *Eugenics and the Progressives* (Nashville, Tenn.: Vanderbilt University Press, 1968); Daniel Kevles, *In the Name of Eugenics: Genetics and the Uses of Human Heredity* (New York: Knopf, 1985).

13. Michael B. Katz, *Poverty and Policy in American History* (New York: Academic Press, 1983), 157–81; Erik H. Monkkonen, *Walking to Work: Tramps in America, 1790–1935* (Lincoln: University of Nebraska Press, 1984); Paul Ringenbach, *Tramps and Reformers: The Discovery of Unemployment in New York* (Westport, Conn.: Greenwood Press, 1973).

14. Susan Tiffin, *In Whose Best Interest? Child Welfare Reform in the Progressive Era* (Westport, Conn.: Greenwood Press, 1982), 130–34; Roy Lubove, *The Struggle for Social Security, 1900–1935* (Cambridge, Mass.: Harvard University Press, 1968), 91–112; Winifred Bell, *Aid to Dependent Children* (New York: Columbia University Press, 1965).

15. For instance, see David J. Harding, Michel Lamont, and Mario Luis Small, "Reconsidering Culture and Poverty," special issue, *Annals of the American Academy of Political and Social Science* 629 (May 2010). See also James T. Patterson, *Freedom Is Not Enough: The Moynihan Report and America's Struggle over Black Family Life from LBJ to Obama* (New York: Basic Books, 2010).

16. Oscar Lewis, *The Children of Sanchez* (New York: Random House, 1961); Oscar Lewis, *La vida: A Puerto Rican Family in the Culture of Poverty—San Juan, and New York* (New York: Random House, 1966); "The Culture of Poverty," *Scientific American* 215 (1966): 19–25; "The Culture of Poverty," in *On Understanding Poverty: Perspectives from the Social Sciences*, ed. Daniel Moynihan (New York: Basic Books, 1969), 187–220.

17. Michael Harrington, *The Other America: Poverty in the United States* (New York: MacMillan, 1962).

18. Edward Banfield, *The Unheavenly City* (Boston: Little, Brown, 1970). On the history of the "culture of poverty" idea, see Alice O'Connor, *Poverty Knowledge: Social Science, Social Policy, and the Poor in Twentieth-Century U.S. History* (Princeton, N.J.: Princeton University Press, 2001), 99–123.

19. Patterson, *Freedom Is Not Enough.*

20. The full text of the report, "The Negro Family: The Case for National Action," is in Lee Rainwater and William L. Yancey, *The Moynihan Report and the Politics of Controversy* (Cambridge, Mass.: MIT Press, 1967), 39–125. Moynihan actually grounded his analysis of the development of single-parent black families in the unemployment of black men, a fact most of his critics overlooked. Rainwater and Yancey reprint many of the criticisms. See also Patterson, *Freedom Is Not Enough.*

21. Michael B. Katz, *The Undeserving Poor: From the War on Poverty to the War on Welfare* (New York: Pantheon, 1990), 52–65. See also Robert O. Self, *American Babylon: Race and the Struggle for Postwar Oakland* (Princeton, N.J.: Princeton University Press, 2003); and Thomas J. Sugrue, *Sweet Land of Liberty: The Forgotten Struggle for Civil Rights in the North* (New York: Random House, 2008).

22. Margaret Weir, "The Federal Government and Unemployment: The Frustration of Policy Innovation from the New Deal to the Great Society," in *The Politics of Social Policy in the United States*, ed. Margaret Weir, Ann Shola Orloff, and Theda Skocpol (Princeton, N.J.: Princeton University Press, 1988); Margaret Weir, "Poverty and Urban Policy: Transcript of 1973 Group Discussion of the Kennedy Administration Urban Poverty Programs and Policies" (Kennedy Archives, Boston); Katz, *Undeserving Poor*, 79–123. For upbeat accounts of community action, see Annelise Orleck, *Storming Caesar's Palace: How Black Mothers Fought Their Own War on Poverty* (Boston: Beacon Press, 2005).

23. Robert H. Haveman, *Poverty Policy and Poverty Research: The Great Society and the Social Sciences* (Madison: University of Wisconsin Press, 1987).

24. Charles Murray, *Losing Ground: American Social Policy, 1950–1980* (New York: Basic Books, 1984); George Gilder, *Wealth and Poverty* (New York: Basic Books, 1981).

25. Murray, *Losing Ground*. For a conservative critique of Great Society and other welfare programs from an authoritarian big-state point of view, in contrast to Murray's anti-state approach, see Lawrence Mead, *Beyond Entitlement: The Social Obligations of Citizenship* (New York: Free Press, 1986).

26. Examples of authoritative and negative reviews include Robert Greenstein, "Losing Faith in *Losing Ground*," *New Republic*, March 25, 1985, 14; Christopher Jencks, "How Poor Are the Poor?" *New York Review of Books* 32 (May 5, 1985): 41.

27. For example, see Nicholas Lemann, "The Origins of the Underclass," *Atlantic Monthly* 257 (June 1986): 31–61; 258 (July 1986): 54–68. Lemann offers a more nuanced interpretation in his subsequent book, *The Promised Land: The Great Black Migration and How It Changed America* (New York: Knopf, 1991).

28. William J. Wilson, *The Truly Disadvantaged: The Inner City, the Underclass, and Public Policy* (Chicago: University of Chicago Press, 1987).

29. Ibid., 41.

30. Isabel Wilkerson, "New Studies Zeroing in on Poorest of the Poor," *New York Times*, December 20, 1987; Erol R. Rickets and Isabel V. Sawhill, "Defining and Measuring the Underclass," *Journal of Policy Analysis and Management* 7 (Winter 1988): 316–25.

31. Martha A. Gephart and Robert W. Pearson, "Contemporary Research on the Urban Underclass," *Items* 42 (June 1988): 1–10. The committee's first major "product" was Christopher Jencks and Paul E. Peterson, eds., *The Urban Underclass* (Washington, D.C.: Brookings Institution, 1991). For an excellent brief history of the SSRC committee, see O'Connor, *Poverty Knowledge*, 277–83.

32. William Julius Wilson, "Social Theory and Public Agenda Research: The Challenge of Studying Inner-City Social Dislocations" (Presidential Address, Annual Meeting of the American Sociological Association, August 12, 1990). For a sophisticated attempt to arrive at a more satisfactory definition, see Martha Van Haitsma, "A Contextual Definition of the Underclass," *Focus* 12 (Spring/Summer 1989): 27–31.

33. O'Connor, *Poverty Knowledge*, 282.

34. Ibid.

35. Leila Fiester, *Building a Community of Community Builders: The National Community Building Network 1993–2005* (Oakland, CA: Urban Strategies Council, 2007), 4–5; Kristina Smock, "Comprehensive Community Initiatives: A New Generation of Urban Revitalization," COMM-ORG: The On-Line Conference on Community Organizing, 1997. http://comm-org.wisc.edu/papers97/smock/smockintro.htm.

36. Smock, "Comprehensive Community Initiatives."

37. Two scholars who have successfully combined qualitative with quantitative work are Katherine Edin and Katherine Newman. A superb but isolated example of the use of ethnography, qualitative research, and quantitative methods in one research project is Xavier de Souza Briggs, Susan J. Popkin, and John Goering, *Moving to Opportunity: The Story of an American Experiment to Fight Ghetto Poverty* (New York: Oxford University Press, 2010).

38. Camilo José Vergara, *The New American Ghetto* (New Brunswick, N.J.: Rutgers University Press, 1995).

39. Philip Kasinitz and Jan Rosenberg, "Why Enterprise Zones Will Not Work," *City Journal* 3, 4 (Autumn 1993): 63–69.

40. Ibid.

41. Michael E. Porter, "The Competitive Advantage of the Inner City," *Harvard Business Review* 73, 3 (May 1995): 55–71. The quotations from Porter in the next few paragraphs are drawn from this article.

42. James H. Johnson, "The Competitive Advantage of the Inner City," *Harvard Business Review*, 73, 4 (July/August, 1995): 152–55.

43. Andrea Silbert, Timothy Bates, Paul S. Grogan, Stephen Goldsmith, Gail Snowden, Bret Schundler, Robert Rubin, and Antoinette Malveaux, letters to the editor, *Harvard Business Review* 73, 4 (July/August, 1995).

44. Initiative for a Competitive Inner City online, www.icic.org/site/c.fnj, accessed July 26, 2010.

45. Initiative for a Competitive Inner City, "State of the Inner City Economies: Small Businesses in the Inner City," *Small Business Research Summary* 260 (October 2005).

46. Goldman Sachs, "Goldman Sachs Launches 10,000 Small Businesses Initiative" (press release, November 17, 2009); HighBeam Research, "The Porter Plan," www.highbeam.com.doc/1G1-20484802.html, accessed July 26, 2010.

47. Katz, *Price of Citizenship*, 128–99.

48. Julia Sass Rubin and Gregory M. Stankiewicz, "The New Markets Tax Credit Program: A Midcourse Assessment," *Community Development Investment Review* 1, 1 (March 2005): 1–11.

49. Jeremy Nowak, "Neighborhood Initiative and the Regional Economy," *Economic Development Quarterly* 11, 1 (February 1997): 3–10.

50. David J. Erickson, *The Housing Policy Revolution: Networks and Neighborhoods* (Washington, D.C.: Urban Institute Press, 2009), ii, xix; Christopher J. Walker and Mark Weinheimer, *Community Development in the 1990s* (Washington, D.C.: Urban Institute Press, 1998).

51. Xavier de Souza Briggs, Susan J. Popkin, and John Goering, *Moving to Opportunity: The Story of an American Experiment to Fight Ghetto Poverty* (New York: Oxford University Press, 2010), 13–14. MTO was inspired by the Gautreaux program in Chicago, which reported successful outcomes in education and employment for families that moved from public housing to low-poverty areas. See note 48.

52. Ibid., 223.

53. Ibid.

54. Ibid., 226.

55. Muhammad Yunus, *Creating a World Without Poverty: Social Business and the Future of Capitalism* (New York: Public Affairs, 2007), 247.

56. Ananya Roy, *Poverty Capital: Microfinance and the Making of Development* (New York: Routledge, 2010), 3.

57. Muhammad Yunus, *Banker to the Poor: Micro-lending and the Battle Against World Poverty* (New York: Public Affairs, 1999), 62.

58. Alex Counts, *Small Loans, Big Dreams: How Nobel Peace Prize Winner Muhammad Yunus and Microfinance Are Changing the World* (Hoboken, N.J.: Wiley, 2008), 2.

59. Ibid., 101.

60. Yunus, *Banker to the Poor,* 149.

61. Counts, *Small Loans,* 342.

62. Yunus, *Creating a World Without Poverty,* 18–19.

63. Roy, *Poverty Capital,* 121.

64. Counts, *Small Loans,* 299.

65. Roy, *Poverty Capital,* 5.

66. The Grameen America website no longer contains this statement, but the current language makes the same point. http://www.grameenamerica.com/.

67. Kristina Shevory, "With Squeeze on Credit, Microlending Blossoms," *New York Times,* July 28, 2010.

68. See www.grameenamerica.com, accessed August 1, 2010.

69. Counts, *Small Loans,* 358 (quote from Clinton) and 365.

70. Ibid., 78–79.

71. Ibid., 19.

72. Ibid., 123.

73. Ibid., 278

74. Women's Initiative online, www.womensinitiative.org/aboutus/about-main.htm.

75. Reid Cramer, Mark Huelsman, Justin King, Alejandra Lopez-Fernandini, and David Newville, "The Assets Report, 2010," New America Foundation, April 2010, 11.

76. Association for Enterprise Opportunity, "Overview: AEO Policy," www.aeoworks.org/index.php/site/page/overview_aeo_policy/.

77. Nancy C. Jurik, *Bootstrap Dreams: U.S. Microenterprise Development in an Era of Welfare Reform* (Ithaca, N.Y.: ILR Press, 2005), 70.

78. Jurik, *Bootstrap Dreams,* 72.

79. Asif Dowla and Dipal Barua, *The Poor Always Pay Back: The Grameen II Story* (Bloomfield, Conn.: Kumarian Press, 2006), 137.

80. Dowla and Barua, *The Poor Always Pay Back,* 105.

81. Stuart Rutherford and Arora Sukwinder, *The Poor and Their Money: Microfinance from a Twenty-First Century Consumer's Perspective,* 2d ed. (Bourton on Dunsmore, Rugby, Warwickshire, UK: Practical Action, 2009), 116.

82. Rutherford and Sukwinder, *The Poor and Their Money,* 1.

83. Yunus, *Creating a World Without Poverty,* 12–13.

84. Quoted in Neil MacFarquhar, "Banks Making Big Profits from Tiny Loans," *New York Times,* April 13, 2010, www.nytimes.com/2010/04/14/world/14microfinance.html?sq=savings%20poverty&st=nyt&scp=15&pagewanted=all, accessed July 29, 2010.

85. Counts, *Small Loans,* 6.

86. Roy, *Poverty Capital,* 203.

87. Ibid., 208.

88. Ibid., 218.

89. Ibid., 190.

90. Yunus, *Creating a World Without Poverty,* 65.

91. Roy, *Poverty Capital,* 114.

92. Ibid., 120.

93. Thomas Dichter, ed., "Can Microcredit Make an Already Slippery Slope More Slippery? Some Lessons from the Social Meaning of Debt," in *What's Wrong with Microfinance?* (Bourton on Dunsmore, Warwickshire, UK: Practical Action, 2007), 13.

94. Milford Bateman, "De-industrialization and Social Disintegration in Bosnia," in Dichter, *What's Wrong with Microfinance?* 208.

95. Tazul Islam, *Microcredit and Poverty Alleviation* (Aldershot, UK: Ashgate, 2007), 146.

96. Islam, *Microcredit*, 163–64.

97. Ibid., 142–43.

98. Jurik, *Bootstrap Dreams*, 199–200.

99. Ibid., 217.

100. G. S. Radhakrishna, "Suicide Shock for Loan Sharks," *Telegraph* (Calcutta, India), November 23, 2010, www.telegraphindia.com/1101123/jsp/nation/story_13210331.jsp, accessed December 3, 2010.

101. Lyda Polgreen and Vikas Bajaj, "India Microcredit Sector Faces Collapse from Defaults," *New York Times*, November 17, 2010.

102. Arjun Kashyap and Sumeet Chatterjee, "SKS Sees No Bank Withdrawals; Shares Soar," *Livemint*, November 19, 2010, www.livemint.com/Articles, accessed December 3, 2010.

103. Vikas Bajaj, "Sun Co-founder Uses Capitalism to Help Poor," *New York Times*, October 5, 2010.

104. Amy Kazmin, "Microfinance: Small Loan, Big Snag," *Financial Times*, December 1, 2010, www.ft.com/cms/s/a3edeba-fd85-11df-a049-00144feab49a, accessed December 3, 2010.

105. "Rouge Micro-finance Companies: Naxalites Have No Confusion Who They Are," *Microfinance Monitor*, November 30, 2010.

106. Kathleen Odell, *Measuring the Impact of Microfinance: Taking Another Look* (Washington, D.C.: Grameen Foundation, 2010).

107. Mark Schreiner and Michael Sherraden, *Can the Poor Save? Saving and Asset Building in Individual Development Accounts* (New Brunswick, N.J.: Transaction, 2007), 10.

108. Roy, *Poverty Capital*, 120.

109. Schreiner and Sherraden, *Can the Poor Save?* 140–44.

110. Yunju Nam, Jin Huang, and Michael Sherraden, "Asset Definitions," in *Asset Building and Low Income Families*, ed. Signe-Mary McKernan and Michael Sherraden (Washington, D.C.: Urban Institute Press, 2008), 1.

111. Nam et al., "Asset Definitions," 1–2.

112. Reed Cramer, Mark Huelsman, Justin King, Alejandra Lopez-Fernandini, and David Newville, "The Assets Report 2010: An Assessment of President Obama's Budget and the Changing Policy Landscape for Asset Building Opportunities," New America Foundation, 2010, 1.

113. Ibid., 1n1.

114. Schreiner and Sherraden, *Can the Poor Save?* 20.

115. Ibid., 21.

116. Ibid., 25.

117. Cramer et al., "Assets Report 2010," 3.

118. Ibid., 19.

119. Signe-Mary McKernan and Michael Sherraden, "Asset Building and Low-Income Families: Fact Sheet," Urban Institute Press, excerpted from McKernan and Sherraden, *Asset Building and Low Income Families*.

120. Melvin L. Oliver and Thomas M. Shapiro, *Black Wealth/White Wealth: A New Perspective on Racial Inequality* (New York: Routledge, 1995).

121. Dalton Conley, *Being Black, Living in the Red: Race, Wealth, and Social Policy in America* (Berkeley: University of California Press, 1999).

122. Robert Friedman, *The Safety Net as Ladder: Transfer Payments and Economic Development* (Washington, D.C.: Council of State Policy and Planning Agencies, 1988); Robert H. Haveman, *Starting Even: An Equal Opportunity Program to Combat the Nation's New Poverty* (New York: Simon and Schuster, 1988); Michael Sherraden, "Rethinking Social Welfare: Toward Assets," *Social Policy* 18, 3 (2000): 37–43.

123. Michael Sherraden, *Assets and the Poor: A New American Welfare Policy* (Armonk, N.Y.: Sharpe, 1991).

124. Schreiner and Sherraden, *Can the Poor Save?* 1.

125. Ibid., 7–8.

126. Ibid., 325.

127. Ibid., 4.

128. Ibid., 3.

129. Reed Cramer, "The Big Lift: Federal Policy Efforts to Create Child Development Accounts," Center for Social Development, George Warren Brown School of Social Work, Washington University in St. Louis, CSD Working Papers No. 09-43, 2009; Cramer et al., "Assets Report 2010." See also Ford Foundation, "Building Assets to Reduce Poverty and Inequality" (2002). On the Bank USA Initiative, see http://www.cdfifund.gov/speeches/Gambrell-2010-2-CDFI-Institute-Keynote-Speech.asp,

130. Bill and Melinda Gates Foundation, 2010 Global Savings Forum, November 16–17, 2010, Seattle, Washington, www.gatesfoundation.org/financialservicesforthepoor/Pages/session-briefs-2010-global-savings-forum.aspx, accessed December 3, 2010.

131. Robert A. Guth, "Giving a Lot for Saving a Little," *Wall Street Journal,* July 31, 2008.

132. CFED, "2010 Assets Learning Conference," http://cfed.org/knowledge_center/events/alc2010, accessed August 31, 2010; CFED, "Wal-Mart Grants to CFED and D2D Fund Will Expand Economic Opportunity" (press release, December 16, 2007), www.cfed.org/newsroom/pr/walmart_sponsor, accessed August 31, 2010.

133. Schreiner and Sherraden, *Can Poor People Save?* 6.

134. Ibid., 48.

135. Ibid., 11.

136. Michael B. Katz, *Improving Poor People: The Welfare State, the "Underclass," and Urban Schools as History* (Princeton, N.J.: Princeton University Press, 1995).

137. CFED, "The SEED Initiative," http://cfed.org/programs/abc/seed, accessed August 31, 2010.

138. T. H. Marshall, "Citizenship and Social Class," in *Citizenship and Social Class,* ed. T. H. Marshall and Tom Bottomore (London: Pluto Press, 1992).

139. David Harvey, *A Brief History of Neoliberalism* (New York: Oxford University Press, 2005).

140. Helen Zelon, "Hope or Hype in Harlem?" *City Limits* (March 2010): 15, 30–31. For background on Geoffrey Canada and the HCZ, see Paul Tough, *Whatever It Takes: Geoffrey Canada's Quest to Change Harlem and America* (Boston: Houghton Mifflin, 2008).

141. Zelon, "Hope or Hype," 13–14.

142. Quoted in Sharon Otterman and Robert Gebeloff, "When 81% Suddenly Becomes 18%," *New York Times*, August 1, 2010.

143. Zelon, "Hope or Hype," 28; for a vivid account of the role of test preparation in the daily life of one of the schools, see Tough, *Whatever It Takes*.

144. Zelon, "Hope or Hype," 29.

145. Quoted in Ibid., 37.

146. Matt Katz, "Camden City Council Approves Massive Layoffs," *Philadelphia Inquirer*, December 3, 2010.

147. New York City Commission for Economic Opportunity, "Increasing Opportunity and Reducing Poverty in New York City" (report to Mayor Michael R. Bloomberg, September 2006), 8–9, www.nyd.gov.html/om/pdf/ceo_report2006.pdf, accessed August 31, 2010.. www.cityharvest.org/media/pdf/MayorsCommissionOnPovertyReport2006.pdf.

148. Two of the recommendations for the working poor reflected the influence of the microfinance and asset-building movements: "Preserve assets, improve financial literacy, and encourage capital accumulation" and "Facilitate the Expansion of Small and Micro-Businesses." New York City Commission for Economic Opportunity, "Increasing Opportunity," 22.

149. New York City Commission for Economic Opportunity, "Increasing Opportunity," cover letter, emphasis original.

150. New York City Commission for Economic Opportunity, "Increasing Opportunity," 45.

151. New York City Commission for Economic Opportunity, "Increasing Opportunity," 42–43.

152. "Social Innovation. Let's Hear Those Ideas: In America and Britain Governments Hope That a Partnership with 'Social Entrepreneurs,' Can Solve Some of Society's Most Intractable Problems," *The Economist*, August 12, 2010.

153. Ibid.

154. New York City Department of Consumer Affairs Office of Financial Empowerment, "A Progress Report on the First Three Years, 2006–2009," http://nyc.gov/html/ofe/downloads/pdf/ofe_progress_report_dec2009.pdf, accessed August 31, 2010.

155. Ariel Fiszbein and Norbert Schady, *Conditional Cash Transfers: Reducing Present and Future Poverty* (Washington, D.C.: World Bank, 2009), 1.

156. Laura B. Rawlings, "A New Approach to Social Assistance: Latin America's Experience with Conditional Cash Transfer Programmes," *International Social Security Review* 58, 2–3 (2005): 134.

157. Fiszbein and Schady, *Conditional Cash Transfers*, 3.

158. James A. Riccio, Nadine DeChuasay, David Greenberg, Cynthia Miller, Zawadi Rucks, and Nandita Verma, *Toward Reduced Poverty Across Generations: Early Findings from New York City's Conditional Cash Transfer Program* (New York: MDRC, 2010); MDRC, "Opportunity NYC Demonstrations," www.mdrc.org/project_16_88.html, accessed August 31, 2010.

159. Riccio et al., *Toward Reduced Poverty*, iii.

160. Quoted in Julie Bosman, "Disappointed, City Will Stop Paying Poor for Good Behavior," *New York Times*, March 31, 2010, A-1.

161. Christine Quinn and Kathryn W. Wylde, "Living-Wage Debate Gets Broader, Louder," *Crain's New York Business*, May 23, 2010.

162. Ibid.

163. Peter Goodwin Heltzel, "Why NYC's People of Faith Must Take Up the Living Wage Fight, *Huffington Post,* August 17, 2010 http://www.huffingtonpost.com/peter-goodwin-heltzel/justice-delayed-is-justic_b_684766.html

164. Quinn and Wylde, "Living-Wage Debate"; Katz, *Price of Citizenship,* 392–93.

165. Center for Economic Opportunity, *Evidence and Impact* (annual report, January 2010), iii.

166. "Social Innovation."

167. Mary Jo Bane, "Poverty Politics and Policy," in *Changing Poverty, Changing Policies,* ed. Maria Cancian and Sheldon Danziger (New York: Russell Sage, 2009), 372.

168. Sheldon Danziger and Marie Cancian, "Reducing Poverty in the 21st Century: Lessons from New York City—Foreword," in Center for Economic Opportunity, *Evidence and Impact,* v–vi.

169. O'Connor, *Poverty Knowledge,* 217.

170. Cancian and Danziger, *Changing Poverty, Changing Policies,* chaps. 5, 7, 14.

Epilogue: The Existential Problem of Urban Studies

1. Michael Harrington, *The Other America: Poverty in the United States* (New York: Macmillan, 1962); Alice O'Connor, *Poverty Knowledge: Social Science, Social Policy, and the Poor in Twentieth-Century U.S. History* (Princeton, N.J.: Princeton University Press, 2001).

2. Colin Gordon, *Mapping Urban Decline: St. Louis and the Fate of the American City* (Philadelphia: University of Pennsylvania Press, 2008), 188.

3. Gerald L. Houseman, *City of the Right: Urban Applications of American Political Thought* (Westport, Conn.: Greenwood Press, 1982), 81.

4. T. H. Marshall, "Citizenship and Social Class," in *Citizenship and Social Class,* ed. T. H. Marshall and Tom Bottomore (London: Pluto Press, 1992), 8.

5. Michael B. Katz, "Was Government the Solution or the Problem: The Role of the State in the History of American Social Policy," *Theory and Society* 39, 3/4 (May 2010): 487–502.

6. Nicholas Dagen Bloom, *Public Housing That Worked: New York in the Twentieth Century* (Philadelphia: University of Pennsylvania Press, 2008).

7. Peter Dreier, "Does Public Housing Have a Future?" *TPMCafé,* June 8, 2010, http://tpmcafe.talkingpointsmemo.com/2010/06/08/does_public_housing_have_a_future/, accessed December 9, 2010.

8. David J. Erickson, *The Housing Policy Revolution: Networks and Neighborhoods* (Washington, D.C.: Urban Institute Press, 2009).

9. Guian A. McKee, *The Problem of Jobs: Liberalism, Race, and Deindustrialization in Philadelphia* (Chicago: University of Chicago Press, 2008); Paul S. Grogan and Tony Proscio, *Comeback Cities: A Blueprint for Urban Neighborhood Revival* (Boulder, Colo.: Westview Press, 2000); Annelise Orleck, *Storming Caesar's Palace: How Black Mothers Fought Their Own War on Poverty* (Boston: Beacon Press, 2005); Lisa Levenstein, *A Movement Without Marches: African American Women and the Politics of Poverty in Postwar Philadelphia* (Chapel Hill: University of North Carolina Press, 2009); Robert Gottlieb et al., *The Next Los Angeles: The Struggle for a Livable City,* updated ed. (Berkeley: University of California Press, 2006).

10. *MetroNation: How U.S. Metropolitan Areas Fuel American Prosperity* (Washington, D.C.: Brookings Institution, Metropolitan Policy Program, 2007).

11. Margaret Pugh O'Mara, *Cities of Knowledge: Cold War Politics, Universities, and the Roots of the Information Age Metropolis, 1945–1970* (Princeton, N.J.: Princeton University Press, 2002).

12. Daniel Singer, *Whose Millennium? Theirs or Ours?* (New York: Monthly Review Press, 1999).

13. Ananya Roy, *Poverty Capital: Microfinance and the Making of Development* (Berkeley: University of California Press, 2010), 39–40.

Index

Note: Page numbers in italics represent figures.

Acknowledgments

Eugenie Birch and Susan Wachter, co-directors of the Penn Institute for Urban Research, encouraged me to send this book to Penn Press for the Twenty-First Century Cities Series, which PIUR sponsors. Peter Agree, editor-in-chief of Penn Press, also solicited the manuscript and guided it through the review and acceptance process in record time. Their enthusiasm for the book buoyed my confidence. At Penn Press, Alison Anderson and Julia Rose Roberts prepared the manuscript for the Westchester Book Group, which looked after its production. At Westchester, the book received excellent copyediting while Brian Desmond oversaw an efficient publication process.

The elements from which this book is assembled took shape over decades of reading, writing, researching, and teaching. I cannot begin to remember all the people whose comments along the way helped me refine and develop my ideas. During the last few years, I have been writing for *Dissent* magazine, and the first iterations of some parts of this book first appeared there. I am grateful to *Dissent* editor Michael Walzer and managing editor Maxine Phillips for their willingness to publish my often unconventional pieces and for their editorial advice. In a slightly different form, Chapter 1 appeared in Merlin Chokwanyun and Randa Serhan, eds., *American Democracy and the Pursuit of Equality* (2011). At my request, Domenic Vitiello wrote a superb working paper comparing Philadelphia and Los Angeles, which proved crucial to the chapter. Mark Stern generously prepared the maps. Mark Stern, along with Jamie Fader, co-authored the version of Chapter 2 that appeared in the *Journal of American History*. Mark also was co-author with me of *One Nation Divisible: What America Was and What It Is Becoming*. Mark's remarkable quantitative and analytic skills provided the empirical foundation for our interpretation in Chapter 2. I am also grateful to the Columbia University History Department's seminar for an invitation to present the argument and for participants' comments. Chapter 3 originated as my presidential address to the Urban History Association and, in its original academic form, was published in the *Journal of Urban History*. I am deeply appreciative of the many comments from readers, especially the cautionary note from Loïc Wacquant to avoid facile comparisons between American ghettos and French working-class public housing. The question that underlies the Epilogue grows out of my teaching urban studies over more than three decades; an invitation from Hilary Silver to write a piece for *City and Community* forced me to try to articulate the problem; I appreciate the comments from participants at Columbia University's Urban Seminar where I tried it out.

I owe a special debt to the judge, defense attorney, and defendant, as well as to my fellow jurors, in the trial described in the prologue. For reasons of confidentiality, I cannot name them. But they provided me with an invaluable education and an inspiring example of how justice happens, at least some of the time. Alice Goffman helped me understand what I had heard and witnessed.

Readers familiar with writing on urban studies and urban history will recognize some of the key intellectual influences on this book. Without the work of Alice O'Connor, Jane Jacobs, Mike Davis, Saskia Sassken, Manuel Castells, Thomas Sugrue, Arnold Hirsch, Kenneth Jackson, William Julius Wilson, and Loïc Wacquant, among others, this book would have been impossible. Scholarship is a collaborative and iterative process. I see this book, not as frozen truth, but as a probe into difficult, sometimes mysterious, issues that, with luck, will provoke others to take up or continue the work.

A few people have responded over and over again to my requests for comments on drafts—Eric Schneider, Daniel Amsterdam, and Viviana Zelizer. There is no way to adequately express my thanks for their generous and careful readings. As ever, my wife Edda and children—Sarah, Rebecca, and Paul—have given me unqualified support.

Much of this book was written at Clioquossia in Oquossic, Maine. As always, I treasure the support—and distractions—provided by my friends and family there—and the stimulation of our still unnamed Tuesday breakfast discussion group. We met in the summer of 2011 in sorrow without the presence of our extraordinary founder, Baruch (Barry) Blumberg, to whom this book is dedicated. In the last several years, Barry became my friend, role model, and kayak buddy. The lakes and rivers still will be beautiful, but without him never quite the same.